THE PUBLIC HUMANITIES TURN

THE PUBLIC HUMANITIES TURN

The University as an Instrument of Cultural Transformation

PHILIP LEWIS

JOHNS HOPKINS UNIVERSITY PRESS
Baltimore

Johns Hopkins University Press
2715 North Charles Street
Baltimore, Maryland 21218
www.press.jhu.edu

Library of Congress Cataloging-in-Publication Data is available.

A catalog record for this book is available from the British Library.

ISBN 978-1-4214-4872-5 (hardcover)

ISBN 978-1-4214-4873-2 (ebook)

*Special discounts are available for bulk purchases of this book. For more information,
please contact Special Sales at specialsales@jh.edu.*

CONTENTS

PREFACE

This small book encapsulates and expands on the thinking I did during my eight years (2007–2015) as a vice president of the Andrew W. Mellon Foundation. During its first half century, the foundation was justly noted for its unwavering commitment to the arts and humanities, which it supported primarily through grants to arts organizations and institutions and to colleges and universities. At Mellon much of my work was focused on the latter, American higher education, of which I had considerable, albeit somewhat rarefied, knowledge as a result of my career as a teacher and administrator at Cornell University (1968–2007).

Although the Mellon Board of Trustees had decided to limit the foundation's grants to a relatively small fraction of institutions in US higher education (elite research universities, elite liberal arts colleges, and historically Black colleges and universities), the grant-making over which my colleagues and I presided had to be explained to our trustees and to our academic colleagues who sought grants on the basis of what we knew about the evolution of the entire system and its current needs and problems. Accordingly, I spent a significant amount of time during my years at Mellon groping for insight and guidance in the massive scholarly literature about US higher education. I also assiduously followed the news in journalistic and professional sources about what was happening at the time.

This welcome and stimulating experience of study and reflection did not, however, turn me into an expert on higher education. Nor, for that matter, did it equip me to make unreserved claims about the arts and humanities, whether in higher education or in culture at large. Given the demands of my multifaceted position, academic expertise of the kind that results from extended study in a well-defined domain of research was simply not an objective I could take on. Yet I could not carry out either the specific grant-making tasks that fell to me or my supervisory responsibilities without attempting to understand better than I had previously how the foundation's policies and decisions fit into a broad sociohistorical context. Accordingly, I found myself caught up in an open-ended exploration of trends and issues in US higher education.

This process of continuing education, pursued in dialogues with the foundation's staff and members of appointed advisory groups as well as with actual and would-be grantees, entailed not only reading and discussion but a fair amount of writing as well, often for in-house purposes such as presentations to Mellon's program staff or to the board of trustees, and occasionally for talks to academic audiences interested in the views and plans of the foundation. From this writing produced for the purpose of rationalizing Mellon's ongoing activities, I have extracted and recast the texts that delineate the scope and purport of this volume.

None of this written work has been published previously. None of it was informed by a presumption that the discrete texts intended for particular, intra-institutional audiences would eventually be collected and woven into a coherent, ultimately polemical book that would focus on the development and potential of the public humanities in the twenty-first century. None of it put into practice the professional standards and methodological scruples that I had once espoused as a scholar of French literature or as an editor of an academic journal. These venerable principles of scholarly rigor have to do with meeting the established expectations of erudite readers. One does so by demonstrating mastery of a corpus in a given field of inquiry and constructing an extensive apparatus of documentation—notes and references that position research and argument as serious, substantive, original, and thus publishable. Most of the hundreds of books published each year that deal with aspects of US higher education do meet these expectations; I respect and applaud their authors for attaining such legitimacy. Yet I have decided not to reach for that status, not to overlay the argument of this book with a bulky scholarly apparatus padded with books and articles that I used superficially or not at all.

While this choice is in part a matter of convenience, it also aims to ensure a certain transparency. In composing the drafts of chapters 1, 2, and 3 while at Mellon or during the few months immediately after my retirement, I did not have time to acquaint myself with all—or even a representative sample—of the relevant literature on the various topics I took up. My procedure was rather to gather a discrete number of books and articles that appeared to me to be timely or particularly worthy of attention and to construct a context that would allow me to treat one or two sources of important information or insight as a focal point for reflection. Obviously enough, such a practice, largely dictated by circumstance, excluded any pretension that I had carried out exhaustive or authoritative research.

This ad hoc approach resurfaces in each of my five chapters here. All reflect a strategic decision to construct arguments around a modest body of work that I subject to patient review and in a few cases discuss in considerable detail. With hindsight, I can identify for each chapter a particular study that eventually came to be contextually or argumentatively pivotal: in chapter 1, *The Faculty Factor* by Martin J. Finkelstein, Valerie Martin Conley, and Jack H. Schuster (2016); in chapter 2, *The Humanities and Public Life*, edited by Peter Brooks (2014); in chapter 3, *The Great Mistake* by Christopher Newfield (2016); in chapter 4, *Scale* by Geoffrey West (2018); and in chapter 5, *Knowledge Worlds* by Reinhold Martin (2021). If the amount of attention accorded to each of these works varies in this volume, the trajectory of concern that they trace corresponds closely to the evolution of perspectives that my thinking about the responsibility of the humanities in general and the promise of the public humanities movement in particular has traversed.

The final two chapters, which unveil my views in their urgency, are close enough to the model of the long review article to incline me to wonder if I have not reverted to a form of deliberation for which I advocated a half century ago when I was a member of the team that founded the journal *Diacritics*. In any case, the limited referential apparatus that I furnish here corresponds closely to the material that I actually selected and studied while engaged in the writing. It is supplemented, for better or for worse, by the knowledge I had acquired and opinions I had formed during my four decades as a faculty member at Cornell.

Why, then, have I recently concluded (during the COVID-19 confinement of 2020–21) that I should return to the efforts I launched a decade ago and mold them into a book? One of the presentations I concocted while at Mellon was a short talk for a

symposium about liberal arts education held at Lafayette College in 2011. After listening intently to many excellent presentations over a stretch of two days, I had to admit to myself, not
without embarrassment, that my own remarks and point of view
were not of a piece with the key themes and common concerns
that made for a largely homogeneous discourse on the present
state and future prospects of liberal arts colleges and liberal
education. My somewhat anomalous paper dealt with the contents of the basic curriculum that college students would encounter in the twenty-first century; it emphasized especially the
framework of general knowledge that could or perhaps should be
shared by liberally educated graduates. I proposed to approach
the problem of general knowledge through two turns or currents
or cognitive vectors, the global and the digital, that cut across
multiple fields and affect the pursuit of research in all of the
disciplines. The knowledges these potent, mutually reinforcing
concepts summon us to articulate confront us with a world that
is unsustainable, with a future that threatens life as we know it
with extinction. Liberal learning, I tried to suggest, needs to be
reoriented around the single, overwhelmingly urgent question
of survival on planet Earth, of how a transition to a sustainable
world order might be achieved.

Although my initial, unconvincing effort to promote reflection on this forbidding horizon failed to gain traction with my
fellow advocates of liberal arts education, my preoccupation with
questions advanced by earth system science and debates about
the Anthropocene has intensified over time. It drives the thinking that underlies this book. The context in which I have gradually reworked the inchoate analysis I ventured in 2011 has
veered from that of liberal education and its evolving mission
into the somewhat more focused sphere of what I then took to

be the humanities. This shift occurred largely because, soon after the Lafayette symposium, my work at Mellon became more concertedly channeled into projects having to do with the struggles of the academic humanities in the wake of the 2008 recession.

The first stage of this process was a program of subsidizing non-academic jobs for recent recipients of doctoral degrees in humanities fields that was conceived by the foundation's president, Don Randel, and developed in a collaboration with the American Council of Learned Societies. It was soon followed by a number of related initiatives: invitations to numerous humanities centers on college and university campuses to apply for grants, a series of grants underwriting collaborative research organized on an international scale by the Consortium of Humanities Centers and Institutes, additional funding to endow fellowships at the National Humanities Center, renewed commitments to the data-gathering operations and website of the Humanities Indicators project hosted by the American Academy of Arts and Sciences, substantial backing for the academy's national commission on the humanities and social sciences, and perhaps most significantly a gradually implemented decision both to encourage deliberations on the role of the humanities in the public arena and to nurture experiments in the *public humanities*. This institutional turn to the public humanities became central to my work; it is the dominant motif—initially, retrospective, yet ultimately prospective—that animates the essays collected here.

From the standpoint of the humanities, the pressing questions to be explored in the light of my concern with the future of our planet and the survival of humanity first have to do with the task or mission of the humanities-writ-large, that is, with a broad conception of the humanities allowing them to embrace the arts and many strands of inquiry in the social sciences that overlap with those of the classic humanities fields. From this broader standpoint of the human sciences, the crucial paths to be mapped are those that delineate relations to the more quantitatively oriented academic disciplines—the STEM fields (science, technology, engineering, mathematics) and those zones of the social sciences that have a more quantitative bent. Far from reinforcing divisions between the humanities and the sciences, the point here is to promote their complementarity and interaction. It is to recognize that the advance of scientific understanding confronts human society with vitally important problems, possibilities, and choices on which science itself, as a mode of inquiry and constantly expanding body of knowledge, does not readily pronounce.

Scientists who undertake to address the issues that "hard" science discloses make assumptions and adopt positions that reflect their capacity to think historically and philosophically, to adopt and integrate the perspectives of multiple fields, to participate in the collective project of liberal education. In the specific case of the scientific understanding of environmental degradation, the challenge to scholars in the humanities is initially to assess the grim findings that science makes available to the public at large and subsequently to advocate for a response to them from the scholarly community that is commensurable with the crises that are looming. The essential social, moral, and ethical aim of my concluding chapters here is, in sum, to impel the public humanities as I initially characterized them (in chapter 2) toward a more urgent and specific project, a responsibly radical reckoning with earth system science.

The ordering of the first three chapters complies with a conventional logic that prescribes moving from general background having to do with the place of the humanities in the system of American higher education to a more specific effort to define the public humanities, and then to reflection on the evolving status of public—as opposed to private—universities and the role of the humanities within them. With this framing of the public humanities in place, I then proceed to propose, in chapters 4 and 5, an expansive reconception of the humanities in higher education, evoking a composite of the arts, humanities, and social or human sciences to which I eventually refer as the Humanities with a capital *H*.

The proposal is grounded in the implications I draw from what earth system science is teaching us about the state of the planet. At its core, the point of view I adopt is hardly original. It associates the outlook I have tried to articulate with the views of many educators who seek to re-establish the now-faded concept of the public good as the fundamental basis for rethinking the curriculum and confronting our institutions of higher learning with the imperatives of social and ecological responsibility. In pursuing this tack, I have also appropriated some widely discussed insights of numerous scholars who seek to reframe and rethink our understanding of humanity and human history by integrating it into the much larger context of geological history and planetary dynamics.

My conclusion attempts to suggest what all this implies for the University, a term that I capitalize when I use it to refer to a massive educational complex that embraces all the degree-granting institutions—universities, colleges, professional schools, and so forth—that make up the global world of higher education. The key move is to reposition what I initially presented, in chapter 2, as conventional public humanities, forging paths across the boundary that separates academia from the world at large and building communities in which professional scholars and ordinary citizens can work together; it adjoins to this project of institutional outreach a critical Public Humanities movement that aims to turn the University into an instrument of cultural transformation.

ACKNOWLEDGMENTS

A combination of restraint and confusion prompted by innumerable long lists of names and effusive expressions of indebtedness that I've encountered in academic books over the years inclines me to thank my many colleagues and friends at Cornell and Mellon collectively, but not individually, for their helpful influence and unfailing kindness. I trust that all will understand my reticence and that most will relish the freedom from association attendant to escaping unnamed.

I do nonetheless wish to single out a half dozen individuals whose direct and substantial collaboration was indispensable as I worked on the writings collected here. Four of them were close colleagues at Mellon: Don Randel, Eugene Tobin, Don Waters, and Mariët Westermann. A fifth, Christie McDonald, invited me to a Radcliffe Institute seminar for which the initial version of chapter 1 was composed. The sixth, Catherine Porter, my spouse of fifty-seven years, encouraged me to engage with this project during the blighted years of the COVID-19 pandemic and supported the work from start to finish.

I owe the subtitle of this book to the good advice of the editorial director of Johns Hopkins University Press, Greg Britton, and his team; I am also indebted to Robert Brown for guiding me through the production process. I'm pleased to acknowledge as well the impeccable copyediting carried out by Elizabeth Farry.

THE PUBLIC HUMANITIES TURN

CHAPTER 1

The Big Picture

A History the Humanities Must Face

This chapter attempts to provide a brief, oriented historical over-view of the system of higher education in the United States—oriented toward providing a context in which questions about the current status of the humanities in American higher education should be placed.[1] It also aims to delineate some of the conditions under which answers to such questions might responsibly be ventured.

Since the founding of Harvard College in 1636, higher education in the United States has grown into a massive open system that current observers treat variously as the cornerstone of our culture and as the engine of the information economy. Its size and the pivotal role it plays in all walks of life make it an important object of study for researchers in many fields as well as a frequent, sometimes controversial topic of political discourse. Inevitably it is the subject of an endless avalanche of books and articles, most of which are the work of specialists representing diverse fields and viewpoints who study specific components or problems of the system. By one measure, the domain of higher education studies in the United States grows by some five hundred new books in print each year.[2] It confronts us, like so many zones of interdisciplinary scholarship, with an information explosion that, on the one hand, makes my attempt here to generalize or summarize in broadly historical terms dubious and pretentious but, on the other hand, reinforces the need to grasp the lineaments of the system comprehensively.

Unsurprisingly, there is something of a standard approach to the history of US higher education. Two recent historians who have provided impressive large-scale accounts, Roger Geiger (2016a) and John Thelin (2011), both follow an essentially generational scheme from the end of the War between the States through the first decade of the twenty-first century.[3] Prior to 1860, Thelin identifies two long periods, before and after the American Revolution, whereas Geiger begins with a century-long early period and then proceeds generation by generation from 1745 onward. Both show clearly, moreover, that the decisive long-term phase of systemic development commences during the time of transformation, 1890 to 1920, emphasized in Laurence Veysey's highly influential study *The Emergence of the American University* (1965);[4] they also present the construction of the University as the predominant impulse and tie it to a story of expansion traversing the twentieth century in which the University is, if not all-embracing institutionally, the conceptually primary representative of the system. That expansion and the diversification it entails are the principal phenomena we have to reckon with.

Before considering the lenses to deploy in looking at the twentieth century, however, I should underscore the key feature of the institutional model that was put in place during the prior era, that of the colleges, the vast majority of which were small private institutions established by religious denominations and operating in isolation, most often with little or no support from a state government. The typical nineteenth-century college gradually evolved away from its clerical roots toward a more secular identity. In part in reaction against the traditions of faculty governance at Oxford and Cambridge, the New World colleges were set up with locally selected external boards of governors or trustees that hired their presidents and usually granted them preponderant authority. The faculty's assumption of authority over academic decisions began to be asserted only in the final third of the nineteenth century and took hold strongly once the era of the University was under way. However, the institutional structure of the external board responsible for fiscal oversight and for recruiting the college or university president was destined to remain a defining fixture of the American system. This core structure would be transferred over from the private colleges to public colleges and universities whose overseers would be boards of trustees or regents appointed to uphold the interests of the states.

Now, in order to trace economically the growth and elaborate stratification of higher education from the late nineteenth to the early twenty-first century, I propose to look at four categories of development: institutional types, academic disciplines and curricula, the professoriate, and systemic structure.[5] I place the segment on the system at the end since it necessarily addresses the problem of dealing with the whole conglomeration.

Institutions

In the eyes of the rest of the world, American higher education is marked first and foremost by the variety of institutions it embraces. Concomitantly, the structure of this multifaceted aggregate is open and loose: it subtends a vast universe, at once hierarchic and labyrinthine, that is distinguished by the fluidity that appears when its components are subjected to a scheme of classification. The German model that informed the first American university, Johns Hopkins (founded in 1876), was one that emphasized advanced degrees and research; its importation, by adding the graduate level to the undergraduate enterprise of the colleges, made the university capable of integrating under its umbrella a broad array of scholarly and educational pursuits, including those of previously independent professional schools such as law, medicine, and divinity that would eventually, through association with the University, situate themselves as postbaccalaureate programs.

The system of higher education that began to develop during the final decades of the nineteenth century was able to be receptive to the creation of new institutions and new types of institution because it lacked the centralized control of the national systems in Europe. Indeed, the one significant early intervention of the federal government, the Morrill Land-Grant Acts of 1862, was stimulatory rather than regulatory. It served to consolidate the authority of the states over higher education and to promote the development of flagship universities that would preside over the state-based systems.

The uncontrolled proliferation of colleges and universities responding to local and regional needs resulted, by the 1920s, in the multiple levels of the framework we now perceive in the latter-day Carnegie classification,[6] which in 2014 covered 4,664 institutions enrolling 20,481,615 students. Whereas private, not-for-profit four-year schools were dominant in the late nineteenth-century beginnings of this now mammoth and heterogeneous academic world, from the turn of the century onward the role of public institutions—including, in addition to the flagships, full-fledged universities oriented toward applied research and vocational training, public four-year colleges that were initially normal schools, and a host of junior colleges that would morph into community colleges in the 1950s—became more and more important. Grasped simply from the standpoint of student and faculty numbers, the ascendancy of the publics was especially notable when the so-called massification of the system emerged after World War II: at present roughly 80% of all students attend public institutions, while the privates take in only 20%.

What the experts regard as the golden age of American higher education was the thirty-year stretch from 1945 to 1975. Initially fueled by the GI Bill, the process of growing the system to make it accessible to masses of students resulted in a vast and rapid expansion while encouraging further diversification of the academic programs offered. A key point to be drawn from the size, complexity, and instability of this higher education universe has to do with the zones of student and faculty concentration. Among the Carnegie classification's typologies of institutions, perhaps the most telling one differentiates them by instructional program focus. Of the 12.5 million undergraduate students attending four-year colleges and universities, 4% are accommodated by the 195 schools with a straight arts and sciences focus; 11% by the 218 schools with an arts and sciences plus professions focus; 42% by the 545 schools with a balanced arts and sciences/professions focus; 30% by the 590 schools with a professions plus arts and sciences focus; and 12% by the 829 schools with a professions focus.

The unmistakable preponderance in this "big picture" is, then, the emphasis on professional programs. The classic liberal arts degree is still the fulcrum in liberal arts colleges and top-tier universities that constitute what is presumably an elite and that profess to sustain what may still be a fundamental model of a well-rounded education. The numbers force us to ask, however, whether it is not to the rest of the system—in which the institutional ethos has been displaced toward the professional or vocational dimension—that the humanities must pay more attention.

Disciplines and Curriculum

Historians of the colonial period and the eighteenth century acknowledge that we have little concrete documentation related to the courses offered in the early colleges and have to infer from students' testimonials what was taught and how. The standard liberal arts core included mathematics, history, natural sciences, political economy, moral philosophy, and continued engagement with classic Greek and Latin texts. During the first half of the nineteenth century, there was at least some talk of modernizing the curriculum, and some institutions did pursue discrete experiments with other subjects: medicine, law, engineering, military science, commerce, theology, and agriculture (see Thelin 2011, 42). There was apparently no widespread deviation from the relatively thin liberal arts core, taught for the most part by generalists.

After the Civil War, on the other hand, active interest in curriculum development spread widely. In addition to the needs of an industrializing economy, the expanding curriculum reflected the mid-nineteenth-century influence of German universities on American students who had gone to study in Prussia at a time of ferment during which the nascent scientific disciplines had begun to shape the organization of faculties and instructional programs.[7] This development established research and knowledge production as required pursuits in the natural sciences and positioned advanced research as the fulcrum of a model eventually to be deployed in all areas of academic inquiry, including the humanities, where the field of philology was a leader in the production of disciplined scholarship.

The structure of academic fields expanding through research and generating specialized knowledge that would be taught in newly conceived courses was conducive to a revised view of the curriculum. It would have to be a dynamically evolving construct embracing multiple subjects and levels of mastery, enabling students to select courses from a large menu on the basis of their interests and qualifications. Accordingly, during the post–Civil War period, the familiar tension between a required course of study in the liberal arts and a program made up of electives chosen on the basis of students' experience, interests, and goals became a prominent feature of American higher education.

In the United States, the formation of the University went hand in hand with concerted growth of the disciplines in the 1880s and 1890s. In a book titled *The Academic Life* (1987), one of the great pioneers in the sociology of higher education, Burton R. Clark, treated the academic commitment to the disciplines as a preoccupation that American higher education would proceed to carry to extremes in the twentieth century—the age of specialization—as a result of its size, its freedom from regulation, and its openness to a myriad of institutional emphases and types. Clark distinguished two kinds of disciplinary development, substantive and reactive. Substantive growth is a product of research and reflection, the ongoing discovery of new subject matter and avenues of inquiry as knowledge advances and as new fields and subfields inevitably emerge. The speed of the process reflects decisions about whether to deal with increasingly specific phenomena or to preserve accumulating knowledge in manageable and teachable forms. By way of contrast, reactive growth is a function of demand, exemplified by increasing numbers of students who require a correlated rise in the numbers of teachers/mentors or by a society in need of problem-solving insights or inventions.

Prior to the era of massification, during which the effects of student demand and new sponsored research opportunities were rapidly intensified, the substantive development of the disciplines was vigorous. It evolved, according to Clark (1987),[8] along four distinct axes:

1. parturition, the division of a discipline like biology into various more specific fields (microbiology, genetics) or hybrids (biophysics, biochemistry);
2. program affiliation, as when professional schools became postbaccalaureate schools of medicine or law within universities;
3. dignification, by which a subject previously unworthy of inclusion in the curriculum became legitimate (the classic cases were technology and modern languages); and
4. dispersion, as when history spread from focusing on the classical world and ecclesiastical matters to covering the entire world temporally and geographically.

In Clark's view, these dynamic processes made the curricular currents—"the contemporary clutter of academic subjects"—in American higher education far more diverse, unsettled, and eclectic than those of its European counterparts. The resulting confusion and disarray were especially pronounced, Clark averred, at the graduate level, where programs leading to degrees in almost any subject, no matter how tangential, could be designed.

On the other hand, by the end of the Great Depression, established American universities did, for the most part, have in common a fairly standard curricular base of roughly thirty fields distributed across a half dozen disciplinary clusters: physical sciences, biological sciences, social sciences, "hard" professional areas (exemplified by engineering, agriculture, and medicine), "soft" professional areas (exemplified by education, business, and law), and humanities. During the first decades of the twentieth century both colleges and universities generally moved to organize their delivery of instruction through academic departments that corresponded to these fields or subjects. A departure from the German model anchored in the authority of a single, long-term chairholder over the university's work in his field, the advent of departments imbued the American approach to disciplinarity with a valuably democratic and meritocratic veer.

By 1920 the disciplinary status of the fields making up the expanded curriculum of the early twentieth century had been reinforced by the establishment of learned societies, national associations of scientists or scholars that often published important field-focused journals. These associations provided to both individual specialists in a given subject and their academic departments a field-based extra-institutional identity. The unending proliferation of such associations during the ensuing decades demonstrated unmistakably the pervasive influence that specialization within established disciplinary boundaries exerted in academic life.[9]

During the period of massification after World War II, the basic curricular structure proved to be quite robust even as the proliferation of specializations persisted, with new academic programs and professional organizations continually being created and absorbed into the existing superstructure. The extraordinary growth in student and faculty numbers of the 1950s and 1960s meant that disciplinary development had to be reactive as well as substantive. In the first place, the interests and career aspirations of students weighed heavily on the expansion of existing instructional programs and the creation of new ones. In the second place, the accelerating development of higher education as a major research establishment took place in an environment heavily influenced by the Cold War. This made for an influx of resources in science and engineering that had dramatic effects on the development of the most influential players, the so-called research universities, and on the shaping of the various disciplines and fields within them.

By 1980, when the golden age of expansion was over and the mature curricular superstructure we continue to work with early in the twenty-first century was largely in place, the distribution of faculty by disciplines thus reflected not only the multiple types of institutions accommodated by American higher education but also the decisive effects of student demand and sponsored research: 20% of the faculty were in science, 50% in professional fields, 13% in social science, and 17% in the humanities.[10] Obviously enough, the disciplinary spectrum of higher education at large is arrayed far differently from that of highly ranked liberal arts colleges or Ivy League colleges of arts and sciences. In these institutions the humanities departments may account for a third or more of the faculty and resistances to the professional/vocational veer remain strong. But their commitments, which reflect perspectives on life and learning, differ sharply from those of more typical, less privileged institutions. To cite just one further illustration of this difference between the universe of higher education at large and the affluent sector of higher education on which the attention of experts and of the public is often concentrated, in 1980 around 28% of the students in the prestigious liberal arts colleges opted for humanities majors, as opposed to around 9% of the students in all four-year bachelor's degree programs.[11]

Before complicating this picture of the relative status of the humanities by looking at trends that are visible in the twenty-first century, we should doubtless recall that in many respects the substantive growth of the humanities disciplines has tended to emulate that of the sciences, most notably through the constant emergence of narrower, more sophisticated specializations, the refinement of research methods, and the search for paradigms or theories that guide work on current interests or objects of inquiry and make for a sense of field-based community. But we also have to ask whether that staid, apparently progressive evolution of the academic humanities was able to withstand the disruptions that accompanied the massification of American higher education after World War II.

In 1997, Princeton University Press published a collection of essays titled *What's Happened to the Humanities?*, edited by the distinguished scholar of English literature Alvin Kernan. This useful, if somewhat exasperating, volume has the signal virtue of looking at the humanities disciplines through multiple lenses and setting them in the context of the major trends in higher education at the end of the twentieth century. With respect to scholarly discipline as an institutional practice of pursuing the orderly acquisition, dissemination, and preservation of knowledge, the overall thrust of the volume is to situate an adverse turning point in the 1960s, a decade of student unrest and methodological upheaval during which the authority of a gradually constructed traditional framework of inquiry, commonsensically objective and broadly consensual, was thrown into question both politically and epistemologically. According to this account, work in the humanities and in related zones of the social sciences could no longer advance in tandem with work in the sciences, where expert researchers would continue to elaborate the communally accepted truths and paradigms that grounded research in their fields on the basis of carefully sustained standards of objectivity and empirical testing.[12] Instead, the humanities lost their bearings, subjecting the claims of scholarship, in the ensuing decades of deconstruction, cultural studies, gender and ethnic studies, postcolonial studies, and so forth, to multiple challenges that left their scholarly communities awash in relativism, theoretical drift, and ideological confusion. Their disciplinary integrity had been weakened, if not definitively undermined.

In his preface to *What's Happened to the Humanities?*, Kernan was nonetheless at pains to provide a capaciously broad introduction to the decline of the humanities at the end of the twentieth century. Despite his own sympathy for the view noted above (the humanities were led astray by their own critique of positivism that ushered in a disabling relativism),[13] he refrained from attributing their problems solely to the intellectual countercurrents that coalesce in what some of the contributors to the volume would have treated merely as intradisciplinary self-destruction. As he noted, the essays collected in the book point to a cluster of invasive factors or trends that have, moreover, been exacerbated over the two decades since its publication: the demographic pressures occasioned by massification, a shift of funding sources away from the humanities, the intervention of electronic and digital media in all facets of our culture, the rise of a rampant vocationalism in all kinds of institutions (including those of the liberal arts elite), and the strong intellectual appeal of problems in the sciences and emerging interdisciplinary areas of research.

At least implicitly, then, Kernan was inclined to describe what's happened to the humanities by invoking a complex set of factors and to grasp in their interaction an explanation of the apparent decline of the humanities in relation to other academic disciplines (notably business, health-related programs, and those we started identifying as STEM fields—science, technology, engineering, and mathematics—in the early years of this century). At the same time, he and most of his contributors would have rejected the arguments that Michael Bérubé has advanced in various venues.[14] Bérubé claims that the multiple, sometimes dissensual, approaches to scholarship now visible on the broad spectrum of the humanities are not assimilable to a compromising relativism or constructivism and that, in their heterogeneity, they are a sign of the healthy interest of the humanities in addressing the complex needs of our world and in forging congenial relations with the social and natural sciences. When we look back at curricular developments during the two decades that separate these opposing takes on the humanities, do we observe either significant adjustments in the overall disciplinary configuration that was visible to veteran observers in the 1990s or further developments internal to the conception and practice of the humanities that affect their problematic disciplinary status?

The prudent answer here is likely to be a qualified *no*. To justify this double (*likely* + *qualified*) equivocation, I propose to consider the effects of some broad, general trends that have surged to the forefront since the start of the century and that will be significant factors in the sections that follow on the professoriate and the system. At minimum, it seems clear that these trends aggravate the pressures on the disciplines that were already manifest in the 1990s. Foremost among them, buoyed by the financial strains incurred by students and their families, is surely the increasing momentum of vocationalism, the always active but now hyperactive push for programs that, ostensibly, lead to gainful employment. Also being reinforced is the tendency, driven by a similar return-on-investment preoccupation, to favor applied over basic research and thus, slowly but surely, to erode the value accorded to basic knowledge in all the disciplines. In the sphere of undergraduate education, the last two decades have been marked by a broadened and sharpened focus on students, their experience as learners,[15] the need to measure their learning outcomes, the value of working in groups and applying lessons learned in community service, and so forth.

So far, the pressure that this emphasis on the ways students learn exerts on the curriculum has been much more pronounced in the design of courses and majors and in a renewed attention to pedagogy than in thinking about fields or disciplines and their scholarly frameworks. Still another influence pervading recent discourse about higher education is that of the globalized knowledge economy, which obviously boosts some disciplines (economics, business, information technology) and areas of inquiry (international studies, foreign languages) more than others.[16] A final major phenomenon, still hard to size up but bearing significant potential for disruption of the disciplines, is the appropriation of digital tools in both teaching and research. The vision of a brave new digital world, already buttressed by burgeoning artificial intelligence, now goes far beyond what was perceptible two decades ago, although paradoxically the prevailing wisdom of the moment cautions us against assuming that it will bring rapid and radical change.[17]

So where have the humanities disciplines stood in relation to these macro-trends that seem dominant at the moment? Unmistakably they have suffered. Following the statistical overview maintained on the excellent Humanities Indicators website by the American Academy of Arts and Sciences,[18] we have to recognize that their place in the institutional and the disciplinary firmaments continues on a trajectory of slow decline, of relegation to a secondary or supporting role in relation to ascendant fields. Moreover, the humanities also appear to be evolving on a path that some would regard as intellectual retreat or insecurity, which is poignantly evoked by the title of Terry Eagleton's book *After Theory* (2003) and by many calls for a return to "close reading."

While it is reasonable to assume that the numerical slippage in numbers of majors and faculty positions has leveled off or will soon do so, a judgment about the strength or weakness of current scholarship in the humanities disciplines is hardly a simple matter. The "post-theory" era into which, according to various commentators, we have stumbled does indeed appear to have left behind critical schools and interdisciplinary movements with wide appeal (the likes of structuralism or poststructuralism or new historicism or postcolonial studies). As Vincent Leitch shows in his *Literary Criticism in the 21st Century* (2014),[19] such "twentieth-century schools and movements of theory," after subsiding, now linger as influences from the past to be studied critically and perhaps appropriated punctually, but with their polemical edge and ideological trappings muted or discarded. Yet we are witnessing a staggering proliferation of approaches and positions presented in more or less theoretical terms, as if a certain ethos or mode or perspective inherited from the lapsed age of theory were still orienting much work in the humanities.

Drawing on the topographical account of this state of things provided by Leitch, we can appropriate the blandly conventional tag "studies" to designate this early twenty-first century post-theory period. Of the 94 terms arrayed under 12 general headings on Leitch's labyrinthine map of "topics" and "subdisciplines," 50 already modify the word *studies* while many more could have the studies label (the fact that all but 4 of the 50 modifiers are adjectival nouns suggests that essentially the map collects objects of inquiry). Among the 106 items (categories and subdisciplines), only 2 are presented as theories, affect theory and cognitive theory; the former is one of Leitch's 12 general categories and lists "affect studies" as an item under that heading, while cognitive studies could doubtless be substituted for or perhaps preferred to cognitive theory.

The variety and specificity of all these studies defy homologation or even coherent classification, just as they dispel—this is Leitch's main point—the notion that humanities scholarship has fallen into an intellectual vacuum. We are observing a somewhat turbulent scene of experimentation that is rather more energized by concerns stemming from the world at large or from prevailing interests within the academic enterprise than it is programmed by methodological positions or by resistance to prevailing models of disciplinarity or interdisciplinarity. At this moment, then, the humanities disciplines appear to be far more susceptible to the effects of those social, economic, and institutional forces than vulnerable to their own internal flirtations with philosophical relativism.

The Professoriate

In the foregoing discussions of institutions and disciplines, it is already evident that the history of the faculty's role is crucially tied up in the processes of growth and specialization that took hold strongly in the final third of the nineteenth century, when the university as we know it emerged. Prior to the age of the university, small colleges and their small student bodies made for small faculties—consisting typically, in the first half of the nineteenth century, of a few (perhaps senior) professors supported by a few (usually young and temporary) tutors—whose members were subservient to trustees and presidents. By and large the modest and stable liberal arts curriculum was subject to mastery by the cultivated intellectual, a "Renaissance man" in the classical mold. To appoint a qualified instructor was, then, to hire a versatile employee who could teach many, if not all, of the subjects offered and who could also be called on by those in charge to carry out multiple duties, including extracurricular supervision of student life.

As soon as the curriculum began to open to new disciplines and courses that required the specialized knowledge of experts, the subservient and at times para-parental status of the teaching corps began to change. It made sense to grant to members of the faculty intellectual authority over the courses and programs in their fields of competency and to give them a voice in decisions about standards for admitting students and about graduation requirements; as fields of study expanded and departments became responsible for them, administrations were behooved to hand over to faculty an important role in the recruitment of new colleagues as well. By the turn of the twentieth century, the hierarchy of instructional ranks and the concept of a career course allowing junior faculty to ascend to full professorship were becoming the dominant infrastructure. Concomitantly, the temporary position held by tutors was being phased out; it was destined to be succeeded in the ensuing decades by a cadre of non-academics serving under a dean of students and shoring up the concentration of faculty responsibilities in the academic domain.

Under such circumstances, in a period of only a few decades (those between the Civil War and World War I), college and university faculties were gradually transformed into organized bodies with the power to claim rights and privileges appropriate to their roles. For the faculty, then, the age of university formation was the decisive period of *professionalization*, marked historically by the founding of the American Association of University Professors in 1915. At the outset, the AAUP's agenda was focused pointedly on the protection of academic freedom in three fundamental domains: research and publication, teaching, and citizenship in the public arena.[20]

While this commitment has remained central and vehement, the university professors' organization moved smartly to embrace a set of interests and prerogatives that would position the academic occupation as a profession endowed with its own ethos or culture: faculty autonomy in their areas of expertise, faculty participation in institutional governance, a career-defining framework for faculty appointments and promotions that academic tenure would eventually consummate, self-established and self-regulated standards of training and conduct, and societal recognition of the professoriate as the guardian and guarantor of an essential public service that cannot be understood as merely a purchasable commodity. Even before the Manhattan Project of the 1940s, professorial prestige attributable to highly specialized expertise rose markedly in the eyes of the general public thanks to the extensive and highly visible deployment of faculty in the service of the federal government during the Great Depression.

It is doubtless reasonable to link the full achievement of the professorial faculty's professional status to the 1940 promulgation of the AAUP's *Statement of Principles on Academic Freedom and Tenure*, which officially refers to college teaching as a "learned profession." In any case, strongly anchored in the institutionalized specializations that were represented by the national disciplinary associations and field-based academic journals, and reinforced by the remarkable growth of PhD-granting graduate programs between the two World Wars, the fully professionalized faculty infrastructure was solidly in place when higher education entered into the period of massification after World War II. The breadth and depth of support for the structure were such that the three postwar decades can rightly be cast as an era when both faculty influence in the operation of colleges and universities and the attractiveness of the professoriate as a profession reached a zenith that has since proved to be unsustainable.[21]

In important respects, the explosive growth and constant diversification of higher education during this golden age contained the seeds not only of the faculty's upward trajectory in status and privilege but also of its subsequent reversal. The forces of expansion that occasioned the extraordinary increase in faculty numbers (from approximately 120,000 in 1940 to 450,000 in 1980) broadened substantially the range of student preparedness as well as that of institutional missions that the army of newly trained teachers produced by thriving graduate programs would confront. The flow of faculty into public institutions with no graduate programs, into two-year colleges, and into institutions with a professional or vocational orientation increased steadily while the percentage of faculty absorbed by traditional liberal arts institutions dropped. This redistribution of scholarly talent made the already significant stratification within the profession still more pronounced.

At the same time, however, in the graduate schools where the flood of new PhDs was produced, the thrust of training programs was to fortify the hold of the disciplines on students' loyalties and consolidate the ethos in which research, publication, and visibility in one's field took priority over—in the parlance of experts, were "unbundled" from—the chores of teaching and of service to an employing institution or to society. So, when administrative leaders in higher education had to face the trying financial, technological, political, and demographic realities of the late seventies and beyond, they had to reckon with the pressures at hand while working with a model of faculty positions and commitments that often appeared to stand in the way of needed change.

As for the story that has unfolded during the last four decades, it is one that has been traced in its depth and complexity in a magisterial study, *The Faculty Factor* (*FF*) by Martin J. Finkelstein, Valerie Martin Conley, and Jack H. Schuster (2016). In examining curricular evolution above, we encountered some prominent recent themes or trends of this story: vocationalism, globalization, digitization, student learning. One additional leitmotif that runs through all facets of the story will be discussed below in the segment on the system. It turns upon a multilayered reversal of the transition from largely private to predominantly public higher education that we have emphasized up to now. Like the other major trends, it reflects a battery of financial pressures that bear down on all kinds of institutions. In most of them, since personnel is the largest item of their budget and faculty costs are the dominant within that item, reshaping the faculty so as to trim costs has been the predictable, doubtless inevitable response.

The statistical markers of the resulting transformation are well known. In 1993, according to *FF*, 51.3% of newly hired full-time faculty were appointed off the tenure track, whereas in 2011, 58.4% were appointed off the tenure track; in 1993, 43.6% of full-time faculty held regular, tenure-track appointments, whereas in 2011 that had dropped to 29.7% (*FF*, 14). It is of course necessary to supplement this picture with statistics on part-time, off-the-ladder faculty. In 1979 about one-fourth of the instructional staff were part-timers, whereas in 2013 the fraction had risen to 43% (*FF*, 58). The educational effect of this shift, moreover, has clearly been to appoint more faculty, whether full- or part-time, exclusively to teaching roles and thereby to entrench a larger proportion of tenure-track faculty in research-oriented activity. The latter trend is aggravated by the increasing numbers of regular faculty who take on administrative functions that reduce their teaching or mentoring responsibilities. Overall, the transition in both appointment zones—tenure-track and off-the-ladder—channels faculty into increasingly specialized roles and thereby reinforces the stratification of the academic labor force.[22] *FF* adds to its account of changing faculty roles a less readily quantifiable but still evidence-based claim that faculty influence in the arena of "shared governance" has declined in recent decades while managerial decision-making, usually advocated by boards of trustees, has gained momentum.

In the broad-based argument developed in *FF*, all of the macro-level trends noted above converge with what strategic planners would qualify as a reengineering of the academic workforce to form the basis of the book's central claim: in the wake of the 2008 financial crisis, the faculty factor—that is, role, influence, status—has undergone an erosion so thoroughgoing that it signals a seismic shift in the higher educational landscape, an irreversible paradigm change that cannot be rolled back, but to which it is imperative for academia to respond constructively. The change heralds the beginning of a new era during which the professional standing of the professoriate will be at risk. Already visible "faculty-*un*friendly developments" have shunted the professoriate from the center to the periphery and made student learning the primary preoccupation. *FF* regards this devaluation of the faculty factor as a menace to the long-term health of American higher education and concludes with some recommendations for reinvigorating the faculty's influence. While we have to ask whether the implementation of such recommendations is either thinkable or sensible at this juncture, we can at least recognize that the book's analytic work with the relevant data provides an essential starting point for debate.

System or Non-system

The preceding remarks about the institutions, curricula, and faculty of American higher education treat the history of these obviously interdependent orders as that of an open, loosely structured, expansive system that has developed in a somewhat haphazard fashion. It can nonetheless be regarded as a system in relation to key stabilizing assumptions woven into the social fabric: a collectively sanctioned framework for human development that includes primary and secondary education, a broad sociocultural consensus about the mission of education, and a certain vision, at once architectural and operational, that suffuses informed discourse about the University. Yet experts on US higher education are not always at ease with the term *system*.

The discomfort derives from historiographic scruples. Since the gargantuan assembly of components we conventionally patch together under the heading "higher education" reflects development that has been uncontrolled and disorderly from the start, efforts to demarcate the jumble's boundaries unequivocally or to explain its evolution coherently have lacked the flavor of a systemic account. They tend instead to consist of collections of factors, sectors, and types that, like the overview I have sketched above, resist ready homogenization. Scholars are thus prone to represent these delineable domains or orders in discrete narratives that proceed item by item; although obliged to allude to the unsettled whole, they incline to do so parenthetically and with duly considered caution. The authors of *FF*, for example, start their first chapter, "Establishing the Framework," by referring to "developments that have propelled the postsecondary system into an unprecedented, new systemic model" (4) only to modalize their assertion on the following page by reminding us of the difficulty of generalizing about "such radically decentralized organizational 'nonsystems' as American higher education." While subscribing to this well-founded caveat, I shall nonetheless presume to discuss below what Burton R. Clark calls, in the title of chapter 3 of *The Academic Life*, "the open system," which he takes up immediately after having situated the professoriate— one component of the far more massive system—as "an enormously complex matrix" of "colossal scope" that is distinguished by "scatteration" and "dispersion" (Clark 1987, 43–44).

A hypothesis that sums up the narratives I've offered above posits two stages of development: initially, a non-system or, perhaps more aptly, a proto-system slowly took shape during the age of colleges, that is, between the founding of Harvard and the War between the States; thereafter, the age of the University ushered in a system with flexible contours and a protean internal logic that would grow in complexity over the twentieth century. Working with such an overview, distinguishing two lengthy phases, we can specify defining features of the proto-system and ask first whether they would be preserved or modified as the system developed, and second by what structures or drivers they would be supplemented. So far we have noted five key features: (1) the absence of central guidance from the national government; (2) the numerical dominance of private over public institutions; (3) the structure of governance that gives priority to boards of trustees and presidents; (4) the traditional, often weakly formulated notion of general or liberal education that was deemed appropriate for young men from the upper classes of society; and (5) the coexistence of nascent state systems, locally oriented and quite independent from one another. If the enduring legacy of this proto-system was its tradition of openness, anchored in operational freedom at the local, institutional level, it also bred a significant secondary tradition, the formation of academic communities in and around the colleges and the cultivation of alumni loyalty to them.[23]

Before examining the distinct forces or organizing principles that intervene to make twentieth-century higher education more systemic than its predecessor, let us review succinctly these inherited traits. First, it is clear that World War II brought the federal government decisively into the world of higher education, both as the framer of the GI Bill and as the principal funder of research in science and technology. Moreover, the second half of the twentieth century witnessed the conversion of the Department of Education, founded in 1867 but largely inconsequential until the 1950s,[24] into a major government agency responsible for collecting data on education at all levels and furnishing it to policymakers and researchers. For higher education in particular, its role in administering the National Defense Education Act (NDEA) of 1955 and the Higher Education Act (HEA) of 1965 is vitally important. The latter piece of legislation and its renewals established programs that now provide grants and loans to some twelve million undergraduate students (Title IV) and subsidize centers for international studies and foreign language study (Title VI). As the celebrated Title IX (1972) of HEA demonstrates through its ban on gender discrimination, the department has also responded to political demands for regulation of higher education. Recent moves to make institutions accountable for educational outcomes take it further into the realm of oversight.

While the shift from private to public dominance of higher education was the major trend of the twentieth century, one can argue that an ironic reversal of that trend has occurred in recent decades. The elements of this re-privatization, as it were, can be noted in a few propositions, all of which have to do with income streams:

- Private for-profit institutions have become a major sector of higher education and, thanks to federal financial aid programs, highly visible beneficiaries of public support.
- Private funding in the form of rapidly increasing tuition charges to students is the principal means of filling the

budgetary gaps encountered by nominally public universities that state appropriations no longer support adequately.[25]

- In both the public and private sectors, research—while still heavily dependent on grants from federal agencies[26]—is turning increasingly to corporate subvention, and universities face increased pressure both to generate income through technology transfer and to back research with their own privately raised funds.
- Public institutions, by dramatically ramping up fundraising efforts with alumni and other private philanthropic sources, have become less dependent on public resources.
- In both public and private institutions, the understanding of education as a public good has lapsed since students and their families are forced to treat it as a private good, a high-priced commodity to be acquired by clients entitled to hold the purveyors of education accountable for the product they purchase.

In sum, the hold of a gradually generated neocapitalist model,[27] over the vast subsystem revealed by even a rudimentary look at the financing of higher education, has become undeniable.

At its core, which is fiduciary responsibility exercised by a board of trustees that appoints a president or chancellor and that assumes an oversight function in some facets of administration, the mainstream structure of governance in four-year colleges and universities has been a pillar of continuity in American higher education, even if does not extend to certain parts of the system (the for-profit sector, some professionally or vocationally oriented institutions). As the influence of the faculty rose over the first three-quarters of the twentieth century and as the growing size of most colleges and universities converted them into large businesses equipped with intricate, sometimes massive bureaucracies, the structure had to morph into more elaborate arrangements that we associate with the notion of *shared governance*.[28] This concept recognizes that three power centers—governing boards, presidents and the administrations over which they preside, and the faculty—have joint interests that require cooperation and that documents spelling out principles and procedures pertaining to the distribution and exercise of institutional responsibilities should be disseminated to all the concerned parties. For many observers, the re-privatization noted above—understood more generally as the adjustment to financial exigencies and other external pressures that contribute to the slippage in faculty authority and influence in recent decades—has diluted the commitment to shared governance and edged institutions toward degrees of managerial control that are at odds with an earlier, less corporate academic tradition.[29]

The future of general or liberal education was thrown sharply into question when higher education's devotion to disciplinary specialization took hold during the final decades of the nineteenth century. The cause of a prescribed core curriculum lost out to the elective system, distribution requirements, and the idea that individuals could achieve a respectable level of acculturation in a variety of ways. If a semblance of debate about a core curriculum continued thanks to well-publicized commitments at the University of Chicago, Columbia University, and eventually at St. Johns College, the case for liberal education anchored in the reading of key classic texts that was typically espoused by purposeful representatives of the humanities was simply swamped by the burgeoning curriculum, episodic calls for its revival notwithstanding. The locus of debate, moreover, has shifted because the erstwhile majority of institutions with programs justifying their asserted allegiance to the production of cultivated, civically responsible graduates has withered into a shrinking minority. At present the central issue is to what extent liberal education should and can be woven into curricula that prioritize vocational/professional training.[30]

Along with the core structure of institutional governance, the early priority accorded to state systems of higher education remained intact throughout the twentieth century. Comparing the various departments of education and the systems they manage reveals significant variation from state to state. This occasions in particular much discussion of the glaring differences between high-flying flagship universities that bank on their capacity to charge high tuition to students whose homes are not in the state and lesser state institutions that lack the power to lure affluent out-of-state students. Nonetheless, there has been, over time, considerable standardization that is national in scope.

In the first place, numerous national organizations of higher education professionals have been established, and for the most part they promote the spread of common practices in the various zones of institutional operation.[31] In the second place, a far-reaching system of accreditation has been put in place. In its original design, accreditation was a peer-review process organized by nonprofit colleges and universities, both private and public, that joined regional organizations. These agencies first sought to establish sufficient uniformity in the standards for high school diplomas to allow tertiary institutions to assume the parity of applicants from various states; subsequently they moved on to establish standards for college-level work that would allow for the transfer of course credits from one institution to another. The effort succeeded, without intervention by the federal Department of Education, in generating a system of academic standards that has by and large been beneficial to American higher education.

In 1952, however, the Department of Education began to assume a significant role on this horizon by endorsing accrediting agencies and requiring accreditation of institutions that receive federal funds. More recently, the department has asserted its interest in a form of accreditation that would hold schools accountable for the education delivered—its cost should be justified by demonstrated financial returns to graduates—and make information about students' outcomes (what they learn and earn) public.[32] While a push for more federal regulation may be looming, it will not occur without resistance from the existing state and regional systems.

The foregoing remarks amount to a predictable general observation that the basic features of the decentralized, predominantly private, and largely uncontrolled proto-system of the nineteenth century were subjected, once growth and specialization became the dominant trends, to considerable complication early in the twentieth century. As the telling complications imply, it was incumbent on the many participants in higher education who were aware of the proliferation of institutions with common purposes and structures to recognize these shared features as constitutive of a system, however open, loose-jointed, and adaptive it may have been. But simply pointing to its major components and enabling conditions fails to disclose either the dynamic forces—the incentives, tensions, initiatives, drivers, logics, and contradictions—that energize and propel an evolving system or the nature of the linkages that allow it to be perceived integrally, that is, to be grasped as a socioeconomic organism or an organized zone of restless institutional activity that has to be understood in functional terms.

Scholars intent on grasping this systemic dynamism historically are wont to focus on the period from 1945 to the present. Given the comprehensive account of Burton R. Clark, it is hard not to fall back on the interplay of two familiar concepts: on the one hand an academic marketplace characterized by multiple zones of intense competition, and on the other hand the mobility of both individuals and institutions that is accommodated by the hierarchic superstructure within which the marketplace functions. To conclude this overview of the system, a remark on the state of the market and a sketch of the strains now visible in that hierarchy are in order.

When sociologists introduced the idea of the academic marketplace in the 1950s, the narrowly delimited phenomenon initially studied was that of a small but intriguing labor market, made up of faculty members in top-tier universities who moved from one institution to another in return for better remuneration and/or working conditions.[33] Until the period of strong growth and relatively encouraging financial conditions ended in the 1970s, there was some concern in the academic world about competition for desirable faculty and students. This disquiet was hardly comparable, however, to the preoccupations that emerged in the 1980s, a decade of rising costs and budget shortfalls that forced fiscal austerity (of which a tight job market was a conspicuous symptom) on public and private institutions at all levels of the hierarchy. The resultant belt-tightening occurred at a time when the infamous *U.S. News and World Report* rankings (launched in 1983) and widely disseminated appeals to the benefits of free or minimally controlled markets became significant factors in the strategic thinking of trustees and administrative leaders about how institutions of higher learning should be evaluated and managed.

If the institutional hierarchy had long existed in the minds of observant educators and indeed, less distinctly, served as a kind of pecking order to which the broad constituency of actual and potential graduates casually referred, the elaborate numerical rankings made it more prominent and influential even as they reconfigured it with fine-grained distinctions of dubious validity. Yet the die was cast, the broadly marketized dynamics of the system we now navigate is the motor of an interinstitutional competition that, when viewed through the lenses of the international rankings produced in the United Kingdom, borders on the caricatural.[34] But in US higher education, that competition is the deadly serious factor that, in the hierarchical setting of a huge marketplace of great economic, political, and social import, explains, if not what a given institution does, where the system is heading.

The imperative to compete strongly with peers derives its poignancy from the possibility of moving up or down in the hierarchy on the basis of performance factors. The relevant criteria, which are not exclusively quantitative measures but do privilege them, have extended intercollegiate rivalry into a host of areas reviewed by vigilant trustees: student recruitment and retention, faculty recruitment and retention, campus facilities and technology support, ratings of graduate fields, various income streams (but especially research grants, private gifts, and where relevant, endowment earnings), various expenditures, reputation, service to the public, success in athletics, and so forth. Managing a college or university with strategic acumen therefore entails not only determining and pursuing an advantageous combination of competitive edges vis-à-vis carefully identified peers but also attending internally to the competitive relations among these spheres of activity and setting priorities for allocating resources in a way that will enhance the institution's overall competitive position, or at the very least enable it to occupy a viable niche vis-à-vis its peers. Traditionally, such management is practiced with sufficient transparency to allow the competition among the numerous internal constituencies to be overt and thus to fuel friction between the administration and its many suitors, both academic and non-academic.

By no means does the market, with its daunting set of competitive pressures, marginalize the importance of academic programs. Rather, it recognizes their importance for key "stakeholders" (students, parents, and alumni as well as faculty and staff). The pressures that it exerts on academic leaders, however, favor almost automatically what the potential sources of revenue appear to demand or at least, when peer practices are taken into account, allow. For administrators, these strains that emanate from the external constituencies appear rather more to be ongoing conditions than solvable problems. Consider a typical set of stresses and trade-offs faced by classic four-year colleges and universities: tension between support for research and support for teaching, between financial aid for students and faculty salaries, between merit and need-blind financial aid, between the benefits of holding tuition down and letting it shoot up, between program support and capital projects, between investments in athletics and favoring nonathletic extracurricular activities, between protecting the liberal arts and building programs in business, between hiring regular faculty and hiring contingent faculty, between imposing measures of learning outcomes and resisting them, between promoting experiments with new instructional platforms or technologies and letting peer institutions be the first adopters, between prioritizing support for apparent educational strengths and holding to a quality-across-the-board commitment, between restraining the search for external research support and allowing it free rein, between raising restricted and unrestricted gifts from alumni, between recruiting senior stars and imposing junior hires, and so forth.

However one constructs the package of conundrums, the administrative response is sure to factor in the institution's position in one or more zones of the academic marketplace and the effects of decisions at hand on revenue generation and resource allocation. For better or for worse, from the standpoint of the system as it operates, it is in this context, not in the rarefied domain in which higher education's social and moral responsibilities are at issue, that thinking about models for disciplines has to begin.

Questions for the Humanities

In light of the stories about the system's development recounted above, representatives of the humanities in a typical institution of higher learning would appear to have cause to be discouraged about their capacity to negotiate for more resources or more favorable program status. The evolution of each of the four headings we have examined does, in effect, raise questions for the humanities themselves to address:

- Fully developed programs in the humanities appear to be concentrated in the tier of universities that offer PhDs in humanities fields and perhaps the top fifty liberal arts colleges. What should humanities programs look like in institutions below this level? Given the history of increasing stratification in the institutional hierarchy of higher education, for what educational goals should the humanities stand? Should the humanities explicitly support efforts to resist this stratification and reduce institutional inequality?

- The decline of the humanities in recent decades coincides with the rise of vocationally oriented fields, such as the health sciences, that benefit from students' preoccupation with future earnings. Can the humanities regain energy by demonstrating the need for what they study and stand for in the vocational/professional fields? Just what can they contribute to the curricula of institutions that emphasize preparing for gainful employment?

- The substantive development of humanities fields or disciplines does not appear to be neatly comparable from field to field (history, literature, and philosophy would have distinct narratives), although all fields have arrived at a high degree of specialization that sometimes gives advanced research and writing an esoteric, inaccessible quality and that often lacks compelling interest for many undergraduate students. Does the problematics of advanced work in the humanities need to shift away from hyper-specialization and toward more engagement with broad historical and social questions? If it does, how could this be achieved?

- The reshaping of the professoriate by the influx of non-tenure-track faculty is especially pronounced in humanities fields such as English, where adjuncts who specialize in teaching composition and introductory literature courses abound, and foreign languages, where language-teaching specialists are in demand but the appetite for literature and culture courses has declined. Should such fields take this to be a fait accompli and rethink their advanced programs accordingly? Should the humanities advocate in favor of the proposal by Bowen and McPherson to develop a faculty corps of teaching specialists whose career trajectory would differ from that of research-oriented faculty?

- Liberal education and courses of study labeled "liberal arts" have occupied a somewhat marginal, defensive position since the beginning of the twentieth century when the advance of ever more specialized, discipline-focused research took over the development of curricula in higher education. The humanities have been the principal guardian of liberal education, and even under the pressure of globalization and the digitalized economy of knowledge they are still able to make a cogent case for it. Should liberal education, including a continuing commitment to cultural breadth and interdisciplinary inquiry, be the cause around which the humanities seek to reassert themselves?

- The humanities that are favored to at least some extent by the marketized system of higher education elicit a so-called instrumental justification, that is, they are useful tools needed for satisfying self-expression and effective communication but will rarely have the kind of market value that matters in an economy that equates success with earning power and wealth. Is there an approach to higher education for large numbers of students that can elevate the value of inquiry in the humanities? How might the existing humanities contribute to a renewed understanding of higher education as a public good?

- To date, the critique of academic capitalism has developed largely in the field of education and in the social sciences, and its focus has been on research in the STEM fields where opportunities for commercializing new knowledge appear to be concentrated. Yet the humanities fields are no less complicitous in the systemic hold on higher education that academic capitalism exercises than all the other fields. Given their scholarly concerns with historical and philosophical issues that pertain to human relations and social organization, they must ask whether they have a special responsibility to study higher education's entrenchment in the contemporary knowledge economy, articulate its implications, and stimulate debate about possible reforms. Is such a critical posture the outlook the humanities should adopt in pursuing productive relations with the sciences and social sciences?

CHAPTER 2

Paradigms for the Public Humanities?

This chapter moves between two dimensions, one conceptual and the other programmatic. Conceptually, it attempts to dissect the key terms of my interrogative title, *paradigm*, *public*, and *humanities*. Programmatically, it provides an account of issues and approaches connected to the *public humanities* project that preoccupied me during my last two years at the Andrew W. Mellon Foundation. The bridge between these two dimensions is an essentially practical question about philanthropic practice: Why and how should a private foundation devoted to the arts and humanities support the public humanities? What objectives are realistic? To what extent can we rationalize public humanities grants when we can't really predict their effects or claim that they will have "impact"? I shall return to this concern and try to refine these panoptic questions in my conclusion. Initially, I shall focus on the three heavily loaded terms in my interrogative title: paradigm, humanities, public. In commenting on each one, I aim to delineate an overarching rationale for my attempt to define the public humanities.

Paradigm is, of course, a term with a history.[1] It was propelled into prominence in the 1960s by Thomas Kuhn's *Structure of Scientific Revolutions*, which disputed—or at least complicated—the idea that science advanced in a linear progression that was incremental and cumulative by describing paradigm shifts: decisive, thoroughgoing displacements of one framework of understanding by another. The idea carried over into diverse disciplines or fields in which the paradigm was taken to be a kind of conceptual and procedural funnel, a structure or superstructure of intelligibility on which research and theory in a given area depend for their coherence and sense of direction.

Obviously enough, overlaying the paradigmatic onto a horizon as broad, amorphous, and, some would say, elusive as the humanities, which I generally take to include the arts and ethnographically oriented social sciences, is a questionable move. Just as obviously, if it were possible to make that move, if we could constitute a paradigmatic dimension or topological grid that would serve as a frame of reference presiding over propositions about the humanities or particular strains of the humanities, the heuristic value of the exercise could be considerable. If, for example, the humanities were experiencing something on the order of an identity crisis, an uncertainty about what values and forms of knowledge belong to the humanities and concomitantly what belongs to the social sciences, reference to a paradigm could help solve the problem; it could identify the humanities with a stable set of cognitive and evaluative practices and priorities.

Now, does this not really amount to gesturing toward the framework of a discipline, as the title of an essay by Geoffrey Harpham, "Finding Ourselves: The Humanities as a Discipline" (2013), might seem to suggest? Initially I would have to say that it does, but only partially. One of the key, long-term projects pursued in the world of interdisciplinary centers in recent decades has taken the academic disciplines—their history, their structure, their operations, their objectives—as its focus. The conception of the discipline—whether that of the humanities vis-à-vis the social sciences and the natural sciences, or of the various disciplines within the humanities (such as history, philosophy, literary studies, classics, and so on)—does generally include an account of research paradigms that focuses on the delineation of objects, scholarly practices, and assumptions about verification or validation. It is not limited to this type of cognitive or epistemic framing, however, because the disciplines are simultaneously understood to be institutional formations that include arrangements for distributing resources and responsibilities, designing curricula, educating specialists, managing accumulated knowledge, and constituting professions.

So, the paradigm, however inclusive, can be regarded as a more narrowly methodological construct than the discipline. Indeed, Harpham demonstrates this abundantly in his essay, which emphasizes the openness of the humanities to the extraneous, their resistances to disciplinarity, their "amateurism," their entrenchment in subjectivity, and their pursuit, by means of liberal education, of an elusive and unstable wisdom. Over against this turbulence—a specter of indiscipline that hovers over the discipline—exploring the possibility of constructing a paradigm, however daunting, is presumably a more limited, less retorsionary project than that of reckoning with disciplinarity.

The less ambitious alternative to such a paradigm would be a taxonomy of the kind that is developed in a remarkable book, *The Value of the Humanities* (2013), by Helen Small. I propose to draw on this book in order to situate the idea of the humanities in relation to the author's interest in public advocacy for the humanities, and then to draw on another book, *The Humanities and Public Life* (2014), which collects the contributions to a symposium organized by its editor, Peter Brooks, in an effort to position the term *public* vis-à-vis the edifice of higher education and prepare us to ask whether a paradigm for the public humanities might be thinkable, or whether constructing a taxonomy is the best we can do.

In *The Value of the Humanities*, Small undertakes to improve the way scholars in the academic world make the case for the humanities when "facing outwards to the general public" (2013, 2) and arguing for the value of work in the humanities both for the individual and for society. Her basic thesis is that the definition of the humanities inevitably involves a complex representation of multiple approaches and activities and thus that support for the humanities has to be pluralistic. No single, overarching claim, she asserts, can defend the humanities adequately against all the attacks and complaints heaped on them, but a well-crafted account of the diverse contributions of the humanities to the public good, while composed of multiple arguments, can be coherent and persuasive. In presenting this set of complementary defenses, Small does make use of an abstract definition of the humanities that is worthy of reflection and comment: "The humanities study the meaning-making practices of human culture, past and present, focusing on interpretation and critical evaluation, primarily in terms of the individual response and with an ineliminable element of subjectivity" (23).

This proposition makes an interesting contrast with what I take to be the standard definition or description or approximation, which consists in listing a series of fields that the humanities include. An apt example of the latter is provided by a re-

markably capacious essay titled "Where the Humanities Live,"
by Edward J. Ayers, which appeared in the 2009 issue of *Daedalus* that bore the less than pointed title "Reflecting on the
Humanities." By tracing the formation and evolution of the humanities in North American colleges and universities and describing their current situation, the essay at once discounts the
idea that they are in crisis and grants that, owing to the roles
they play in academic institutions and to the dynamics of competition in the disciplinary system, they are perpetually in crisis
or at least associated with crisis. Here is the definition of the
humanities that Ayers ventured in his first footnote: "The humanities are generally considered to include English language
and literature, foreign languages and literatures; history; philosophy; religion; ethnic, gender and cultural studies; area and
interdisciplinary studies; archaeology, art history, the history
of music, and the study of drama and cinema" (24). Ayers also
notes that various "soft" social sciences that stress qualitative
rather than quantitative analysis are often associated with the
humanities.

This type of definition by way of institutional or curricular
geography contrasts sharply with the epistemological cast of
Small's definition, which evokes the individual subject studying
"meaning-making practices." At a pivotal point about a third of
the way through her book, as Small concludes her discussion of
claims about the differing outlooks or cultures of scholars in the
humanities, social sciences, and natural sciences, she refines her
definition. She does so in response to pressures, which she takes
to be a constant in learned discourse about education, to relate
the work of the scholar or teacher in the humanities to her or his
attitude or mindset, to character or lifestyle. Following closely
the subtle articulation of the characterological turn elaborated

by Amanda Anderson in *The Way We Argue Now* (2005), Small remarks that a more aggressive or defensive view of the humanities is made possible and necessary when political discourses in countries like the United Kingdom and the United States are hostile to or dismissive of the humanities and when the non-humanities disciplines in the academy press for priority at the expense of the humanities. Here is the substantial paragraph she appends to her single-sentence definition:

> In the main the humanities value qualitative above quantitative reasoning; they place greater faith in interpretative than in positivistic thinking; unlike the sciences and the scientific wing of the social sciences, they do not have a dominant methodology and many of their truth claims are not verifiable as those of the natural sciences are verifiable; they tend, accordingly, to distrust proceduralism and to value independence of thought. They are orientated as much toward historical analysis as toward synchronic structural analysis, and as much toward the medium of expression as towards its content (tending to see the form/content distinction as itself problematic). They attend to the role of the perceiver in ascertaining even the most philosophically secure of knowledge claims; and they have an interest, often they also take pleasure, in the specificity of the object of study and the specificity of the individual response (its content and its style) over and above the generalized or collective response. Not least, they respect the products of past human endeavours in culture, even when superseded. (57)

In this deftly composed characterological supplement, we encounter a proliferation, here of comparisons and contrasts, there of allusions to tendencies and attitudes, that constitutes simultaneously a register of assertion and one of caution, if not of indecision. Two of its assertive features deserve to be underscored. First, it continues to emphasize approaches to the constitution, interpretation, and evaluation of knowledge even as it opens up space for a variety of methodologies and objects of inquiry, a range of truth claims, and persistent attention to individual experience. Second, the claims it adds about habits of mind and intellectual priorities are consistent with Small's thesis that a defense of the humanities in their breadth and variety has to be pluralistic: their multiple approaches, interests, and cognitive claims cannot not have multiple functions and values in multiple contexts. To appreciate their value adequately one thus needs to examine the main arguments, assess them one by one, ask whether or how they relate to one another, and position them in relation to the public interest or to public goods. This is what Small does by constructing a taxonomy of the claims made by the defenders of the humanities and then returning to the problem of linking epistemology to characterology, of correlating intellectual formation with an "ethical mode of living in the world" (55).

I do not propose to delve into the dense elaboration of five claims about the value of the humanities that Small sets forth with consummate skill and acuity in her book. It will not be unduly reductive simply to qualify lapidarily the five arguments, which are for the most part familiar:

1. The argument for a distinctive form of understanding that attends to human subjectivity and creativity, which is reinforced by the cautious articulation of the intellectual posture I have just outlined with modes of living— ethical or political—in the real world.
2. The instrumental argument, which claims that human-

ities are useful to society and make significant, measurable contributions to the economy (especially the contemporary economies of knowledge, culture, and education).

3. The life enrichment or epicurean argument, which links the benefits of education in the humanities to individual and collective quality of life, to gratifications such as those encountered in complex thinking or esthetic insight.

4. The public benefits argument, or to use Small's phrase, the "democracy needs us" argument, which stresses the role of the humanities in bringing informed and critical perspectives into social and political life and in asserting the priority of public over private goods.

5. Finally, on a different register, the self-justifying or autotelic argument according to which the humanities matter, not because of their effects or benefits, but for their own sake, for their commitment to knowledge as an end in itself, as its own reward, as a good that is neither intrinsic nor subjective, but an objectively grounded common good for humanity.

Now, what is perhaps most intriguing about this taxonomy of arguments or values is that it presents no cross-cutting thread or unifying principle. Rather, in her conclusion, titled "On Public Value," Small recognizes that the taxonomy of five arguments is marked by the incommensurability of the five values she delineates. She also insists repeatedly that in none of the five cases can she subscribe to a heavy-duty, unequivocal assertion of the argument; rather, in each case she holds to a carefully modulated, prudent version of the argument that recognizes the limits of its validity. One has to assert all the values and draw on all the arguments because none is sufficient by itself; the defense of the humanities relies on the complementarity of their diverse and divergent approaches.

Such realism, Small acknowledges, makes for constraints when one advocates for the *public value* of the humanities. All the arguments are worthy in certain circumstances, yet even when asserted together, in combination, they cannot override the priority of the most basic human and social needs. Civil and civic rights grounded in rational thinking about social justice are important, but they do not trump the needs for clean air and water, food, shelter, and medical care.

The various specifiable public goods that correlate with the values of the humanities are caught up inextricably in a competition with other public goods and abstract values to which they are not readily comparable. A firmly grounded formulaic approach to deciding what values should take priority under complex and changing conditions is beyond our reach. The conundrum calls for negotiation, for an appropriation of the critical, historical, philosophical, experienced-based reasoning that resides in the humanities. The ultimate argument is thus that above all else the contribution of the humanities to the public good derives from their thoughtful and historically mature ways of thinking about the relations between private experience on the one hand and public institutions and policies on the other. Surely there ought to be a place for such capacities in dialogue about public goods and public policy.

The thrust of Small's taxonomy is clearly to deny the possibility of a paradigm for the humanities at large and thus to suggest that the only possibility for constructing one for the public humanities will depend on the import of the term *public*. Before turning to its acceptations in *The Humanities and Public Life*, I should like to take note of a strategy for portraying the public humanities that, in redeploying Small's account of the humanities, I tend to set aside, although not at all to dismiss. It is aligned with the institutional definition of the humanities and will allow me to orient my account of the public humanities around an activity the higher education program at the Mellon Foundation has supported.

The strategy is ably enacted in a 2009 essay by Kathleen Woodward in same issue of *Daedalus* that contains the piece by Edward Ayers mentioned earlier; its approach resembles that of Ayers in that it charts a landscape of institutional activity. The institutions in question are university humanities centers that bring together diverse fields and perspectives. In recent years the centers have come to aim not only to sponsor interdisciplinary activity internal to the university but also to open up the communities they constitute to interactions with individuals and communities external to the university.

There are at least three models of engagement with the extramural publics that thus come into play: community-based projects of research, dialogue, and social activism; presentation of knowledge through publications or events designed to interest non-academic groups; and provision of opportunities for intellectuals to advocate for their positions on issues of public policy. As Woodward observes, these strains of public outreach can be reinforced by an alliance with the so-called digital humanities in two obvious ways: by enabling online interactions with work carried on in the humanities centers, and by involving unlimited numbers of participants located outside the university in the kinds of collaborative scholarship that typify the digital humanities.

When the Mellon Foundation restored its practice of making grants to humanities centers in 2010 after having allowed it to lapse for a few years, it did so with an explicit shift of emphasis—away from bolstering interdisciplinary programs inside particular university settings and toward a new project with two axes: first, promoting the public humanities defined in accord with Woodward's description, and second, supporting a compatible extra-institutional endeavor, the collaborative networking of humanities centers committed to working on major problems of public interest. The rationale for this move in 2010 was that it would mobilize the centers in a combat against ivory-tower insularity, increase the pressure on interdisciplinary scholarship to make its insights accessible to an educated but not specialized public, and perhaps allow university administrations to glimpse the capacity of the humanities to represent higher education in the world at large. While the quick and strong receptiveness to this move by the humanities centers that stood to benefit from it was gratifying, the long-term concern it put into play is of another order.

For the question now before us bears on a rather more critical reflection on the idea of the public, as it relates to the public sphere, the public good, public interest, public opinion, and the role of the humanities in defining and shaping them. Is the public for the public humanities all-encompassing? Is it the world at large, whatever is outside, whatever does not lie in the order or orbit of the private audience for the humanities within the academy? Or does the public of public humanities merely designate an object of inquiry, the public dimension, as the literary of literary criticism designates literature or the environmental of environmental humanities or environmental studies designates the environment? Does it simply position the public order as a crucial object of inquiry not simply for political science or political history, but for the full range of scholarship in the humanities at large?

In *The Humanities and Public Life*, the keynote essay by Judith Butler moves into its final and most compelling segment with the following assertion: "In thinking about the humanities and the public sphere, we need to move beyond the idea of the public intellectual and to a broader reflection on the humanities in the public sphere" (2014, 28)—which is to say that the public is the former, an extra-academic order, a field of real-world engagement rather than merely an object of inquiry; it is thus to say that the question is how the humanities as a sphere of inquiry and body of knowledge can intervene out there in the world at large.

It may seem ironic that one of the few scholars who is able to wear the mantle of a public intellectual and represent the humanities polemically makes this point, but it is an apt introduction of her line of argument. The public sphere described in the early work of Jürgen Habermas was an open place for dialogue among bourgeois intellectuals in which heroic interventions by leading thinkers could animate influential political discourse. But that erstwhile public sphere became a counterpoint to which Habermas would contrast the media-shaped, state-dominated public order of the modern era.[2] Clearly that eighteenth-century public sphere is far removed from the massive and chaotic communicative spaces the world of higher education has to reckon with today. The broader reflection Butler calls for is one that confers on the university or higher education, on the community of scholars rather than the public intellectual, the responsibility for thinking through the status of the public good and the dialectics of private and public interest.

Butler takes the essential activity of the humanities to be the exercise of critical judgment and claims that the exercise of such judgment in the practice of citizenship "establishes an important link between the humanities and public life" (2014, 30). The main focus of her reflection is the instrumental argument for the value of the humanities. She alludes, in particular, to the opinion expressed by Geoffrey Harpham, which is largely of a piece with that of Helen Small, that the academy has to make some accommodation with instrumentality as a measure of value even though the infamous metrics of evaluation are often grossly inadequate and have to be correctively supplemented by other viewpoints.[3]

Butler's worry is that complying with that evaluative system, however cautiously and conditionally, might entail forfeiting the task of thinking critically about values and schemes of evaluation. She asks whether our defenses of the humanities may in fact compromise them by going along too far with a variety of instrumental justifications or value judgments shaped by peripheral metrics that fail to capture central objectives or results. Such complicity risks taking us inside the system or the discourse that would, in matters of public policy, relegate critical judgment from the standpoint of the humanities to a minor role, if not to oblivion. Her question, in sum, is how critical judgment—how questioning the value of values—can be reinvigorated in the face of a dominant public discourse that marginalizes it while asserting the primacy of hard data, quantifiable outcomes, and discrete deliverables.

Here I should doubtless note parenthetically that Butler's concern is relevant to a project I supported vigorously during my time at the Mellon Foundation, the Humanities Indicators, a website maintained by the American Academy of Arts and Sciences that collects, cleans, and presents skillfully whatever data it can obtain from serious sources for the purpose of informing the public about the current state of the humanities. It is a form of compromise, akin to those defended by Small and Harpham, that the foundation deems valuable, helpful to the cause of the humanities in the sphere of public life, which the site helps us define. But as the "humanities report card" issued by the academy in 2013 on the basis of the indicators showed, it can result in a reductive view of the humanities that borders on caricature.

The book Butler's essay kicks off proposes to respond to the question about the link between the humanities and public life by exploring the possibility of an ethics of reading, a concern that Peter Brooks has often highlighted in his teaching and writing. In his introduction to *The Humanities and Public Life*, Brooks situates disciplined reading at the very core of the humanities and argues that a serious, responsible practice of reading is in effect an ethical act, an experience of scrupulous attention, respectful dialogue, and good faith that entails an appreciation of otherness, a fidelity to other voices, to what the text means on its own terms (2014b, 11). Can one extrapolate from this core experience of intellectual honesty to an ethics that humanities training and knowledge can foster in the public realm? The question is taken up, sometimes directly and more often tangentially, in the book's other essays and in the discussants' comments. Multifaceted skepticism is the note most often sounded. In an eloquent essay titled "On Humanities and Human Rights" (2014), Paul Kahn offers a particularly salient articulation of that skepticism. Let me cite just one exemplary paragraph that conveys the thrust of his reservations:

> The problem is not that the study of texts in the humanities ignores values of recognition and dignity. Rather, there is no

single message in these texts. Great works are, almost by definition, morally complex. At the center of the Western imagination
is not just the peaceable kingdom of love, but the act of sacrifice
for the sake of love. Inclusion is never without boundaries, and
thus it is unavoidably tied to exclusion. Violence is as much an act
of meaning creation as lawmaking is. Contemporary aesthetic
productions frequently take up the question of what we will give
for love. When we read violence as sacrifice, we begin to approach
the complex character of the modern, political imaginary. (119)

The complications of reading are doubtless the main source
of the skepticism about an ethics of reading that permeates *The
Humanities and Public Life*. The humanities pursued in their density, depth, and complexity produce interpretations of texts and
behaviors that grapple with changing historical contexts, ex-
pressive ambiguity, and intractable personal and political dilemmas. Resistances to their values and insights are as inevitable as
the search for simple truths; they underlie the doubts of scholars who ask whether an ethics of reading would suffice to deal
with them.

So just where does Butler's admonition to broaden the reflection on the humanities in the public sphere leave us? The essays
and discussion in *The Humanities and Public Life* do tell us something about the public that humanities scholars of a certain generation have in mind, even though there is little agreement about
the kinds of relationships they ought to have with it or how
they might be forged. Clearly the public in question is a public
deemed to be in need of enlightenment, and the questions about
the value of scholarly pursuits for that public have to do not
only with the various benefits an educated public may derive
from research in the humanities but also with the kinds of work

in the humanities that we can usefully take out into a broader public domain and promote as essential practices in and for public life.

For answers to these questions, it makes sense to look not only at a landscape that sometimes seems hostile to the humanities (or at least hostile to humanities that cannot be linked to measurable effects such as gainful employment) but at the public humanities as they are actually developing in the academy and, to use a phrase that Michael Holquist deployed as his presidential theme for the 2008 Modern Language Association convention, are being put to "work in the world." When we make this move and consider what programs in the public humanities do, ask into what kinds of study and dialogue they aim to draw the citizenry at large, I think we can construct something of a rudimentary paradigm for the public humanities, albeit one that for now, while thematically coherent, is not susceptible to a strongly epistemological characterization.

Given this still-emergent status of the public humanities, I would contend that in their current phase they are, like the digital humanities, a movement, yet one that differs significantly from the digital humanities to the extent that the latter have pursued a more concerted effort to constitute themselves as a scholarly field or subfield and are more engaged with the discourses of theory and method and with the development of analytic techniques that have a scientific bent. The difference is even more pronounced vis-à-vis the environmental humanities,[4] an institutionally well-established constellation of vibrant interdisciplinary programs in a great many colleges and universities around the world. While the concerns about nature, culture, justice, and value characteristic of the environmental humanities obviously intersect with those of the environmentalist movement and its diverse interests in public policy, the movement's immersion in the multifaceted study of the environment, anchored in subfields such as environmental history, environmental philosophy, and ecocriticism, situate it on a horizon far more fully elaborated and research focused than that of the relatively nascent, necessarily much broader yet at present more diffuse public humanities that I am undertaking to define anticipatorily.

I shall suggest, in chapter 4, that public humanities and environmental humanities are behooved to recognize climate change—both the study of it and action to thwart it—as a crucial priority, as a crucial factor that will often bring them to make common cause. If they are destined to remain distinct movements, it is because the traditional agenda of environmental appreciation and protection incorporates neither the commitment to democracy and equal educational opportunity that distinguishes the public mission of the university nor the breadth of sociopolitical and cultural concern that I shall ascribe to the public humanities in the schematic account that follows.[5]

Among the vectors or premises I would include in the construction of a paradigm or, perhaps better, a problematics for the public humanities of the future are the following seven observations about what they can or should do:

1. They attend to a horizon of *public scholarship*, already well illustrated by the subfields of public history and philosophy, that makes a strong assumption about the role scholarship can play in understanding and promoting the public interest.

2. They resist the model of the solitary scholar writing for a professional audience of specialists and support a *collaborative model of research, teaching, learning, and*

creative activity that has the capacity to draw a non-academic public into dialogue with academics.

3. Whether the emphasis falls on individual or collective experience, they are *content oriented* because the choice of objects of inquiry is driven by concepts such as *public interest, public good, public perception, public issues, public policy,* and *public decision-making.*

4. The horizon of public interest and societal well-being fuels a consensus about the importance of studying collectively and from multiple perspectives what we commonly term the *grand social, political, and environmental challenges,* such as poverty, inequality, energy, pollution, climate change, health care, population growth, the knowledge explosion, and so forth—vast and complex problems that make it necessary for the humanities to collaborate with the social and natural sciences and pursue the kind of *interdisciplinary* understanding and problem-solving in which humanities fields play a crucial role of translation and communication for the public at large.

5. Since this broad interdisciplinary horizon of grand-challenge questions implies a global public and a transnational concept of public interest, the public humanities clearly need to be *international in scope,* and as they evolve, they will have to craft a language and an organizational structure that extend across linguistic and cultural divides.

6. If the public humanities are democratic, as the idea of opening up an increasingly privatized university to the public suggests, it is because in civic society they ascribe to the key fields of history, literature, and philosophy a

responsibility for shaping what we can loosely term *public discourse or vision, a sociopolitical imaginary*, and they ask how that responsibility can be enacted in a world that has been reordered by digital technology, by the global economy, and by multidisciplinary recognition of the Anthropocene, the geological epoch in which human activity has become a decisive influence on planetary ecosystems.

7. While the public humanities acknowledge the fundamental importance of reading texts critically for intellectual life and for constructive dialogue about the uses of knowledge, they situate both the public and the humanities in a *world of objects, media, and emotive or sensual experience* that is not always subject to textualization and critical reading, a world that calls for creative work and artful response for which language is only one of the vehicles.

This set of guidelines for engaging in the public humanities defines them as a project of collaborative public scholarship with a necessarily interdisciplinary and international research program and a socially constructive agenda. We could argue over whether such a schematic account could be refined into a paradigmatic structure or whether it is merely a taxonomy of current activities that falls short of providing a framework for homogeneous scholarly endeavors. We can probably agree, however, that the academic status of the scheme deserves less attention than the questions Judith Butler's critique of instrumentality generates and those that Helen Small's account of the characterological turn projects back on that critique.

Do we find or can we elaborate an important place within the public humanities for the practice of critical judgment and for countering demands from institutional and economic quarters for demonstration of their instrumental value? Are the public humanities unduly complicitous with ideological and axiological pressures with which, to put it in an overly glib but understandable shorthand, the global system of neocapitalism confronts them? And do the public humanities incorporate a principled basis for what I shall call here, again in shorthand that is too facile, the turn toward ethics or altruism that Small envisages for the humanities at large?

These are, I submit, important questions that that intellectuals from all areas (not just from the humanities) can usefully discuss and to which the public humanities, in order to thrive, will have to devote some long-term self-critical work. The public humanities also face somewhat less theoretical, more conjunctural questions that beckon toward support that will have to come from philanthropic sources external to the institutions that harbor them. If support for developing them seems unlikely to come in a vigorous and timely fashion from either public or private universities, it is because both are too dependent on the system of interests and values that threatens the humanities at large to risk committing significant resources of their own to the effort. For the administrative leaders of both public and private research universities, who deal with a constituency committed at least to higher education and often to liberal education, the evident imperative is by no means to degrade or suppress the humanities. It is rather to forge a compromise, protective of the university on all fronts, that keeps the humanities in a safe place, that accords them the status and the platform they need in order to exercise guarded critical judgment and to carry out their instrumental function, which we might call literacy and cultural competency training. The compromise does not, however, allow the humanities to assert moral or institutional authority over decisions about priorities or resource allocation—decisions in which, one could plausibly argue, their historical and analytical judgment, thanks to its breadth of vision and its minimal entrenchment in conflict of interest, should be primary. At the same time, the compromise does keep a damper on any temptation the university might experience either to educate the public in the fundamental or transcendental value of the humanities or to mobilize the humanities strongly in their outreach to the public. Overwhelmingly, owing to the institution's perceived interest, that outreach emphasizes natural and social scientific research and the economic benefits of that research.

A coherent case for supporting the public humanities emerged in the work of the National Commission on the Humanities and Social Sciences, organized by the American Academy of Arts and Sciences and funded by the Mellon Foundation. The commission issued a masterfully written report called *The Heart of the Matter* (2013).[6] The report makes the kind of compromise with instrumentalism that Helen Small and Geoffrey Harpham are ready to tolerate and that Judith Butler resists. It builds the compromise around appeals to national security and to the need for a competitive edge in the global economy that thoughtful observers at various points on the American political spectrum would doubtless wish to challenge. It also brings into focus the failure of American education at all levels to sustain a bonding narrative of American history and culture to which a broad cross-section of informed citizens must subscribe if our democracy is to work well.

One question it thus raises for the public humanities is what the movement can contribute to the reinvention of a public narrative or discourse, a constructively critical activity of art and science that my generation was prone to regard as an essential and renewable product of the humanities: it was a social body's story, at once enduring and evolving, about a revolutionary experiment in democracy that shapes its public and political mind, making for a bipartisan solidarity that our recent descent into polarization belies. Have we, in the academic humanities, deprived ourselves of the very possibility of sustaining that critically creative narrative function? If not, if we have distanced ourselves from what was once a polity-forming national story without allowing it to disappear from memory, what could—or perhaps should—we be advocating in order to give the humanities an opportunity to reinvent and stand for it?

The idea of a national narrative that makes for social cohesion, for a collective sense of inclusion or belonging, for a common political discourse, is one that my own scholarly experience as a citizen of my country of birth and as a student of the society and culture of France has repeatedly put forward and into question. In the mid-twentieth-century United States, we unquestionably had a widely proclaimed "save the world for democracy" narrative, tied to our role in World Wars I and II and in the Cold War, briefly embellished in the 1960s by an unrealized vision of the Great Society. That narrative seemed to unravel during and after the Vietnam War. In twentieth-century France, a traditional narrative treating the assimilation of French identity by every citizen as a responsibility of the educational system seemed to contribute to the solidarity required for maintaining a viable welfare state until well after the Algerian War; however, it, too, has fallen into disarray in recent decades. In both cases, one has to ask whether the issue at this juncture is not how best to account for the earlier narrative's dissolution or demystification rather than how to reconstitute a unifying view of the national identity or purpose.

The task of the humanities in general, both Butler and Small would acknowledge, is to tell the truth about what has happened in plain, accessible language and then to analyze cogently the very conditions that make the work of imagining a renewed national narrative exceedingly difficult, if not impossible. Is it nonetheless thinkable that the *public* humanities, via their specific project, could move beyond the analysis of those conditions toward the invention of another discourse, collective but not necessarily national, and narrative but not necessarily traditional, pointedly forward looking, critical but also creative? And if such an aspirational public discourse is thinkable, inventable, by what principle—by what vision of the future or by what public imperative—would it be animated?

These all too familiar current conditions that have to be understood critically are of course what *The Heart of the Matter*, like the Office of Science and Technology of the Obama White House and countless other authoritative sources, have designated as the grand challenges of the twenty-first century; they are the very problems I take to be the intellectual impetus at the core of the public humanities. *The Heart of the Matter* carefully points to global examples of these challenges: "the provision of clean air and water, food, health, energy, universal education, human rights and the assurance of physical safety."[7]

Were we to insist on calling out the rather less abstract challenges confronting our own society, we would doubtless add equal opportunity, educational achievement, and social mobility since these appear to have waned in recent decades; and we could add the exorbitant gap between haves and have-nots, the unsustainable consumption of the planet's natural resources, and perhaps above all the massive scale of the solutions to all these enormous national and global problems. Our perceived inability to carry out the solutions we can devise becomes paralyzing; it contributes here to political gridlock and there to visions of planetary catastrophe; it is hardly the stuff of an uplifting narrative at this juncture, and yet it is clear that we will not overcome the impasse unless we make it the stuff of concerted public dialogue.

The authors of *The Heart of the Matter* understood this. It is not hard to distill from their report an implicit national narrative of future renewal that could be constructed as a process of recognition: a consensus would form around the benefits of liberal education, the value of cultural institutions, the importance of responsible citizenship, and the contributions of the humanities and social sciences to our competitive strength in the global marketplace.

Such a potential narrative would be remarkably compatible with the "national strategic narrative" advanced by two military strategists, Mark Mykleby and Wayne Porter, who argued against a vision of American hegemony in a closed system of power relations and for a position of credible influence in an open global system.[8] According to Mykleby and Porter, the national interest should be defined less as a regime of military defense and protective security and more as a regime of cooperation-based prosperity in a knowledge economy. In such a regime, marked by investment in education, the narrative of an imagined present-to-future trajectory accords a key role to the humanities and social sciences. The highly regarded political scientist who prefaced the essay by Mykleby and Porter, Anne-Marie Slaughter, summed up the proposal in this single sentence: "The strategic narrative of the United States in the 21st century is **that we want to become the strongest competitor and most influential player in a deeply inter-connected global system, which requires that we invest less in defense and more in sustainable prosperity and the tools of effective global engagement"** (3; bold type in the original).

Here one has to cringe, since the nationalist and neocapitalist overtones remain so forceful in this proposition. Yet the question is clear: it is indeed what story we wish to be able to tell about ourselves, and Slaughter's projection of a patriotically reassuring tale about the strongest competitor and most influential player, when nuanced by the very complex set of interests and investments prescribed by Mykleby and Porter, is largely of a piece with the savvy perspective adopted and the recommendations advanced in *The Heart of the Matter*. Both rearticulate our national interest capaciously and for the better while appropriating the instrumental value of the humanities. But is that implicit narrative, which derives from a realistic consensus outlook that can seem reasonable and plausible to an enlightened public, a story to which the public humanities can also be expected to subscribe?

To this final question a confident conclusion is doubtless not in order, but a hypothesis based on the work now under way in public humanities projects on the grand-challenge questions can be ventured. In my account of the problematics, the two premises that follow upon the linkage of public interest to the grand challenges—one underscoring an international trajectory, the other incorporating a critique of the new world order from the standpoint of the Anthropocene—bring into play the exercise of critical judgment that Butler emphasizes. Both move in the direction of confronting the public with questions about the priority of national identity, competitive advantage, and prosperity dependent on economic growth: they ask if these value-defining concepts, which are fundamental to the compromises that make room for the instrumental argument for the humanities, do not have to be contested, contextualized differently. They ask if awareness of the Anthropocene does not compel us to reach for a narrative of humanity in which limits on the concentration of wealth and the consumption of resources will be the central thread of the story, in which a broadened ecocentric conception of public interest—transcendent, as it were—will loosen the hold of self-interest on our thinking about the good life.

My hypothesis is not that the public humanities movement grasps the possibility of supporting the invention of such a story as it takes the work and values of the humanities into real-world communities beyond the walls of the academy. It is rather that the institutions in which the public humanities originate grasp instinctively the veer of the public humanities toward unsettling the compromises that serve both their institutional self-interest and the larger national interest as they are now understood. The fortunate lot of major philanthropies is to be free of the constraints that make for those compromises, free to support an experiment that might give the humanities a greater purchase on public opinion, free indeed to beckon them toward a narrative of humanity that our anthropocenic twenty-first century is destined to need.

CHAPTER 3

Public Humanities and the Privatized Public University

In preparing this chapter shortly after my retirement from the Mellon Foundation in March 2015,[1] I've had occasion to ask myself over and over whether I once had a handle on current issues and discourses in the humanities and simply could not sustain it after I went into academic administration and then into the world of twenty-first-century philanthropy. Since the last decade of the twentieth century, my perspective has devolved into that of a retired scholar/teacher, retired administrator, and retired grant-maker—which is to say that I have considerable distance from the various trends and perturbations within the humanities in the early twenty-first-century University.

My recent experience has been channeled by what was probably the single most interesting effort for which I was responsible at Mellon, where I was actually driven to reflect on the term *public humanities* by a significant intra-institutional change that occurred during my eight years there. Since 2012, all members of the foundation's nine-member board of trustees, save one,[2] were replaced as a result of the mandatory retirement policy that also imposed my own departure in March 2015. The members of that renewed and younger board expressed considerable interest in the connotations of the term *public humanities* as opposed to the relatively loose notion of the humanities with which they were familiar. Initially, at least, that interest—driven by a concern with the impact of the foundation's grant-making in support of the humanities—focused on a less broad and capacious idea of public humanities than the one that has become current in the scholarly world. Inside the academy, the notion is likely to be associated with master's programs like the one at the Center for Public Humanities and Cultural Heritage at Brown or in the Humanities Division at the University of Chicago. Alternatively, it may conjure up books like those published by the University of Iowa Press in its Humanities and Public Life series. For other scholars, it may beckon toward a disciplinary horizon that emerged in the fields of history, philosophy, and American studies during the second half of the twentieth century and be connected to scholarly practices termed public history, public philosophy, public arts, and so forth.

In any case, before Earl Lewis took office as president of the Mellon Foundation in March 2013,[3] some members of the board had begun expressing concerns that beckon pointedly toward so-called impact philanthropy. This approach to grant-making differed from the foundation's predominant strategy for supporting the arts and humanities, which had been to invest in the long-term programmatic work of trusted cultural and educational institutions by encouraging them to seek resources for their basic needs or critical priorities as they themselves perceive them. Impact philanthropists, by way of contrast, deploy metrics and analytics in order first to choose grantees and then to make their own judgments on an organization's needs and capacities and on the kinds of activities they might choose to support. Like venture capitalists or entrepreneurial investors, they seek out projects that will have measurable results in an established time frame, placing a premium on grantee accountability and on the leverage a grant may bring to bear on other donors.

The general question about grants to higher education that arises when this interest in demonstrable impact comes into play has to do with public perception and public policy: have Mellon's grants, for example, been sufficiently visible and concerted to have an effect on current discourse about higher education and on deliberations by state and federal policymakers? The attempt to articulate a view of the public humanities, which in 2015 became one of the four cross-cutting foci delineated by the foundation's strategic plan, was rather more a response to this concern about impact than to any claims about a crisis in the humanities or glaring stresses in the system of higher education. During my last two years at Mellon, which coincided with a protracted exercise in strategic planning, I undertook to elaborate a relatively wide-ranging and multifaceted vision of the public arts and humanities that, while cautiously accommodating the concern with impact, also subjected it to some critical resistance and sought to integrate it into a larger set of commitments to the causes of education and cultural heritage. The immediate purpose of the exercise was to establish a framework for use in our discussions with representatives of cultural and educational institutions about public humanities activity.

The seven premises or guidelines for a schematic account of the public humanities that I formulated in chapter 2 were conceived in the context of grant negotiations I was pursuing with the roughly two dozen campus-based humanities centers we had worked with at Mellon as well as that of conversations with the Consortium of Humanities Centers and Institutes. The background against which I projected those seven premises or vectors was, as I indicated in chapter 2, the set of rationales for defending the humanities, pointing toward a broad Anglo-American horizon, outlined in *The Value of the Humanities* by the British scholar Helen Small (2013).[4] For the purposes of the argument I want to sketch in this chapter, however, I propose to invoke a different, essentially American context for my line on the public humanities. A quick way to do so is to recall the claims advanced in two influential studies, one from the 1970s and the other from the 1990s.

The first of these, Richard Sennett's *The Fall of Public Man* (1974), makes a historical case against the thesis developed by David Riesman in *The Lonely Crowd* (1950). Whereas Riesman saw citizens of the United States caught up in a society evolving toward other-directedness, that is, toward conformity with mainstream or peer-group norms at the expense of personal, inner-directed views and values, Sennett saw essentially the opposite: a society veering away from the public values and collective commitments that are essential to a robust democracy and toward the exaltation of personal identity, self-absorption, and relations of intimacy, toward dealing in terms of subjective, individual experience or self-fulfillment with matters that can only be addressed through impersonal, objective codes of meaning that are social rather than psychological, broadly consensual rather than egocentric. Sennett's book describes the erosion of public life, the emergence of what he calls "dead public space" (1974, 12), the dissipation of the claims of convention, civility, and worldly experience, and a concomitant reinforcement of the claims of family and personality. In sum, he invoked a shift in the balance between public and private life that tended to blur the vital distinctions between them and ultimately to devalue the public, sociopolitical order. An overarching task of the public humanities as I conceive of them is to rearticulate the balance of the public and private in terms that accord to the public—to the common good or collective interest—a certain primacy that has to be rethought collectively in the brave new world we inhabit in the twenty-first century.

The second frame of reference I would like to invoke encompasses a much wider, more diverse, complex, and critical view of the public sphere than that of Richard Sennett. It is delineated in a collection of texts edited and introduced in the early 1990s by Bruce Robbins. The volume titled *The Phantom Public Sphere* (1993) gestures toward Walter Lippmann's *The Phantom Public*, which appeared in 1925, to which John Dewey replied two years later in *The Public and Its Problems* (1927). Lippmann attributed to theories of democracy the presupposition that the public as it is commonly imagined—the body politic or voting citizenry—can act competently to direct public affairs in accord with the will of the people. He dismissed that notion of a competent public as historically naive, insisting that democratic societies were largely made up of weakly interested and marginally informed spectators and that at best public opinion could sometimes, though not consistently, serve as a corrective in moments of political crisis. Hence the claim that by and large the public was an illusion or phantom. This view positions various narratives of the loss of the public sphere or the ascendancy of the private over the public as unrealistic fictions and takes the private as always already dominant.

In the collection of essays gathered and presented by Robbins, the project is not so much to answer Lippmann's conservative critique more convincingly than Dewey did,[5] nor to respond to the latter-day deconstruction of the public/private dichotomy that problematizes the private sphere no less than the public sphere; it is rather to recognize the necessity and multiplicity of the publicities and privacies we have to reckon with and in particular to specify lineaments and components of a public sphere or features of public value that remain socially and economically indispensable. It is a matter, in sum, of moving "away from the universalizing ideal of a single public" (Robbins 1993, xii). The project Robbins envisages would involve attending to the actual "multiplicity of public discourses, public spheres," public opinions and public geographies; it would seek to mobilize concepts of public interest and engagement oriented toward the challenges humanity must confront in an age of mass media and global capitalism.

So, a second overarching task of the public humanities as I conceive of them at this juncture, in an institutional and philanthropic context, is to work with a complex and fluid notion of publicness that requires us to deal with a multiplicity of publics and to relate the issues we confront to particular publics that they concern or call for. From the standpoint of the public university, it is a matter of understanding what its publics are and how the needs and expectations of the various publics will be prioritized, conciliated, and in some cases ignored.[6]

The set of guidelines for positioning the public humanities that I proposed in the course of 2014 delineates the mission of the public humanities movement in terms that situate it very close to the mission of the public university. The guidelines are aimed at an academic public willing to exit from the proverbial ivory tower and to engage with non-academic publics in the world at large. They define the public humanities as a project of collaborative public scholarship with a necessarily interdisciplinary and international research program and a socially constructive agenda. While the immediate purpose of constructing them as a paradigm or, more loosely, as a set of features, was to provide a heuristic framework to which humanities faculty and students can refer in an academic setting, I shall defer comment on its historical and theoretical implications until after an attempt to situate the second member of my title, the privatized public university.

The Privatized Public University

In the fall of 2010, the Mellon Foundation received an invitation to participate in a conference hosted by the Townsend Center at the University of California–Berkeley on "The Remaking of the Public University." This topic resonated for the participants with the title of a very fine book published in 2008, *Unmaking the Public University*, by Christopher Newfield, who was one of the key speakers.[7] Don Randel, who was then president of the Mellon Foundation, dispatched me to represent our interests there, notwithstanding the widely recognized commitment of the foundation to channel most of its grant-making resources for higher education into elite private research universities and private liberal arts colleges. To be sure, the organizers of the conference had noticed that in the wake of the Great Recession of 2008 the officers and trustees of the foundation had become alarmed by the situation in the great public universities of the United States and had substantially increased the proportion of our annual budget that we put into a group of flagship universities in state-supported systems. The group in question was something of an elite in the public sector of higher education. It included University of California–Berkeley and UCLA, Michigan, Wisconsin, Virginia, North Carolina, and a few somewhat less prominent R1 research university peers such as the City University of New York, Rutgers, and the Universities of Illinois and Washington.

At Mellon at that time, in 2010, we had two dominant concerns: the need to preserve academic strengths in the humanities that it would be difficult, if not impossible, to reconstitute and the slippage of top public research universities into a cost structure more and more like that of private higher education, where high tuition and dependency on private donations underpin the dominion of an affluent establishment and make for a quite limited, increasingly fragile commitment to equal opportunity and diversity. In my remarks at that 2010 conference, I felt obliged to underscore what might be regarded as the tokenism of the stopgap measures the foundation was able to consider: more grants for humanities programs in a small number of highly reputed public universities, while they doubtless had some symbolic value, were obviously not commensurable with the huge systemic need that state legislatures generated by cutting their budgets for higher education. Our rationale for doing what little we could—we had actually issued bonds in 2009 in order to maintain our own grant-making budget at 2007–8 levels and avoid reducing our contributions to grantee institutions—was an awkward one since it amounted mainly to signaling a concern rather than dealing strongly with the problem and since we understood full well that making a dozen or so grants to a privileged subset within the public university system could actually exacerbate some of the financial inequities within the research university sector that we hoped to combat.

The discussions that were occurring in 2010 seemed signifi-

cant because, in many quarters, and especially in the philanthropic world and much of the academic world, they reflected
what was experienced as a moment of crisis, a turning point
when the gradual drive toward privatization of the public university was intensified and rendered irreversible. The recent
history that I shall now recall briefly is one that resurfaces over
and over, ad nauseam, in the enormous flood of publications on
US higher education—a perpetual avalanche whose innumerable producers are curiously prone to assume their own originality, the importance of their intervention in the debates about
higher education, the interest of a broad, attentive audience,
the theoretical and practical value of their contribution, and so
forth. Having immersed myself in this vast sea of redundancy
during my time at Mellon and having learned much from it, I am
intent on acknowledging that what I have been able to distill
from it is not—cannot be—original, surprising, or unorthodox.
Yet its familiarity does not make it insignificant or unworthy of
further reflection. For a large professional community, the massive discourse on higher education and the research underlying
it do subtend a set of widely shared insights and judgments that
I take to be a mainstream outlook or ideological construct that
we need to discuss critically.

The part of this picture painted by the higher education literature that concerns us most immediately situates the golden
age of the public university—indeed that of research universities (public and private) in general—in the quarter century after
Sputnik.[8] This golden age of the US system was a period when
state appropriations for higher education were strong, federal
funding of scientific research abetted robust institutional growth,
and expansion of the state university systems made it possible
for the public sector to accommodate the growing student de-

mand for postsecondary education that could not be met by the relatively static private sector. During this period of expansion the distribution of matriculants in public and private institutions went from 50% in the publics and 50% in the privates to 80% in the publics and 20% in the privates.

So, the public university's distinguishing feature was unmistakably its contribution to access, which was of course dependent on its affordability for lower- and middle-class students. According to the mainstream narrative, of which an authoritative short version is presented in the chapter on public research universities in *Knowledge Matters* (Calhoun and Rhoten 2011), the decisive reversal—the sharp swerve into full-fledged privatization—occurred during the 1980s. It began with the passage of the Bayh-Dole Act in 1980 that transferred the intellectual property rights to techniques and inventions produced by federally sponsored research from the government that funded the work to the universities and the researchers who received the funds. The bolstered incentive to pursue technology transfer and collaborations with industry gave an impetus to profitable applied-side research that pushed public universities toward a mission shift. Their commitments both to access and to service to their localities, regions, and states lost ground while income-generating ventures on a national and international horizon were proliferating.

One conception of this mission shift, propounded by the British analyst of higher education Ronald Barnett (2011), positions the research university in its basic, first-order incarnation as an institution in which academic freedom protected the disinterested production of knowledge—especially in the STEM fields—for its own sake. Yet this relatively independent, self-regulating university that understood the knowledge it pursued as a public good eventually became a transformative historical agency. Applications of the technologies it spawned led to the emergence of the "knowledge society" or "knowledge economy" in which the research university itself was an important player competing with other knowledge producers and users for resources and status. It thus evolved into the entrepreneurial university, an institution that values knowledge in terms of its impact and its exchange value in the real world and that reorganizes itself as a dynamic business changing in response to market conditions. The entrepreneurial university, dealing in commodifiable knowledge and purveying education as a product, is now dominant, Barnett claims. By stressing applied rather than basic research, it has backed away from forms of knowledge that are "formal, propositional, disciplinary, universal and public" (444) and advanced what some sociologists of science have termed Mode II knowledge, exemplified by the work of multidisciplinary teams that come together for short periods of time to work on specific problems in the real world.

In the United States, the University that understood itself explicitly as an entrepreneurial organization emerged during the decade of the Reagan presidency that followed on the heels of Bayh-Dole. It was a period of economic stringency when the financially strapped states generally recoiled from the per capita increases to their education budgets that marked the sixties and seventies, allowing the dollars per student allocated to their universities to decline. For the public university, the principal pressures that accompanied this waning of support were, naturally enough, to raise tuition charged to undergraduates and to chase after private donations, whether for building endowments or for covering operating deficits.

Both of these responses, in seeking to compensate for inadequate state support, moved the public research universities closer to the budgetary models and practices of the private sector. Moreover, a number of the differences between public and private research universities had been dissolving for some time since, in competing with the privates for students, faculty, and research funding, the publics were already imitating them, already operating in a higher education market in which the values of the private sphere, derived from the conception of education as a salable commodity, are paramount.

In crucial respects, then, privatization is a function of marketization and the competitive environment that it entails. In the public sphere of higher education, a particularly telling case is the market for places in a flagship state university. Here and on numerous other robust research-1 campuses, the effects of privatization and marketization are especially prominent. In some of the distinguished flagship institutions, the demand for admission has become so heated that out-of-state tuition levels for undergraduates can be set as high as those of elite private institutions. Unsurprisingly, the substantial income that derives from that high-end market position is a major factor in the impressive success that many of the flagships have achieved. On the other hand, in the education budgets of most if not all states, the flow of money required to support the research missions of these top institutions introduces pressures that ramify across the entire public system. The funds made available to lower-tier master's and comprehensive universities and to community colleges are typically held flat or reduced. Whether encouraged or merely permitted to compensate for reduced subsidies from the state, these predominantly undergraduate institutions, for which tuition and fees constitute the main revenue stream, are in turn forced to raise the amounts they charge to students and reduce services that help the students to succeed.

Thus, despite their presumed responsibility for democratizing higher education by opening it to masses of students, the middle- and lower-tier members of the public system have little choice but to acquiesce to cutbacks that dilute the public sector's defining commitment to access. They are caught in a classic pricing squeeze, needing to raise tuition in order to budget for their academic needs, yet also needing to hold it down at more affordable—thus less forbidding—levels that won't deter potential students from attending. At the local level, their problem can be further compounded when states that defund higher education systems retain their role in regulating the prices charged to students. By restricting tuition increases, state governments can and often do force institutions of their university system to make damaging cuts that increase their faculty-to-student ratios and reduce the academic assistance and cultural enrichment they offer their students.

The difficulties occasioned by government-imposed budget cutting coupled with price control underlie a claim articulated insistently by the Australian scholar Rob Watts in *Public Universities, Managerialism, and the Values of Higher Education* (2017). In his view, it is important to recognize that higher education in the United States, the United Kingdom, and Australia is not fully marketized, even though university administrations have come to treat students as paying customers, to commodify the knowledge they produce, to regard high-stakes, multilevel competition as a central preoccupation, and to adopt the language of financial interest and market values in managing and representing their institutions.

For according to Watts, the public system does not really—or not quite—function as a market. In the first place, the dynamics of an open market are impossible since to some degree the public university has remained faithful to academic traditions that resist change in response to external conditions, has held on to the ideas of education and knowledge as values in themselves that cannot be adequately understood in economic terms, and has been insulated from the profit motive that pervades a classic commercial market. In the second place, and perhaps more vitally, state governments, through their annual appropriations and rules propounded by their departments of education, continue to subject public colleges and universities to a great deal of control. They have less freedom than private institutions to set their own prices and priorities in response to market conditions. Even head-to-head competition among institutions trying to attract students from the same pool of potential matriculants doesn't allow the market to do the corrective work that neoliberal theory credits it with doing in the business world. At all levels of the system, the search for advantage is impeded or muted by the practice of groups of competing institutions that carefully track the tuitions of their primary peers. On the basis of perceived self-interest and widely shared commitments to the maintenance of the larger system in which they participate, they proceed to construct annual budgets with a view to keeping their tuition and fee levels in parity.

From Watts's standpoint, one can also perceive the typical not-for-profit residential university's limited capacity for growth as an impedance to full-blown marketization:[9] rivalry with peers cannot focus on increasing market share, but rather has to aim at performing strongly in head-to-head competition for student recruits or for star faculty or for philanthropic support. Thus we have to grant that the business of higher education is a somewhat peculiar operation. It seems unreasonable, however, to deny that the processes of competition, pricing, and developing a variety of income streams situate the public university, no less than ostensibly less constrained private institutions, in a complex market that is readily perceived as such by all of the key constituencies.

The extensive and calamitous effects of privatization on the American system of higher education are studied intensively in an important book by Christopher Newfield, *The Great Mistake: How We Wrecked Public Universities and How We Can Fix Them* (2016a). Newfield's purview in this work is broader and somewhat more historical than that of his *Unmaking the Public University*, in part because he aims to address long-term socioeconomic issues that were brought into sharp relief by the aforementioned financial crisis of 2008. His hefty diagnosis of the American public university's ills—massively documented—dovetails with the review of recent history sketched above on at least five major counts.

1. As Barnett and Watts both assert (along with many others), there has been a mission shift away from claims that education is a public good supportive of important social and cultural values and affording students many worthwhile benefits that are not economic.

2. This shift is concomitant with a veer away from knowledge understood as the product of disinterested research that is valuable in itself and toward the pursuit of knowledge as a commodifiable asset that deserves priority because of its exchange value.

3. An altered funding model transfers much of the cost of

education in the public sector from society to individual students and their families, subjecting these clients of the education business to exorbitantly high tuition levels and creating a huge student debt problem.

4. This transfer of cost subverts the public university's key function of providing access to higher education for a large portion of high school graduates; it thereby dissipates the capacity of the public system to serve the interests of democracy by enabling students of all backgrounds to achieve upward socioeconomic mobility while learning, as participants, to appreciate and take on the ethos of an enlightened university community.

5. The increasingly large and management-oriented leadership of the entrepreneurial university, characterized by Watts as preoccupied with competition, fundraising, performance measurement, and business transactions, has generally gone along with a shift of resources into administration and away from the academic core of teaching and learning.

These components of Newfield's indictment, already very substantial when viewed in combination, are largely consistent with a broad critical consensus that one can derive from the massive literature on higher education that I mentioned earlier. However, at this juncture it is crucial to take note of further insights set forth in *The Great Mistake* that sharpen the distinction between the public and the private university, thereby making Newfield's theses on the public university original and exceptionally telling.

In the first place, I would stress the way Newfield's complex account of privatization incorporates the insights of work on academic capitalism launched by Sheila Slaughter and her collaborators in the 1990s.[10] Newfield locates the shift of costs from public funds to individual students' tuition payments within a larger framework that favors private interests, whether those of affluent students whose families can afford to pay, for-profit external vendors to whom formerly internal functions of an institution are outsourced, wealthy donors whose gifts enable them to influence institutional commitments, corporations that back University researchers so as to make use of faculty, graduate students, and facilities at a discount, or widely diffuse players in the world at large who recognize and value the University's role in a far-reaching political and economic structure, a distributional order that sustains the power and enrichment of a well-educated elite. In this broad context of activities that often seem natural and are largely inconspicuous, privatization realizes a culturally significant promotion of private interest that quietly reframes what it means to be an educated person. In lieu of the broad set of goals articulated by proponents of liberal education, it channels the process of learning toward a preponderantly economic slant that privileges efforts to maximize human capital, understood loosely as the individual's capacity for production, innovation, and enrichment, and ultimately for achieving wealth and status in a hierarchic society.

In the second place, Newfield looks at sponsored research through a lens that sharpens trenchantly the distinction between the public and the private university. Unlike commentators who sympathize with the public university's predicament vis-à-vis a state government it needs to please despite the budgetary austerity that results from legislated budget cuts, he forcefully criticizes state universities for their complicity or submissiveness. They have, he suggests, taught state legislators that they can get away with annual cuts by allowing tuition increases to make up for them. Simultaneously they have failed to explain to representatives of the state why various newly adopted business practices have increased costs rather than efficiency, and why curricula designed to equip students with specialized skills that could be sold to purchasers (including employers) as commodities need to be replaced by customized programs in active or experiential learning that foster the development of research and problem-solving skills and of creativity.

An especially troubling concern stems from the comparison of the ways in which sponsored research costs are handled in public and private universities (Newfield 2016a, 90–113). In both sectors, universities subsidize externally sponsored research with institutional funds since they routinely accept grants that do not cover their full indirect costs. Finance officers build such subsidies into their general budget through the mechanism of cross-subsidization (typically a portion of the tuition income provided by students taking courses in fields where costs generated by sponsored research are low or nil[11] is used to cover losses incurred in STEM fields where the costs associated with sponsored research are high). By this expedient, they effectively deploy resources that might have gone into teaching and learning for the support of expensive research.

As state budget allocations in support of research have declined, public universities have relied more heavily than their private counterparts on the use of their own discretionary funds (notably tuition income) to make up the deficit in indirect cost recovery.[12] As Newfield and others note, private research universities have a significant advantage here not only because they do not have to make up for lost state research funding but also because they are better positioned to call on private donors to support particular projects, to reserve a portion of their endowment income for opportunistic investments, and even to reject outside grants that refuse to cover indirect costs and thus require supplemental monies from the institution's general expense budget.

Thirdly, and perhaps most importantly, Newfield focuses vigorously on the issue of educational attainment, which he depicts, as do Richard Arum and Josipa Roksa (2011), in alarming terms. Newfield's central claim is that wealthy, highly selective colleges and universities have recognized the need, spawned by globalization and the information economy, to adopt new, customized pedagogical practices that ensure subject mastery and provide for the cultivation of creativity and networking skills. Their students, a majority of whom are advantaged by their affluent backgrounds and have internalized the values that make for the perpetuation of a socioeconomic elite, benefit from their institution's investments in education per se and graduate with good prospects for success.

By way of contrast, the vast constituency of students in the public systems come from lower- and middle-income groups. They both lack these advantages and face a battery of socioeconomic obstacles to an effective learning experience. Their educational attainment has declined during the privatization period since the public systems have had to lower their standards and often can deliver little more than a weak credential to those who do manage to graduate rather than drop out. In sum, the disparity between public and private universities—or at least between public university systems and a relatively privileged group of elite liberal arts colleges (not specified) and about twenty universities that Newfield terms the Double Ivies (top privates along with roughly a half dozen flagship publics) (2016a, 123)—underlies a pronounced socioeconomic divide.

That this situation contributes to growing income inequality and intensifies doubts about the twentieth-century vision of public higher education as a force for democracy can hardly be denied. It is therefore a credit to his remarkably deep store of optimism that Newfield ends *The Great Mistake* with a chapter titled "Reconstructing the Public University." His admirably capacious utopian vision of a "recovery cycle" (309–40) is built around a call for paradigm change that he summarizes as follows: "We are now undoing the pieces of the great mistake. The recovery cycle sketches the working principles: a public good vision focused on nonmarket and social educational benefits; zeroed-out private subsidies and their replacement with equitable partnerships; rebuilt public funding that eliminates student debt; elite training on a mass scale for regular students; and the reconstruction of the productivity wage.[13] If you think all this is impossible, you are right—inside the current paradigm. We can't get there from here" (339).

In the final chapter of *A New Deal for the Humanities* (Hutner and Mohamed 2016), titled "What Are the Humanities For? Rebuilding the Public University," Newfield—perhaps gesturing toward Bill Readings's remarkable 1996 book, *The University in Ruins*—veers slightly away from the reconstruction motif, pronouncing the public university dead and calling for the construction of a nascent "postcapitalist university" on the basis of these same five principles, stated in perspicuously prescriptive terms as measures to be enacted (Newfield 2016b, 176).

Among the many difficulties to be confronted by advocates of such a thoroughgoing systemic transformation, the most immediate is doubtless not that of the institutional "repositioning" (changes in goals, values, assumptions) that Newfield envisions in "What Are the Humanities For?" (2016b). It is rather that the sociopolitical barriers to the far-reaching funding measures that would be required appear to have hardened during the initial decades of this century. Indeed, it seems reasonable to suggest that, in the near term, the lot of the public university system is likely to worsen. In the next chapter, I shall undertake to explain why enactment of the type of reformist program or paradigm change that Newfield maps out is an even less plausible prospect for the future than he would like to believe. At this point, however, holding to the standpoint of the public humanities that numerous colleges and universities have begun to put in place, my task is to take stock. It is to stand back from the overview of the privatized public university that I first drew from the literature back in 2010–11 and have now fortified by appropriating some key critical strands of Newfield's formidable analysis, and to ask just how do the humanities figure in this picture.

The Humanities in the Public University

Given that privatization continues to erode the commitments to access and affordability that have heretofore distinguished the public from the private university, does privatization—the multifaceted drift of the public university toward the operational model of the private university—make a significant difference when we focus on the humanities writ large (by which I mean the humanities and the arts in their symbiotic relations with the other academic disciplines)? Here I take two observations, which are again anchored in the higher education literature, to be immediately relevant.

The first is that the account of recent history I've sketched above invariably takes the evolution of the University's research function as its core and for the most part treats that research as the domain of science and technology. The standard, oft-repeated national interest argument is familiar to all of us: cutting-edge research, whether basic or applied, is essential to the nation's competitive strength in the global economy and requires large-scale investment of both public and private resources. In accounts of what higher education contributes to society, the applications of constantly advancing scientific research, including some developed in the domain of the social sciences, are all important—so much so that quite often the story omits the humanities or includes them only as an afterthought: yes, they promote useful communication skills and critical thinking, and yes, by sustaining the classic exemplar of the liberally educated individual they provide for enjoyment or embellishment of the human experience. However, in relation to the research machine, which brews life-changing material progress for the populace as a whole, their largely instrumental and relatively static, if not stagnant, position is subordinate, marginal, taken for granted; the research they pursue, the knowledge they produce, the funding they require, the professional opportunities they open up are not comparable to those of science and technology. While the humanities are certainly not expendable, and while their instrumental value may be enhanced by the importation of technological tools, new media, and the development of the digital humanities, for universities under financial strain, big science and commercially exploitable technology take priority.

My second observation about the lot of the humanities as privatization has proceeded involves a more immediate temporal frame. It bears upon a trend that, according to most observers in and of higher education, has rapidly become much more pronounced in recent years. Given the high price students and their families have to pay for undergraduate education and the difficulty of finding employment that graduates encountered during the years after the 2008 recession, university education is increasingly regarded as training for a career, and student curricular choices are increasingly oriented by professional prospects and financial goals.

Privatization and marketization go hand in hand with vocationalization. Since lucrative job prospects are not all that plentiful in the humanities, we commonly assume that the tendency to privilege career choice is unfavorable to the study of the humanities and to the appreciation they are accorded in universities' understanding of their values and priorities.[14] To some extent, this assumption is borne out by the fact that between 2009 and 2014, degree completions in the core disciplines of the humanities (English, history, non-English languages and literature, classics, philosophy) fell from 8.0% to 6.5% of the total number of degrees awarded; recent surveys showing a sharp drop in the numbers of English and history majors convey a similarly disconcerting message (Flaherty 2018a, 2018b).

Yet the comprehensive long-term statistical picture is far more complex than the ebb and flow of undergraduate majors would suggest. It does not demonstrate that the humanities are either more or less in crisis than they have usually appeared to be. Their problem, which is not so much a punctual, eventful crisis as it is a worsening condition of competitive disadvantage and misrepresentation in the face of the dominant neoliberal orthodoxy, is their peripheral status in the entrepreneurial research university; and as Michael Bérubé has repeatedly insisted, the problem looks far more acute when examined in the context of graduate programs and the academic workforce.[15] If, for example, the likely academic career path for the doctoral student in English or history devolves into an insecure, weakly remunerated position of teaching required basic courses to freshmen, will advanced work in the humanities remain an attractive option? Will there be a place for high-level scholarship in the humanities in the public university beset with privatization?

Against this background of concern with the status of the humanities in an environment that favors investment in science and technology disciplines and vocationalization of the undergraduate curriculum, could the problem of the humanities somehow be more amenable to a solution in the public university? Or does the privatization of the public research university mean that in the publics and the privates the humanities face essentially the same problem? A data-based answer to the question is not readily available. The Humanities Indicators report that the proportion of humanities degrees awarded by public colleges and universities rose from 57% of the national total in 1987 to 67% in 2013 and, more significantly, that the proportion of humanities majors in private institutions, which was 4% greater than in the publics in 1987, had dropped to less than 1% greater in 2013. While this is not fine-grained information, we can safely conclude that in the humanities, the publics and the privates have been moving toward a certain parity at the undergraduate level and that interest in the humanities has held up about as well on the public side as on the private side.

At the graduate level and in the sphere of research, where assembling all the relevant data and establishing the basis needed for serious comparisons would be an almost insuperable hurdle, it seems necessary to resort to structural analysis of a passably tendentious, albeit quite familiar, variety. Precisely because research costs in the humanities are modest, the advantages the privates derive from long traditions, robust library collections, higher faculty salaries, and more generous graduate student support packages have not prevented the strong publics from competing successfully with them in the various humanities fields.[16] But what would happen if a new agenda, featuring the public humanities and perhaps along with them the digital and environmental humanities, were to become the institutional priority? How would the privatized public university fare?

A first way to approach this question would be to draw on my limited experience with grants to humanities centers. State-of-the art initiatives in the public humanities have generally been concentrated in public universities (notably those of Texas, Wisconsin, Washington, and the City University of New York, among others). The least we can say is that public universities have been in the forefront of the public humanities movement, as they have also been when it comes to the digital and environmental humanities, and their administrations have been supportive. But such anecdotal observation is of limited purchase on the question at hand. A second, more broadly comparative way to approach it is to ask whether the privatization of the public university has left it just as distant from the social and intellectual horizon of the public humanities as its private university peers or whether, instead, public higher education has preserved an allegiance to the public interest that continues to distinguish it from the private sector, on which the ironclad hold of the market and of the drive to accumulate intellectual capital is irrefragable. Indeed, could the public humanities assume a role in the public university that would reinvigorate some of the features that once distinguished it from the private university, or even enable it to take the lead in pursuing an enlightened research and public service agenda that private institutions might eventually be compelled to emulate?

This query points, I believe, if not to the question, at least to the horizon of questioning, with which representatives of the humanities in the public university should grapple. It takes us back to the notion of the University's publics—specifically, to the implications of the divergent publics that preoccupy the leaders of public and private universities, to what views the humanities in particular might bring to bear upon them. The public that matters to the public university is clearly larger, more complex, and less homogeneous than its private counterpart. Its most vital component is precisely the massive assemblage of lower- and middle-class citizens that it is supposed to serve by providing affordable access. If a suitably educated citizenry is an essential ground of durable democracy or a condition for the sustenance of a flourishing economy, it is with the interests of this dominant layer of the body politic that the public university should rightfully be aligned. An obvious correlate of this connection to the public at large is a special relationship with the state government, the elected governor and legislators who also serve this general public—the voting public—and whose work with their university system is a part of that public service. In short, the responsibilities of public higher education entrench it directly in the world of politics.

By way of contrast, the responsibilities of private colleges and universities are plainly focused on a narrower set of interests that are heavily concentrated in and influenced by the more affluent strata of society. The numerically smaller but economically powerful public at issue here enables the privates to charge high prices, secure large donations, and maintain thriving networks of supportive alumni and friends.[17] Thus the attention of the private university administration goes predominantly to a public made up of alumni and others whose allegiances to the values of private wealth are deep-seated and who are attuned to the advantages of reserving the lion's share of institutional resources for an elite at the high end.

While by no means totally homogeneous[18] or immune to altruism and while committed to a certain limited but much hyped diversity, for the most part this privileged public does not link its interests to the societal imperative to scale up higher educational opportunity for the public at large, and of course the scale of private higher education is incommensurable with the massive and necessary expansion that has had to be a public university project. Moreover, the dynamics of elite higher education are not unlike those of a high-end commercial market: the value of the product—a prestigious degree—depends on its relative scarcity, on maintaining the experience of privilege by a practice of exclusion that restricts its availability to the proverbial "chosen few." The elite university serves an astute public that understands why leading institutions prize its selectivity.

To appreciate fully the implications of these distinctly different publics for the effort to develop the public humanities, it is crucial to reflect on the compromises that research universities are prone to make as organizations caught up in the system of academic capitalism. The task of academic administration is one of constructing elaborate institutional accommodations in a process of dealing with multiple interests, expectations, obligations, and publics, thus one of trying to manage a set of complex interactions among them. During the past few decades, both public and private universities have become too dependent on the system of interests and values that threatens to reduce the humanities to their practical utility and measurable achievements to risk asserting on their own recognizance a strongly innovative commitment to the public humanities of the kind I began to envision at Mellon in 2012–13.[19] If only because their constituencies expect it, the administrative leaders of both public and private research universities are well advised to preserve humanities programs and to represent them as fundamental to an academic enterprise in which they are responsible for maintaining an invaluable cultural continuum. Thus, as I noted in chapter 2, the administration upholds a prudent compromise, protective of the university on all fronts, that keeps the humanities in a safe and constructive place.

While this intra-institutional expedient disallows a flatly dismissive view of the humanities, it keeps a damper on their capacity to assert critical judgments while highlighting the easily defended instrumental function that I have termed literacy-and-cultural-competency training. In the case of public university systems that the "great mistake," to use Newfield's phrase, has subjected to a severely disruptive austerity, the safe-and-secure position commonly occupied by the humanities is compatible with a vital managerial effort to preserve an income stream that, even when reduced, is invaluable. This effort has typically entailed a dual posture: on the one hand, administrators reckon with the need to demonstrate or at least assert their institution's commitments to public service and to access for the state's students; on the other hand, they bow to the necessity of going along with decisions of the governing authorities on whom they depend for a nontrivial piece of their budget.

In sum, since both incentives and constraints inhere in the structure of this political relationship, the public university has been inextricably involved in assent to co-optation as well as worthwhile cooperation. The question now before us is whether, for the public university, this rational compromise that preserves the humanities while allowing them to languish is still, in the harsh light of current conditions, defensible. The question is also, from the standpoint of the public humanities, whether those conditions point to a menace that has become urgent enough to justify a less collusive, more dissensual, more confrontational strategy. If it is time to adopt a more aggressive, openly critical, and activist posture that many would take to be typical of the humanities, what should such a strategy look like?

In the 2014 talk that morphed into chapter 2 of this book, I claimed—not conclusively, but with some confidence—that no research university, public or private, would be able to adjust its compromises with all the forces it has to confront to the point of making an unequivocal commitment to the public humanities on its own, through a concerted and overt reallocation of resources that it controls. In my 2015 talk, which is largely reproduced in the first two-thirds of this chapter, I maintained that claim, asserting a second time my belief that universities, in order to stay afloat, were compelled to uphold a restrained, steadfastly judicious compromise. Such a strategy would normally consist, I suggested, in treating the humanities with deferential respect but would stop short of publicizing them—that is, of prevailing on them either to represent the public and its interests within the institution or to speak and act for the university in the public sphere. Kept in check, the humanities would comply with the university's sense of its own needs, interests, and risk-management requirements and thus, in reaching out to the general public and to the political establishment, would echo the standard institutional line that emphasizes research in the STEM fields and especially the economic benefits of that research.

Upon reconsidering five years later the compromises forged by the public university, and upon thinking about the effort to educate the public that is central to the public humanities agenda, I have come to a different conclusion. While it takes into account the many problems of the University and of the humanities I have noted, my change of perspective is based above all on the decline of the public university's capacity to enroll and educate productively the massive cohort of high school graduates from the middle and lower classes. The state systems that American higher education has developed, ostensibly for the purpose of guaranteeing access and sustaining over the long term a linkage between learning and social mobility, are increasingly unable to claim that these students are being well served. In recent years the percentage of secondary school graduates who go on to the tertiary level has been declining,[20] and all too often the quality of education made available to students who are not welcomed into elite colleges and universities falls short of what they need to match the standard of living achieved by their parents.

What Christopher Newfield represents as a devolutionary cycle in all but the uppermost tiers of the public sector is not a temporary aberration that the system, as currently constituted, will seek to reverse; it is a fait accompli visited on an enormous number of students who are pawns in the schemes of innumerable institutions that seek not so much to educate and empower as merely to survive. Overall, the majority of students have experienced, often unwittingly, the withering of their prospects for upward mobility. The scenario of disaffection is hardly consonant with the system's goal of serving democracy by preparing an enlightened citizenry for allegiance to the common good and by forming responsible individuals capable of flourishing in a world that values personal freedom and benevolence as much as—if not more than—material wealth.

From the standpoint of the public university's core social and cultural mission, which is to broaden and level the playing field so as to promote equal opportunity, the regressive trend is an untenable development that must be challenged. It puts the humanities—and perforce the public humanities—in a position that requires them, on social and moral grounds, to criticize the public and institutional policies that condone the devolution; it beckons toward a responsibility to advocate for the humanities both within the public university and in its interactions with the non-academic public outside the university. For the public humanities specifically, the regress unsettles the compromise articulated in *The Heart of the Matter*[21] between two perspectives on the humanities, one that stresses their instrumental value by invoking our needs for national security and for a competitive edge in the global economy, and another that underscores their critical function and their association with ethical and political modes of living in the real world.

Within the university, the urgent task of the public humanities—the promotion of knowledge by and for the public—is to contest the multifaceted mission shift that has decimated the commitment to equal opportunity; it is to pressure the institution to take a political stand for the cause of democratized—as opposed to privatized—higher education. Beyond the university, in their encounters with a multitiered external public, representatives of the public humanities must insist on attending to the educational plight of the majority that is being shortchanged by the hierarchical system. Their mission is to enable the public to understand how that system privileges the private sector and reinforces the advantages its affluent public seeks to maintain. The task, in sum, is to assert the priority of the critical and political cutting edge of the humanities over the more assimilable instrumental functions that lend themselves to co-optation.

In the previous chapter, by suggesting that the grand challenges facing humanity preclude a defense of the humanities anchored in a narrative of national interest and economic advantage, I was, in effect, pushing back against a familiar Western cultural narrative focused on what the advances of knowledge and technology have contributed to the formation of human societies and their gradual consolidation of control over nature. Insofar as that narrative of progress, as we have come to know it since the eighteenth-century Enlightenment and the nineteenth-century Industrial Revolution, constructs a certain coalescent triumph of science, capitalism, and democracy, it retains an understandable traction in the life of institutions such as the University. Yet in the light of the current foundering of public higher education and the apparent efficacy at least of the upper crust of private higher education, we have to assume that the private sector is more clearly and determinedly aligned than its public counterpart with the interests such a narrative expresses.

The public university, I now submit belatedly, needs to assume responsibility for representing the interests of its broader constituency through a different narrative of what research and higher education have accomplished, one that will highlight not only their laudable values and achievements but also the reasons for which the system in which we are entrenched is imperiled and must change. In the final chapters of this inquiry into the public humanities, I shall undertake to describe the underpinnings of such a story and to suggest the directions in which it would lead us.

CHAPTER 4

The Real Humanities Crisis

Reckoning with the Anthropocene

Among the grand challenges to which I alluded in chapters 2 and 3, the advancing climate change occasioned by global warming is clearly overarching and, from the standpoint of humanity at large, primary. Put baldly, the issue is the survival, not of the earth or of life, but of the human species as we have come to characterize it in recent times. More and more often we grasp the knowledge in question here through the geohistorical lens of the Anthropocene. This is to say, again in blunt, unapologetically general terms, that henceforth the context of reflection on the human and the humanities has to be contemporary, that it is subtended by the so-called Great Acceleration that took hold, according to scientists who study the earth system, after World War II.[1] From the 1950s on, the impact of human activity on the state of the planet has grown so rapidly and produced such major environmental changes that a new geological era has begun to take shape: after the Holocene, the Anthropocene. At the dawn of this era, human activity has emerged as the dominant driver of change in the earth system. For many observers, realistic predictions about the changes now in store for us suggest that we are perilously close to, if not beyond, a tipping point after which humanity will be unable to forestall the collapse of the civilization it has developed over the last ten thousand years.[2]

From the standpoint of the humanities in general as well as that of the public humanities in particular, the questions with which the Anthropocene confronts us are numerous, complex, and urgent. To summarize them exhaustively is beyond my power and pretense. It is, however, possible to delineate a set of recurring motifs that preoccupy scholars laboring in the vineyard of the environmental humanities and to ask how these questions or concerns or issues relate to work in the public humanities. Provisionally, I would array them under the following headings:

- environmental protection as an obligation to future generations
- explanations and implications of political inaction on climate change
- revised understanding of relations between the natural world and human inhabitants
- rationales for urgent action to limit climate change
- measures required for limiting and adapting to climate change
- connections between environmentalism and socioeconomic justice
- potential impact of technologies on the future of environmental and human evolution

Although I shall not take up these concerns as separate topics to be treated in discrete segments, the argument that follows will eventually touch on all of them. My premise here is that there is a need to grasp them synthetically as interlocking components of an all-pervasive problem and that the humanities have a vital role to play in engaging the public at large with the issues at hand.

To start exploring this far-reaching problem, let me revert to a moment near the turn of the twenty-first century when it was possible to envisage the mitigation of global warming—for example, possible to recommend measures that would limit it to an increase of 1.5° or 2° C. Two very serious, capacious books seem to exemplify the pellucid calls that were then coming from science and social science to address the problem while it may not have been too late. The first of these, *Fragile Dominion: Complexity and the Commons* by Simon Levin (2000), offers the general reader an account of the earth as a complex adaptive system and explores the ecological consequences of the loss of biodiversity; the second, *Collapse: How Societies Choose to Fail or Succeed* by Jared Diamond (2005), sets off, against explanations of why some past societies collapsed and some others were resilient, a comprehensive set of environmental problems distinctive of our era that threaten us with an all-embracing tragedy of the commons, the global collapse of human civilization.

Both of these books appeared at a time when it was possible for their authors to conclude their works with reflections on what humanity must do in order to ward off terminal decline and develop a sustainable regimen for the long term. In the case of Levin's extrapolations, anchored in scientific understanding of the biosphere, this meant elaborating a set of geopolitical principles and policies for managing the environment at a planet-wide level; achieving compliance with them would require a spate of international agreements on the order of the 1987 Montreal Protocol for the protection of the ozone layer that has largely succeeded in suppressing the use of chlorofluorocarbons. In the case of Diamond's anthropological account of cultural success or failure, hope for the future was deemed possible because certain societies had understood the need to act on the basis of long-term planning and found the courage to pursue the painful but necessary revision of core values.

Stopping short of invoking insuperable obstacles to mitigating action, both of these eminent scholars recognized, in similar terms, the difficulties to be overcome. For Levin, the heady obstacle is the distance of the global threat from local problems that people experience as urgent and worthy of their direct attention; for Diamond, it is the firm resistance of inhabitants in the prosperous, industrialized world to the imperative to lessen their impact on the planet by consuming much less than they do now. In sum, while it is human nature, as it were, to discount the future (Levin) and to shirk sacrifice (Diamond), early in this century a collective turn toward survivability could still be imagined even when forceful warnings about looming catastrophe were the dominant message.

At this juncture, however, nearly two decades after the publication of *Collapse*, such cautious optimism has become hard to muster. The point is uncannily illustrated by a common feature of two noteworthy books of the last decade, *Hot: Living through the Next Fifty Years on Earth* by Mark Hertsgaard (2012) and *We're Doomed. Now What?* by Roy Scranton (2018). At key moments both of these knowledgeable and astute authors chose to set their reflections on the climate crisis in a highly personalized context, their relations to their young daughters. Hertsgaard's epilogue is a letter to his daughter, Chiara, in which he tells her, "I wrote this book for you." Scranton's final chapter is titled "Raising a Daughter in a Doomed World." Both fathers are preoccupied with the living conditions their daughters will experience in midcentury and beyond when, as mature women, they and the members of their generation will have to reckon with the failures of their elders. For each of these men, I surmise, the interests of their daughters—future judges doubtless not so much of relatives such as their politically engaged fathers as of far-flung collectives, notably the recent generations of ancestors who ignored their responsibility for combatting climate change—underlie a halting and strained imperative to confront forthwith the likelihood of planetary catastrophe and what it implies for procreative attachments. We must respond, they submit, by rejecting apocalyptic despair and by rationalizing a certain vision of human survival in a torrid world for which we must help our children and grandchildren to prepare.

The personal disquiet expressed by Hertsgaard and Scranton when they evoke the hardship and suffering likely to be experienced by their children stems from an understanding of what has happened since the Great Acceleration. They share this concern with innumerable fellow citizens and scholars who take seriously the findings of earth system science.[3] The basic point is quite simple: modern society's technologically enabled growth has resulted in what many happy participants in the industrial and digital revolutions have experienced as progress, yet it has also, unmistakably, resulted in an irreversible devolution of Earth toward a state of massive devastation that will make it largely inhospitable to humans, if not totally uninhabitable. Various components of the emerging ecological crisis have been detailed ad nauseam, and for decades.[4]

The account starts with warming temperatures that, by compromising agriculture in many parts of the world, will occasion famine while elevating the incidence of death by hyperthermia, abetting the spread of disease, and accelerating destruction by fires, floods, and storms; it continues with rising levels of acidified oceans that, while debilitating coastal cities and imposing unprecedented migrations, will make for a dwindling seafood supply; it goes on to such phenomena as frequent droughts, melting polar ice caps and glaciers, chronic freshwater shortages, the multiplication of severe storms and natural disasters, mass extinctions of plant and animal species, and a complex amalgam of geopolitical stresses conducive to deadly warfare, if not to nuclear conflagration.

Forceful warnings from scientists have emphasized from the start the long-lasting effects of carbon dioxide in the atmosphere and the consequences of delaying measures to limit greenhouse gas emissions. The warming trend, they remind us year in and year out, is bound to continue for a very long time; it is too late to avert a major crisis. This warning is reinforced by the compelling argument we hear from economists, often associated with the work of Sir Nicholas Stern: the cost of acting to stem global warming now would be far less than that of repairing the damage after a crisis occurs.[5]

In light of this grim situation, what messages should practitioners of the humanities be articulating? Perhaps it is necessary to initiate reflection on the possible answers by recognizing that the ongoing concern within the academic humanities and other cultural institutions about the crisis of the humanities is no longer a front-burner question. In the preceding chapter, I alluded in passing to the commonplace notion that humanities are always in crisis, that their well-being or their very survival is perpetually imperiled, that crisis talk or discourse is a defining feature of their institutional existence that reinforces their marginalization. The issue has not been whether crisis is engrained in the humanities, but how leaders in the field of higher education should understand it. The perspective on the issue that seems most persuasive to me actually emerges from the predominantly historical accounts of well-established authorities such as Roger Geiger and Geoffrey Harpham. In the first chapter of *A New Deal for the Humanities*, "From the Land-Grant Tradition to the Current Crisis in the Humanities," Geiger discusses (often critically) four sources of the sense of crisis commonly voiced by humanities professors: waning student interest evidenced by enrollment declines, restricted funding along with muted institutional support, the veer toward vocationalism, and a lack of public understanding (2016a). Geiger contends that the last of these irritants, public disaffection, is a consequence of implausible and incompatible rationales for study in the humanities and an inherently conformist faculty culture that justifies public skepticism or indifference. The ebb and flow of these multiple interacting factors fuels the discourse of crisis, which tends to become one of chronic malaise and detrimental complaint.

In the keenly insightful first chapter of *The Humanities and the Dream of America* (2011), "Beneath and Beyond the 'Crisis in the Humanities,'" Harpham also emphasizes, citing the critique ventured by Louis Menand in *The Marketplace of Ideas*, the "crisis of rationale." He then proceeds, in an argument that concludes with a remarkably original commentary on Gustave Flaubert's *Madame Bovary*, to articulate an artfully woven, thick rationale for an inescapably dual "humanistic understanding": "On the one hand, a liberation from the confines of the mundane self through an immersion in the lives and thoughts of others, a loss of bearings; and, on the other, a vicarious or secondary participation in the author's act of creation that enhances and strengthens our imaginative powers" (39). Owing to this unsettling duality positioning humanity as their overarching subject and making each humanities discipline partial or fragmentary in relation to it, "the humanities represent by their very nature a crisis in that institution dedicated to research and knowledge, the academy" (39). For both Geiger and Harpham, then, the crisis of the humanities is an inescapable condition of knotty complexity, at once engaging and disconcerting, that requires multiple explanations. Unlike an emergency or turning point that requires an immediate, decisive response, the condition of crisis is a restless constant, a recurring encounter with an ever-changing flow of challenges and opportunities. While imbued with a certain urgency, the situation calls for persistent commitment and promises duration rather than resolution.

The question I am raising here obviously assumes the validity of Harpham's recognition of humanity, understood in its density, as the subject—the crux—of the humanities.[6] Its focus is precisely the commanding crisis of that subject—of humanity—that the humanities, no less than all other areas of inquiry, are summoned by current experience to confront. In chapter 2, in the fourth, fifth, and sixth of my premises for the public humanities, I linked their focus on the grand challenges to a broad consensus about the value of public goods that would, in the final analysis, be reflected in a universally shared normative vision of the human condition.

My proposal on imperatives to be formulated and communicated at this point in time (2022) obviously relates to a mission or educational project that starts with a wide-ranging emphasis on public interest and ecological responsibility by the arts and humanities disciplines inside of academic institutions; it proceeds to advocate the translation of that work into a reasoned and willful common commitment to human well-being and survival that will achieve traction in society at large. Yet we hear constantly from acquaintances in all walks of life the salient counter that brings responses to the urgent questions at hand up short: Why bother to combat environmental degradation since we have failed for decades to heed the warnings issued by scientists? Are there not insuperable obstacles that make it impossible to overcome the inaction, or at least impossible to take action that would be commensurable with the threats we face? Indeed, will it not turn out to be true that the changes we have to envisage are so forbidding that the concerned publics simply will not entertain them even if the alternative is conducive to the extreme outcome, extinction of the human species?

To respond to these questions it is necessary to consider both what our evolving planet will impose on its inhabitants in response to the dramatic human modification of its environmental systems over the past two centuries and the many changes we will have to make in the way we live in order to give future generations a chance to survive. As Bill McKibben in numerous books from *The End of Nature* (1989) to the recent *Falter* (2019), Clive Hamilton in his *Defiant Earth* (2017), and many others[7] have argued, claims that we can conceive of the planet as a fecund and resilient natural world that humans can continue indefinitely to domesticate, exploit, and govern are belied by the realities that now confront us. Their portrayals of a wounded, reactive, unpredictable, sometimes retributive nature resonate with a central anthropological claim elaborated in the work of Bruno Latour, the influential French proponent of actor-network theory. From his *We Have Never Been Modern* (1991) onward, Latour tirelessly endeavored to displace the dualist outlook that, in his view, informs the science-and-technology-driven culture of modernity toward an alternative that neither can nor should cleanly separate nature from culture, the human subject from

nonhuman objects, rigorously constituted knowledge from belief, or necessity from freedom.

Across the wide net cast by Latour in a voluminous corpus, he
consistently campaigned for rethinking the concept of nature
that, he averred, has anchored the thinking of post-Enlighten-
ment modernity about the human habitat.[8] During the last two
decades, he sharpened his position with an innovative adoption
of James Lovelock's Gaia hypothesis: "The Earth is a totality of
living beings and materials that were made together, that cannot live apart, and from which humans can't extract themselves"
(Latour 2018a). The point here is that humans are agents inside
of, rather than separate from, nature; like other living organisms
they are entangled in the fashioning of nature, which thus has
to be conceived as an evolving interaction of forces caught up
in the multilayered evolution of the earth system; thus they
are subject, not to fixed laws that guarantee nature's integrity
and stability, but to the self-regulating processes and feedback
mechanisms of a planetary dynamics that is not characterized
by linear relationships of the kind we observe in a simple cause-
effect paradigm. Hence a vision of a metamorphic Earth that is,
as its geological history shows, susceptible to abrupt, unpredictable changes, and of a nature that human activity—the interventions responsible for the potent effects of urbanization and
our globalized economy—can destabilize but cannot control.
In sum, our disruptions of the Holocene epoch's homeostasis,
which have produced the Anthropocene, are driving a disfig-
ured, human-appropriated nature—or more to the general point,
Earth—to fight back.

We are, then, discovering a planet—facing Gaia, as Latour put
it—that we can no longer understand in terms of humanity's

triumphant struggle for dominion over nature.[9] If we take earth system science seriously, we have to anticipate a reckoning with environmental changes, starting with the all-encompassing effects of global warming, that will force us to forge new and different relations with nature. More broadly, life on a parching planet will force us to come to grips with a complex world in which what we previously separated into nature and culture has to be grasped integrally as part of a biogeophysical framework of interconnectedness and feedbacks.

The challenge before us is not limited to the effects of global warming triggered by the burning of fossil fuels and adjacent human-induced biophysical trends such as biodiversity loss, pollution of air and water, deforestation and desertification, spoliation of arable land, and exhaustion of vital resources for manufacturing and agriculture; it also extends, perhaps more dauntingly, to human and societal issues that have been usefully integrated within the conceptual framework of the Anthropocene, a horizon that merges human history and natural history into a single construct.[10] These latter issues include such phenomena as a global economy built on an almost sacred requirement of permanently growing consumption, a massified human population concentrated in urban environments that has outgrown the planet's carrying capacity, and an international sociopolitical stage, pervaded by cultural difference and disparities in power, on which world leaders ostensibly well informed about looming ecological crises nonetheless give priority to short-term nationalistic interests and to upholding anachronistic disagreements.

Ultimately, facing up to these components or drivers that constitute the Anthropocene beckons toward broadly critical questions about the implications of human being and humanity that some will surely dismiss as pretentiously or naively metaphysical. Yet perhaps such questions about what is at work or at stake in a collective body's desecration of its own invaluable habitat have to be confronted before major remedial measures can even be contemplated. As Clive Hamilton argues in making the case for a new anthropomorphism (2017, chap. 2), such potentially apocalyptic considerations can also have a practical and perhaps constructive edge precisely because they sharpen our awareness of the demonstrably formidable power of humans to build their environment and to influence the functioning of the earth system. Should we not at least look for realistic ways to fit these human capacities into an updated account of our place in the world that the state of the global environment summons us to construct?

Of Risk and Uncertainty

It is widely recognized that the most telling horizon on which to anticipate the earth's response to two centuries of industrialization and vast increases in human population is that of energy, the life-giving force we derive from the sun and use for what we do and create. Scientists assure us that the quantity of relatively constant energy we receive from the sun—a reliable external source expected to continue for upwards of four billion years— far exceeds what we need or could conceivably use.[11] During the past two hundred years, however, we have moved to meet most of our needs by harnessing the sun's energy long ago stored underground in coal, oil, and natural gas; we have thereby tied our supply of fuel for essential systems of heating, transportation, and electricity to an expendable source that is both hostage to changing market forces and productive of harmful by-products (principally cardon dioxide) that cause global warming. While it is impossible to forecast with confidence the date by which coal and petroleum will no longer be deemed available, it is reasonable to assume that by the end of this century our descendants will be able to survive only if they obtain most of the energy they use from sources other than carbon-laden fossil fuels.[12] At the same time, we have to assume the necessity of adapting to temperatures averaging 2° to 5° C higher than those that prevail now, an increase that will have devastating climatological and ecological effects. That these two overarching developments will make for major changes in the physical and economic environment seems all too evident; moreover, if they occur too rapidly or chaotically, they could trigger the implosion of the global socioeconomic edifice.

What, then, can we say about the adjustments that human populations are likely to have to make upon facing an energy shortage, a crumbling of essential infrastructure in zones such as transportation, telecommunications, sanitation, water supply, and agriculture, and resultant economic and political breakdowns of varying forms and intensities? Here the answer has to be a guarded one. While the necessity of adapting to a gradual climate change that can no longer be prevented has become a widely recognized certainty, the situation is paradoxical to the extent that it entails an imposition on all of Earth's societies of unprecedented uncertainty about the future. No one can determine when a particular episode of calamitous disruption will occur or when a given trend toward deprivation will become widespread and irreversible. This unpredictability is double-edged. On the one hand, it puts into play an awareness of the risks we are running that breeds confusion and anxiety; on the other hand, it functions as a hindrance to action, as the nebulous origin of an ignorance-based excuse—"we don't really know what the future will bring"—for neglecting signs of danger.

For individuals, retreat into ignorance and inaction often seems integral to the drift of everyday life.[13] When groups of concerned citizens—for example, the "green" political parties in Europe—advocate major policy reforms reflecting the urgency and magnitude of the climate change problem, they typically have to recognize factors of commonsensical reason and natural human self-interest underlying their failures. A first-world assumption, whether implicit or explicit, that almost automatically informs the thinking of members of the majority (whether vocal or silent) and of the politicians who represent them accredits the likelihood that, when tomorrow comes, both the general conditions of life as we know it and the problems requiring immediate attention will largely resemble those of today. This year's climate may not seem more than episodically different from last year's. Thus, for the most part the ongoing assumptions we make and the terms we use in thinking and talking about passing time and coming events or changes will continue to be essentially the same, consistent with past practices and attuned to short-term needs, desires, possibilities, and risks.

Accordingly, most of us, as individuals busily living our lives, are reluctant to take into account the long-term eventuality of disaster. Rather than face up to warnings about unprecedented danger or brewing catastrophe, we switch back to imagining the contours of the future as incremental improvements on those of the present; they evolve, precisely, on a manageable horizon of continuity. For those of us who live in areas of relative prosperity, this is a valued stability that we take to be open to palatable changes—progress—made possible by technological innovation. Schooled to invest in comfort, wealth, status, and security, we are intent on preserving and enhancing them. Thus, to repeat the already noted concern voiced by Diamond, we recoil from sacrifice. A reckoning with cataclysmic change caused by an unsettled earth system simply does not enter into our congenially normal picture of a future unfolding from the present as the present unfolded from the past. Instead, our protective propensities for self-interest and indifference incline us to revert to a sense of history's lessons oriented by predictability. It tells us to anticipate what ordinary past experience has taught us, day in and day out, to expect, and also to assume that the evident risks we rationally choose to run are acceptable ones. This reassuring structure of foresight has been a confident supposition— a relative certitude—built into the language of common accord that we speak.[14]

Climate change and global economic crises have already thrown into question this reasonable certainty—an experience-based faith in progress—that has buoyed our Western sense of the modern human condition since the Enlightenment. Parallel to the more complex view of nature that the study of the earth system proposes, there is now a sense, at least among a modicum of thoughtful observers, that our collective view of history and culture must also undergo a shift—not only a move, imposed by rapid technologically spawned change, away from planning for a future anchored in repetitions of the past, but toward confronting long-term large-scale risk urgently. The challenge is to do so no longer from the confining standpoint of individuals or interest groups but at the scale of the entire geophysical planet and of the entire global population. For all concerned— individuals, governments, international organizations, humanity as a whole—such a reckoning would entail a turn toward coming to grips with complexity and discontinuity, toward anticipating a future marked rather more by insecurity than by stability, by necessity than by opportunity, by limits than by new vistas, by contraction than by expansion.[15]

The key concepts pervading and problematizing the hypothetical history of our environmental future are, then, risk and uncertainty.[16] The degree and type of uncertainty are of course crucial factors affecting perceptions of risk and approaches to it. In the case of climate change, the picture is dauntingly complex insofar as the increasingly elaborate and irrefutable scientific account of global warming and its probable effects is at once conclusive and inconclusive. It makes for confident predictions about problems to be encountered sooner or later, but without information about the precise forms they will take or the time frames within which they will become acute.

Such uncertainty perturbs the familiar methods of quantitative risk assessment that take patterns observable in the past as a basis for predicting the future. This classic approach yields estimates of the magnitude of possible adverse consequences or calculations of probability or frequency of occurrence of events. Such probabilistic analyses inform the qualification of risks as acceptable or unacceptable and allow for a notion of managing risk that mutes or conceals the uncertainty factor, enabling the kind of confidence achieved by individuals when they make decisions about liability protection or by businesses when they weigh the costs and benefits of safety measures or compare the outcomes of multiple possible scenarios. But when unprecedented effects of climate change or unexpected phenomena such as the 2008 global financial crisis or the 2019 pandemic come into play, the uncertainty factor becomes radical: planning based on the past no longer works for want of precedent and calculable risk is no longer the relevant concept. In the case of climate change, the impairment of rational risk management can coincide with untimely pressure to determine how the responsibilities for dealing with crises should be distributed.

In situations of this kind, where deliberations seem to be stalled by the multiple and elusive complications attendant to uncertainty, is it necessary simply to abandon the development of rational responses to risk? The so-called precautionary principle, which has often been a reference point in international deliberations since the 1970s, stipulates that when decisions in response to threats to the environment or public health cannot be based on full scientific knowledge or statistical calculation, lack of certainty should not be used as a reason for doing nothing to prevent harm. In this abstract, question-begging formulation, the principle invites obvious objections: it is vague, impractical, inattentive to possible tensions between environmental needs and public health, and potentially at odds with the pursuit of technological innovation.[17]

Over time, however, it has been rearticulated, notably by policymakers in the European Union, in more concrete terms that provide a framework of deliberative practices for implementing it. This expanded version of the principle typically stipulates that its appropriation in regulatory contexts must be grounded in standard procedures such as cost-benefit analysis incorporating Bayesian risk assessment[18] and comprehensive descriptions of the scope and likely consequences of potential degradation. Under the conditions of uncertainty, moreover, these exercises are to be carried out as extensively as is possible; they feed into a practice of elaborating future scenarios that entails specification of the uncertainties in question and scrupulous discussion of their significance. Similarly, current protocols associated with the principle provide for thorough review of proposed or adopted risk-reducing actions by qualified experts. Their task is to ascertain that the measures under review address potentially irreversible harms without resulting in unacceptable side effects or unforeseen new risks. In sum, with its substantial refinement of the precautionary principle, the decision-making model adopted by the European Union's regulators has demonstrated the feasibility of a relatively scientific approach to some forms of uncertainty.

Another theoretically powerful demonstration of the possibility of rational risk management under uncertainty is provided in a remarkably forceful treatise by philosopher Toby Ord. In *The Precipice: Existential Risk and the Future of Humanity* (2020), Ord focuses determinedly on the ultimate risk identified by his subtitle. Existential risk is defined as any risk—nuclear war, climate change, engineered pandemics, advanced artificial intelligence, and so forth—that threatens to destroy humanity's long-term potential, whether by simple extinction or by irrecuperable transformation of living conditions. While granting that the complex, unprecedented nature of the risks (they are all-encompassing matters of life and death, unlike the small- and medium-scale risks to which we are accustomed) prevents precise mathematical analysis, Ord contends that quantitative estimates of probability are needed, shows skillfully that they are, if speculative, at least possible, and argues insistently that humans have both the cognitive capacities to understand the estimated risks and a moral obligation to future generations to act so as to reduce those serious risks—anthropogenic rather than natural—that technology and/or wisdom equip us to confront.

Yet *The Precipice* appears to be ultimately at odds with the framework I've begun to erect. This has to do with its estimates (based on relatively weak data and requiring significant guess-work[19]) of the likelihood of existential catastrophe during the next one hundred years. They situate climate change and nuclear war as relatively unlikely causes (one in one thousand), whereas engineered pandemics (one in thirty) and artificial intelligence unaligned with human values (one in ten) lie in a far more con-cerning order of magnitude. In assessing major effects of climate change, Ord forges unmistakably rational claims for asserting that none of them "threaten extinction or irrevocable collapse" (110). Yet how confident can we be in the adequacy of the evi-dence and the validity of the assumptions underlying them? In particular, we must ask whether Ord is right to set aside Martin Weitzman's claim that standard economic models of cli-mate change, anchored in cost-benefit calculations, mistakenly ignore the risk of low-probability but high-impact scenarios that would be catastrophic.[20]

Over and beyond the uncertainties about the geophysical effects that crossing various tipping points might have, the im-mediate difficulty this reasoning occasions for me concerns what it implies about the relative urgency of climate change and the imminent humanitarian need to forestall its harms. Set off against the long-term impact of biological warfare or runaway artificial intelligence and their potentially radical harm to hu-manity, should climate change have lesser priority or be deemed less urgent because risk analyses can conclude that it is much less likely to result in a sixth mass extinction? Should the risk of climate catastrophe not be perceived as more urgent than that of runaway artificial intelligence because the development of the latter, while alarming and rapidly intensifying, is still subject to decisive human regulation, whereas climate change is bound to happen and its influence on the future cannot be predicted and limited?

Ord's subtle and capacious discussion, which eventually advocates looking at the whole package of serious risks together and maps out a complex "grand strategy for humanity" (189–99), scrupulously avoids the pitfalls of prediction. He argues that all of the "five big risks" (169) warrant major global efforts, and he factors into his optimistic assessment of the climate change scenario the expectation that effective public policy measures and strong societal commitments to mitigation efforts will eventually lessen the risk of catastrophe. My main reservation about his approach is neither with his premise that makes safeguarding the long-term potential of humanity a fundamental value[21] nor with his elaborately delineated method for analyzing risks and identifying priorities. It derives precisely from my firm skepticism about his optimistic judgment that the gap between human wisdom and technological ingenuity, which he recognizes along with many others, will be closed in time to thwart ecological devastation and about his expectation that the numerous major changes to our norms and institutions he deems necessary will be carried out before it is too late. Can we, in other words, conclude—or at least hope—that confronting the predictable consequences of climate change—or at least those likely to cause irreversible harm—through enlightened public policy judgments will move us onto a new and different cultural and ecological trajectory?

The case for deploying frameworks such as those subtended by the precautionary principle in the sphere of environmental regulation or by Ord's relatively technical analysis of existential risk is at once logically compelling and deceptively reassuring.

As Langdon Winner points out (1986, chap. 8), when the danger of severe harm that calls for decisive preventive measures is treated as a risk subject to scientific analysis and expressed in calculable odds, the decision about what to do is diverted away from straightforward avoidance into a realm of uncertainty, a discussion about what risks it makes sense to run and what gains and losses will result from possible risk-reducing actions. The risk-analysis approach tends to complicate the issues, to veil the immediacy and urgency of the problem, and thus to prolong the status quo. In a culture that tends to appreciate risk-taking positively in the economic sphere, the inducement to accept risk as necessary for a desired return is unmistakable; risk-running is by no means devoid of a rational veneer.

In all events, in the particular case of climate change it remains far from evident that approaching risk and uncertainty rationally can be a successful strategy for achieving two goals of most international proposals that aim to limit global warming to temperature levels we are not far from reaching (increases of 1.5° or 2° C figure in the well-known schemes such as the Paris Accords that have been promoted by the United Nations). One of these goals is to go beyond responses to specific problems such as air and water pollution at regional scales and to pursue measures for protecting the earth system at the global scale; the other is to construct plausible scenarios for societal transformation that, while continuing to promote sustainable development, eradicate poverty, and reduce inequality, will result in modified lifestyles and altruistic human behaviors compatible with long-term survival.

These sensible, laudable goals come up against what the 2020 IPCC special report *Global Warming of 1.5°* terms "knowledge gaps"[22] as well as exceedingly robust cultural obstacles. The knowledge gaps that interfere with establishing feasible prevention measures are particularly acute in the case of high-impact events such as a shutdown of thermohaline circulation,[23] an extreme sea-level rise that could be triggered by ice sheet melting, a massive release of methane from melting permafrost, and a huge cascade of species extinctions that could result from habitat loss. As for dealing with broadly and firmly entrenched cultural norms and socioeconomic aspirations, rare are the parties to climate change negotiations whose presuppositions allow them to deviate from the dominant progressive view of modern human history, relayed by contemporary networks of communication and bolstered politically by the strong appeal of the sustainable development paradigm and the human rights movement. Not only is that outlook durable; it has spread far and wide, often reaching well beyond the more affluent strata of global society, achieving a deeply ingrained influence that is hard even to question—and still harder to disown.

I will have more to say about what contesting it entails near the end of this book when I turn to the horizon of higher education. For now, however, I shall assume that, at least in theory, disputes about the wisdom of responding to manifest risks under conditions of uncertainty can be resolved in good-faith negotiations. This implies that the principal obstacles that cripple efforts to impede climate change lie elsewhere, that it is a matter of appreciating major real-world forces that defy the development of reasonable responses to scientifically secure knowledge. How, then, should we understand the misfires of organized attempts to mitigate climate change? What are the overarching problems that, up to now, have appeared to be insoluble or unmanageable to the authorities who are nominally responsible for addressing them? Is there any prospect for tilting public opinion toward support of policies that heretofore have been politically unthinkable?

Understanding Inaction

In the vast literature about climate change, a broad consensus has emerged concerning the primary factors that have inhibited efforts to preserve the hospitable biospheric conditions that have prevailed during the Holocene epoch and in particular to thwart the steady global warming that has been observed over the last century. Rather than attempting a point by point review of the many plausible explanations offered by journalists and scholars, I shall try to summarize key general insights elaborated in the exceptionally discerning works of two philosophers, Clive Hamilton (in *Requiem for a Species*, 2010), and Dale Jamieson (in *Reason in a Dark Time*, 2014). Both of them delve into three overarching theses that seem to me to lie at the core of the problem. First, from the socioeconomic standpoint, there is what we can loosely represent as the system, the complex of societal arrangements underlying the gradually upgraded living conditions to which residents of wealthy countries have become accustomed since the Industrial Revolution and to which people in less developed parts of the world understandably aspire. Second, from the cultural and political standpoint, there is the vast collective action problem, the need to induce the planet's entire population to adopt very substantial changes in lifestyle in order to stem the greenhouse effect. Finally, there is the less frequently discussed issue, the problem of scale. I shall dwell on it at considerable length because, more clearly than the systemic and political quagmires, it opens onto a probable scenario of civilizational decline. The awesome challenge that scale presents results from exponential growth that has elevated the mass of harmful environmental changes to a level that appears to be beyond the reach of existing problem-solving capacities.

While each of these broad explanatory horizons presents specific obstacles worthy of our attention, I shall position them lapidarily as components of the previously noted story of progressive global development, anchored in humanity's achievement of a certain dominion over nature, that climate change subjects to a troubling turn.

The System

A central feature of human civilization as it has evolved since the Industrial Revolution has been the enabling role of science and technology, to which we owe the production of machines that save labor, provide material amenities, and enable travel and communication on a massive scale. By harnessing the power of machinery, technology has both allowed us to assemble the elaborate infrastructure on which organized societies depend and enabled the production of bodies of knowledge, now monumental, that inform and enhance all kinds of human experience.

Using these resources, humans have moved at a rapid pace to construct the infinitely complex world we now inhabit in the era of globalization. If this huge conglomeration of environments, infrastructures, enterprises, institutions, and nations functions as a relatively muted, but incontestable influence, a superstructural background that we usually take for granted, it is nonetheless the controlling systemic guide that makes us what we are. It locates and defines us, orients our thoughts and desires, shapes our spaces of activity, provides the material reality we manipulate and the context in which we identify ourselves and pursue our projects. Caught up in its processes, we are entangled in its dependency on the enormous supplies of energy that are necessary for its operation. To appreciate the strength of the interests behind the continuing extraction of coal and petroleum, it suffices to ask how our society would manage if we suddenly had to do without the fuels that power cars, planes, trains, ships, and electricity generation. The system that undergirds the extraordinary agency our species has achieved would simply disintegrate.

Given all that this world system we have built up does to and for us, given the opportunities for flourishing it offers to those who are capable of navigating productively within it, it is easy enough to understand why its diverse beneficiaries (individuals, publics, institutions, organizations, nations, and so forth) would be reluctant to support measures to reduce or limit the order of sustenance and gratification the system makes possible. Moreover, the system has programmed its subjects, as it were, to support not only its preservation but its continued development. It has formed a society of consumers whose interests lie in the always expanding process of acquiring capacities, possessions, and privileges. In societies that prize competitive success, the drive to accumulate wealth and advantage—for some who are already well-off, it amounts to "luxury fever"—expresses itself in the tenets of neoliberalism. This much reproved yet still presiding credo associates devotion to the accumulation of material wealth—consumerism—with an established socioeconomic commitment to the dynamics of growth.

During the second half of the twentieth century, and especially during the Reagan era, as globalization of the world economy was taking hold and staking claim to its positive status in the neoliberal orthodoxy, an imperative to achieve constant growth was reinforced and became a leitmotif of macro-level policy. According to the well-known rationale for what we label loosely as neocapitalism, an essential, indisputable value of economic growth is that it benefits everyone, from the bottom of the financial ladder to the top. It thus makes for improved conditions at every level and at times, perhaps, for a more equitable distribution of wealth overall. The framework that serves as the open space and efficacious instrument of this broadly beneficial economic growth is the free market. Protected from undue regulation, the market is a field of competitive activity on which the players assume that the processes of expansion, innovation, and adjustment to evolving conditions will continue indefinitely. Maintaining measurable growth, as indicated by the gross national product, gross domestic project, or other statistical indices, is the paramount imperative in this consumption-based economic system.

The system, in sum, is essentially the capitalist economy as we have shaped it in the era of globalization. Many authorities regard capitalism as the only instrument with sufficient strength and adaptability to save us from the disaster that climate change portends.[24] Rather than dwell on the apologies for and critiques of capitalism here, I shall simply note in passing that its requirement of permanent economic growth is incompatible with any plausible political program for ending planetary devastation and converting human societies to long-term sustainability. My concern is rather to underscore its extraordinary power. Its ascendancy is such as to endow it with an aura of indispensability. It prevails largely unscathed even when its judgments are challenged by practitioners of the very sciences and technologies that made its development possible.

A flagrant case in point was the deliberate effort by the leaders of the fossil fuel industry to represent the research of climate science as inconclusive while they knew full well, thanks to studies they had themselves funded and directed, that the findings were accurate. While the impregnability of their position derives in part from their capitalist commitment to exploitation of the underground resources they control, it derives ultimately from the dependency of the entire global system on the usable energy they supply. Like the big banks that had to be bailed out during the 2008 financial crisis, the system is, so to speak, too big—too necessary—to fail. Nearly all of its components depend on the operability it ensures in much the same way that businesses count on the banking system to facilitate their transactions. Given that dependency and the system's dependency on energy, for the time being there is no alternative to going along with the continued use of fossil fuels.[25] The risk of systemic collapse is an invincible obstacle to doing otherwise.

This same risk pertains, to be sure, to capitalism as a whole. For progressives who advocate for the "Green New Deal," this is hardly a welcome proposition. Yet as Noam Chomsky observes, the enormity of the challenge has to be confronted in terms of the problem of scale that I shall take up below: "A good argument can be made that inherent features of capitalism lead inexorably to ruin of the environment, and that ending capitalism must be a high priority of the environmental movement. There's one fundamental problem with this argument: time scales. Dismantling capitalism is impossible within the time frame necessary for taking urgent action, which requires a major national—indeed international—mobilization if severe crisis is to be averted" (Chomsky and Pollin 2020, 102). A key upshot of this understanding is that Chomsky and his coauthor, Robert Pollin, have to conceive of a Green New Deal that, rather than overturning capitalism, seeks to transform it from within. Pollin goes so far as to assert that, "if successful, a Green New Deal might also 'save capitalism' in the sense that it will abort the suicidal tendencies of 'really existing capitalism' and lead to some viable form of social organization that might fall within the very loose spectrum of what can be called 'capitalism'" (Chomsky and Pollin 2020, 72).

Collective Indecision

All governmental bodies, whatever their type, level, or size, face a collective action problem: policies adopted and enforced have to be accepted by the affected populations. Since climate change concerns all of the earth's inhabitants and since its mitigation will not occur unless all nations and all people—world citizens, as it were—accept and implement policies that limit emissions,[26] the problem is a strategic one: by what approach in the spheres of international relations and global sociocultural convention could agreements to institute and enforce such limits be achieved?

During the second half of the twentieth century, at least two international responses to major, highly publicized threats to worldwide security, nuclear arms proliferation and depletion of the stratosphere's ozone layer, gave us some cause to hope that multilateral agreements on a retreat from fossil fuel use would be possible. As it happens, however, the value of these nominal precedents seems limited. In the first place, the parties to the agreements on nuclear arms have been backing away from them, and leakage from the chlorofluorocarbon banks that were not disallowed by the Montreal Protocol of 1987 has slowed the restoration of the ozone layer. In the second place, as Robert Jay Lifton has pointed out forcefully in *The Climate Swerve* (2017), both of these dangers could be addressed by the articulation of clearly necessary common objectives that the negotiating parties could reach by sharing the relevant facts and making the appropriate decisions. If this is not the case with discussions of climate change, it is because such clarity of objectives and the feasibility of attaining them are missing.

Looking back from the decades of the 2020s at the various serious efforts to avert climate change that have been pursued, we have to grant that the diplomatic record so far is unpromising. To be sure, many meetings have taken place, principally under the auspices of the United Nations Framework Convention on Climate Change. Established at the 1992 Rio Earth Summit, this arm of the UN, with 195 member nations, has organizational responsibility for the two major agreements that have been reached to date, the Kyoto Protocol (1997) and the Paris Accords (2015).[27]

Even though they were successful in achieving an essentially universal involvement of the world's countries in negotiations, both of these agreements have been qualified as inadequate by proponents of strong action. In the first place, lack of support from the United States crippled both agreements; the two presidents concerned, George H. W. Bush and Donald Trump, viewed them as economically disadvantageous to American interests, and nonparticipation by the second-largest (after China) emitter of greenhouse gases subverts the entire cooperative scheme. In the second place, the terms of the agreements failed to satisfy experts on climate change since full-blown compliance with them would fall short of the key goal of keeping total global warming by the end of the century below 2° C.[28] Finally, the record of pledges that nations have made but not kept underscores the UN's inability to secure and enforce binding commitments to reduce harmful emissions.

The arduous, perhaps irresolvable, debate in the attempts to construct an inclusive agreement tends to oppose the highly developed nations concentrated in the Northern Hemisphere to economically disadvantaged countries of the Southern Hemisphere. The former pollute and consume far more. Having done so for a long time, they can hardly deny their primary responsibility for the unabatable greenhouse gas contamination of the stratosphere. The latter, victims of a warming due largely to the profligacy of the affluent energy consumers of the north, argue for economic justice, asserting that the massive long-term emitters should play a primary role during the first phase of mitigation and gap-narrowing by curbing their excessive consumption. This would, they contend, allow development in the poorer countries to continue, bringing them closer to parity in living standards before they have to join in the carbon-cutting endeavor. The term climate justice is often used to refer to this objective of equitably distributing the costs of mitigation.

If just agreements about climate change are difficult to achieve, a major long-term factor is the diplomatic regime that emerged in the aftermath of the treaties of Westphalia in 1648. The key understanding is structured to favor the perpetuation of national autonomy. In principle, the sovereign state safeguards its own interests and boundaries while eschewing intervention in the affairs of other states. As Paul Harris argues convincingly in *Global Ethics and Climate Change* (2016), insofar as the regime of international arrangements confers upon states the responsibility for dealing with environmental issues, it functions as a context of constraint not unlike that of the fossil fuel–dependent economic system. Ignoring the human rights and responsibilities of persons, it has no purchase on the most consequential factor, which is the behavior of affluent people wherever they happen to live. In compromises such as those that acceptance of the Paris Accords required, respect for the values of sovereignty, nonintervention, and boundary protection means that national interest consistently takes precedence over global welfare. During the current "age of uncertainty,"[29] the prospects for strengthening the authority of international bodies such as the UN are dimmed by evidence that in recent decades public trust in mediating institutions has been declining in democratic societies throughout the world.[30]

In light of the failures to achieve effective climate agreements already noted and the enduring structure of international negotiations hampered by the primacy of national interests, is there simply no prospect of achieving an effective international agreement to pursue mitigation efforts? The one approach I have found at least theoretically plausible is elaborated in great detail and with abundant argumentative power in a book with the promising title *Global Carbon Pricing: The Path to Climate Cooperation* (Cramton et al. 2017). The authors of this collectively articulated proposal purport to draw on Elinor Ostrom's work on cooperation in the management of shared resources.[31] They begin by positing that a common reciprocal commitment—according to which every national government will impose a negotiated minimum global price (a universal floor charge or tax, as it were) for carbon emissions and submit to a cooperatively designed mechanism of enforcement—could serve as a principled foundation on which a successful treaty for protecting the earth's atmosphere could be constructed. Since each country could use the revenues it collects for its own purposes, and since all participants could represent the near-term domestic benefits of cooperation as consonant with their self-interest, the classic free rider problem—the party that fails to pay benefits unfairly from the investment of the party that does pay—would be largely resolved. Moreover, such an arrangement would presumably serve to promote trust and cooperation and thereby serve as a model for the common pursuit of other measures necessary for reducing the risk of harmful climate change.

An at once admirable and problematic feature of *Global Carbon Pricing* is that, in chapter after chapter, it is replete with analysis of the complications and resistances that establishing a global pricing scheme would entail. A particularly robust example of this emphasis on the difficulties of designing and implementing a global system is provided in chapter 10, "Effective Institutions against Climate Change" (2017) by Christian Gollier and Jean Tirole. Their view of the path to cooperation has the feel of a compendium of impediments: "carbon leakages" such as moves by high-emissions industries to "nonvirtuous countries"; the popular preference of present consumption to investment in future well-being; the economic heterogeneity within a very diverse coalition of nations that requires a complex negotiation mechanism; the reluctance of rich countries to establish a necessary system for subsidizing poor ones; disagreement over the design and financing of such a system; the daunting size of the massive wealth transfers to the less-developed world; acrimonious debate over the basis for determining those transfers; tension between ethical and economic imperatives; an "enforceability problem" that "requires a strong international monitoring system"; controversy over both the allowable cost of such an overnight mechanism and the establishment of authority within it; multiple uncertainties that make setting the right initial price for carbon emissions unlikely; and so forth. Skeptics can reasonably doubt that existing institutions such as the United Nations, the World Bank, and the International Monetary Fund are equipped to take on the task of setting up such a complex apparatus expeditiously and managing it effectively.

Since current trends show the north-south disparity to be fading as the developing nations both increase their greenhouse gas emissions and acknowledge the wisdom of pursuing sustainable development and a transition to green energy simultaneously, a good number of informed observers expect the debate about allowable energy sources to become less intense over time. However, there is ample reason to believe that the foreseeable progress will be too slow; the damage that has been done by continuing increases in fossil fuel burning since the Kyoto Protocol and that will unavoidably be done for many years to come will take us well beyond the recommended warming limits of 1.5° or 2.0° C. In addition, the future negotiations between developed and developing countries seem destined to take place under conditions of accelerating global warming and aggravated socioeconomic pressures that will exacerbate the already challenging issues. Such complications are likely to force concessions to weak compromise options at a time when unequivocally strong, indeed drastic, measures are needed. It is thus difficult to imagine how the negotiation of workable agreements can occur until the onset of overwhelming crisis intervenes to force cooperation. Will its advent not simply be too late?

Scale

Distinct stories can be told about growth and scale. From the standpoint of the Anthropocene, however, the narratives deserve to be conjoined since the problem of scale we now face—how to design and implement measures extensive enough to address the enormous, planetwide problems we humans have unleashed—has resulted from multiple forms of growth that we have instigated and promoted. Some of the significant areas of growth—in human population, creation and expansion of cities, use of natural resources (such as coal, oil, metals, fresh water, forests, arable lands, and the marine food chain), living standards, demand for electricity, manufactured goods, and transportation—have resulted in levels of consumption that are patently unsustainable. This becomes all the more evident and ominous when we ponder the global dynamics of consumer demand, which appears to be insatiable.

In the comments on growth and scale that follow, I draw on two extraordinarily illuminating books: *Scale: The Universal Laws of Life, Growth, and Death in Organisms, Cities, and Companies* (2018), by the Anglo-American physicist Geoffrey West, and *Growth: From Microorganisms to Megacities* (2019) by the Czech-Canadian interdisciplinary scholar Vaclav Smil.[32] A plainly reductive, but orientationally useful, way to characterize the complementarity evoked by the term growth in these titles is to treat *Scale* as the source of a general theory of growth and *Growth* as the source of a strategic history of growth. Since both of these resolutely interdisciplinary works weave history and theory together, and since both insist on data-based quantitative analysis driven by established science, the distinction is undeniably a heuristic artifice. It does, however, allow us to ask how West's ambitiously theoretical outlook is positioned and complicated by Smil's empirical accounts of growth as it has actually happened.

Scale presents a general theory[33] of exponential growth, dealing first with biological life and then with collective activity by humans. The theory, anchored in the laws of scaling and the dynamics of network structure, emphasizes the relation of systemic growth to the production and distribution of energy; it treats both biological organisms and social organizations as complex adaptive systems that develop nonlinearly. Growth for plants and animals is sublinear, which is to say that as the size of organisms in the biosphere increases, their per capita energy needs decrease. Thus the metabolic growth of the organism, which occasions economies of scale, has an exponent of less than one; since its growth is bounded, it eventually reaches maturity, and it stays at that size until, owing to its inherent entropy, it dies.

In important respects, this life-course scenario of beings such as humans contrasts with that of cities and economies. As their size enlarges, the growth exponent for such key systemic features as productivity and innovation is greater than one, so the process results in increasing returns to scale. Thus they benefit from expansion of population, territory, or human capital. In light of the benefits of greater size and the presumed open-endedness of the system, the incentive to recognize growth as a positive phenomenon that continually boosts the value of the whole is unmistakable. This propitious dynamic of aggrandizement is reflected in the outlook of mainstream economics, for which the objective of maintaining growth is, as I noted above in characterizing the global system, deeply entrenched as a kind of principle of principles.

West and Smil argue vehemently, however, that the postulate of indefinite growth is untenable. Decrying the linkage of an economy's health to endless exponential expansion of at least a few percent per annum, they press economists to face up to the need to factor energy use and resource depletion into their models. For the uninitiated, there are at least two common-sensical ways of grasping the impossibility of unlimited growth.

The simpler one is to observe that producing the energy needed by a perpetually expanding system would require more and more expendable resources and that eventually the supply would fall short of demand. The other one, also readily apparent, is that the diverse components of the expanding system scale differently as its size increases and that endless growth would gradually modify the relations among them in ways that create disabling asymmetries or disproportionalities.

In any case, West's theory posits that "unbounded growth cannot be sustained without having either infinite resources or inducing major paradigm shifts that 'reset' the clock before potential collapse occurs" (31). Smil echoes both of these points by disputing "claims that ignore long-term trajectories of growth (that is, the requisite energetic and material needs of unprecedented scaling processes) and invoke the fashionable mantra of disruptive innovation that will change the world at accelerating speed" (xxiv).

West reinforces his resistance to the widespread notion that future discoveries and inventions will always turn up to save the system before it reaches its limit by introducing a further theorem: the innovations that reground the system's viability—by changing its "material composition or structural design or both" (60)—have to occur at an exponentially accelerating pace. As the time gap between each vital innovation (examples of key points of renewal mentioned by West include the inventions of printing and computing, the discoveries of iron, steam, coal, electricity, and so forth) and the next one becomes shorter and shorter, the system-saving process will finally run out of room for further paradigm shifts and lack the wherewithal to stave off collapse.[34] A worrisome prospect! For his part, Smil inveighs against futurists who envisage miraculous solutions provided by technology and asserts his agreement with Stephen Emmott, who commented in *Ten Billion* that "technologizing our way out of this does not look likely" (2013, 186).[35]

Yet a remarkable, if somewhat curious, feature of West's formidable study is the deftness with which it equivocates on the urgent questions about climate change, energy supply, and sustainability that it raises with consummate acuity. For example, after noting that significant climate changes are upon us and that we need to develop strategies for adaptation and mitigation, West puts the issue as follows: "The crucial question is not whether these effects [ecological and climatological changes] are anthropogenic in origin because they almost certainly are, but rather to what extent they can be minimized without leading to rapid discontinuous changes in our physical and economic environment and ultimately to the potential collapse of the global socioeconomic fabric" (237). Here, despite the stern alarm signals, mitigation and adaptation may or may not still be open possibilities.

Two hundred pages later, after discomfiting chapters devoted to the Urbanocene, which is the stage of a rapidly advancing, environmentally nocuous takeover of the planet by super-exponentially expanding cities, West comes to equally somber yet still wavering conclusions:

> Nevertheless, exponential growth may very well be unsustainable for the very kind of concrete reasons originally advanced by Malthus, namely, that we will be unable to produce enough food or sufficient energy, or that we will run out of essential resources such as phosphorus, oil, or titanium, and that at the same time, we will have failed to develop the appropriate technology to address these issues. In addition, we may be producing so much

entropy that the resulting pollution, environmental damage, and other induced changes, particularly to the climate, become insurmountable, leading to untold unintended devastating consequences. (423)

If this double bind of scarcity and damage does not exclude saving innovations, they appear to be unlikely because the relentless spread of our modern habitat of municipalities has become super-exponential. It has the effect not only of speeding up the pace of human—that is, urban—socioeconomic life but also of increasing both the rate at which major innovations or paradigm shifts have to occur and the mind-bending scale of change they have to enable. The process would take us precisely to that inflection point that West's theorem about the pace of innovation qualifies as untenable—to what he specifies, in mathematical terms, as an essential singularity.

What strikes an awkwardly improbable note in the passage just cited is the slippage into the conditional mode marked by the auxiliary "may." A similar modalization is articulated in the final paragraph of *Scale*, where the concluding thrust of the argument moves from the conditional ("if nothing changes") to the interrogative:

The increasingly rapid rate of change induces serious stress on all facets of urban life. This is surely not sustainable, and, if nothing changes, we are heading for a major crash and a potential collapse of the entire socioeconomic fabric. The challenges are clear: Can we return to an analog of a more "ecological" scaling and its attendant natural limiting, or no-growth, stable configuration? Is this even possible? Can we have the kind of vibrant, innovative, creative society driven by ideas and wealth creation as manifested by the best of our world's cities and social organizations, or are we destined to a planet of urban slums and the ultimate specter of devastation raised by Cormac McCarthy's novel *The Road*? (425)

The unresolved tension here sets off the option of scaling down to a no-growth, stable configuration against the drive to retain the gratifying features of a dynamic modern society. To the extent that the author's questions are both real and rhetorical, they disclose a lingering, perhaps insurmountable complicity with the very society of consumerism or neocapitalism from which he is nonetheless recoiling. For most readers, however, I believe the balancing act will not obscure the dominant thrust of *Scale*, which advances toward a vision of human society growing steadfastly until it collapses under its own weight.

For Vaclav Smil, who takes the trajectory of Japan since World War II to be an exemplary indicator, the phenomenon of an aging and shrinking Japanese population and of the country's economic stagnation after a spectacular ascent to affluence and socioeconomic acclaim points to the historical necessity of a guarded view of future growth. On the one hand, barring major catastrophe, it is likely that thanks to improved standards of living human fertility levels will wane everywhere and thus that the global population in 2100 will settle back to around nine billion. On the other hand, it is also likely that the upward spiral of global demand for energy and material goods will continue until it becomes unassuageable—at which point economists would have to stop decoupling growth from energy and material inputs. Such an adjustment would entail a shift to multifactor models that could restrict growth or favor "no-growth" stability or even require contraction. But this is by no means a prediction.

Smil remains the spokesperson par excellence for uncertainty.

Lacking even an approximate notion of the kinds and amounts of change that the biosphere will tolerate, we cannot foresee its state, he insists, in either the near or the distant future. Neither can we predict the potentially dire effects on humans and their world that continued growth and mass consumption will cause, nor can we know in advance how human societies will choose among the various options for responding to crises that lie ahead. The upshot of such a multiplication of uncertainties is a daunting escalation of the risk factors to be anticipated. The fully elaborated picture complicates the abstract problematics of risk both by situating it at a scale of incommensurability and by including in the overview of harmful scenarios the possibility of a cascade of breakdowns too concentrated in time to be managed technologically. Paradoxically, the heightened uncertainty makes the mobilization of a precautionary approach more necessary and less feasible.

Far from going along with the tendency to allow such uncertainty about the future to inhibit action, however, Smil tilts decisively toward reckoning with risks and probabilities. Near the end of *Growth* (2019, 503–6), he offers crisply an excruciating review of major anthropogenic impacts of growth that have to be set alongside the most prominent public concern, the link of global warming to the combustion of fossil fuels. Smil and his team of researchers have carefully documented these impacts. They include, among others, light pollution, degraded oceans, decimation of wild animal populations, depleted and polluted freshwater resources, species loss and diminished biodiversity, desertification, deforestation, reduced areas of contiguous wilderness, and loss of arable land, along with increases in population, energy consumption, air pollution, and numbers of ruminant livestock and other domesticated animals. Against this background, the ultimate risk is clear. "On the global level, there is no greater what-comes-after-growth uncertainty than the very fate of modern high-energy civilization with its still continuing population growth, high material requirements, and commensurately high environmental impacts. All of these long-lasting trends will have to end, deliberately or involuntarily" (454).

With this firm diagnosis in place, and working with his judgment that we cannot know whether the end of growth will be followed by a descent to a sustainable level of civilization or by the extinction of humanity, Smil veers in the final chapter of his study toward a posture of judgment and advocacy that in important respects dovetails with West's carefully modulated call, in the afterword to *Scale*, for a certain de-urbanization. West envisages in circumspect terms a retreat from the acceleration of life that technological advances have fostered and toward a worldview centered on a depreciation of consumption, an assertion of ecological responsibility, and a redefinition of progress that makes sustainability the universal goal. For Smil, the accumulation of excesses—in the spheres of economic development, extraction of resources, material consumption, and environmental degradation—appears to make for greater urgency. We face "a nonnegligible probability of some kind of involuntary global retreat—that is substantial prolonged worldwide retrenchment" (498). In the abstract, to face this probability is to grasp the relevance of responsible risk reduction, notwithstanding the insurmountable uncertainty that Smil emphasizes. Concretely, the potential for inescapable regress or devastation forces us to grant that we should already be considering the need for unthinkably anti-growth objectives: "deliberately declining levels and performance (or, in inelegant and inaccurate newspeak, 'negative growth' or 'degrowth')" (510). Smil aligns his ultimate stance on growth with moral imperatives: "to ensure the habitability of the biosphere while maintaining human dignity . . . to preserve our species while inflicting the least possible damage on other organisms with whom we share the biosphere" (512).

Such rays of optimism as one can find in *Scale* and *Growth* are dim and fleeting. The reserved tone and nuanced caveats of their respective conclusions are a function of scientific caution and firm intellectual integrity. Both West and Smil carefully refrain from excluding a universal awakening to danger and a turn away from the worship of growth and consumption. It is nonetheless clear that both are well aware of the three obstacles to action—the pervasive power of the system, the difficulty of collective action, the massive scale of the energy use and consumption spawned by growth—that I have outlined above; likewise, it is clear that both, cognizant of the tenacious social and personal drives fueled by humans' dominant sense of self-interest, regard an about-face at the monumental scale needed for preservation of a viable habitat as an unlikely outcome.[36]

From my vantage point within the humanities, the concern that Smil expresses by positing human dignity, preservation of the human species and habitat, and respect for other organisms as guiding principles has to be understood as a refusal—based rather more in human decency and a mature reflection on the lessons of our recent history than in scholarly scruples or ethical ratiocination—to give up the struggle for ecological enlightenment even though the deck is stacked against success. Given the evidence before us, we are surely behooved to anticipate the continuation of a losing battle against planetary degradation.

In a worst-case scenario, the struggle would finally dissolve into an apocalyptic cascade of severe crises. The global financial fiasco of 2008 and the pandemic that arose in 2020 have doubtless offered us a foretaste of devastating events that lie ahead and that could converge in a paroxysm of global collapse. In the absence of an explosive cataclysm such as nuclear warfare, however, the more likely outcome of global warming would be Smil's "involuntary global retreat," that is, a gradual disintegration of the thermo-industrial civilization we have constructed. It would be gradual because the decline in available natural resources would occur in fits and starts over many decades, because the harmful effects of slowly warming temperatures would take hold in incremental steps rather than suddenly, because intelligent adjustments and savvy technological advances would delay and dilute some of the injurious impacts, and because the accumulating responses to a series of crises would belatedly constitute an airtight case for the necessity of international cooperation.

In sum, a ruinous outcome that I consider more plausible than total extinction would not be far from a possible extreme scenario envisioned by Toby Ord.[37] Rather than a full-blown existential catastrophe, it would be a dark episode in the human story, a collapse of civilization whose survivors would be left to forge another trajectory. Yet whatever the ordeal of reversal and adversity that awaits future generations, and whatever the form of human survival that may emerge in the wake of an inevitable large-scale reorganization of terrestrial life, it is evident that our inherited assumptions about the course of human civilization will have to change.

If this hypothesis is reasonable and commands the predominant, urgent attention that I propose to accord to it, the question before us is whether we should respond to the distressing situation with despair and resignation, or with evasive, puerile escapism, or with an insouciant carpe diem posture amounting to cynical indifference, or with determined efforts at mitigation aimed at overcoming the obstacles that up to now have thwarted the proponents of the environmentalist cause.[38] In the final, brief segment of this chapter, I propose to recount the modern historical overview that I believe the public humanities, and then higher education at large, will need to recognize in order to address the anthropocenic challenge with urgency and efficacity.

Reframing Modernity

In the final pages of chapter 2, I noted the lineaments of a suspect national narrative that once nourished the idea of American exceptionalism but that of late has disintegrated. Here, in discussing the obstacles to action aimed at deterring climate change, I have in effect presented the beginnings of an ongoing international narrative of humanity that I called for there. This much wider perspective underlies the dour story we hear now from the French collapsologists,[39] who situate the epoch of the Anthropocene and the advent of climate change as a turning point that exposes the human species to the grandest of the grand challenges: its survival on a depleted, inhospitable Earth.

Initially it is a Eurocentric narrative that starts in the eighteenth century and proceeds along two tracks, ideological and technological, that are complementary and interlocking. Prior to the Anthropocene, technology was generally welcomed as the instrument of progress. From the Industrial Revolution onward, a steady series of advances in the capture and distribution of energy enabled great increases in human productivity and remarkable, albeit unevenly distributed, enhancements of living standards. After World War II, the Great Acceleration, which boosted the construction of a world order marked by massive growth and consumption, reinforced the economic ascendancy of highly developed nations of the Northern Hemisphere in the global economy that now prevails. A conceptual ally in this enormous anthropocentric adventure, the rationalist ideology of the enlightenment construed the advance of technology as an engine of civilization and liberation that demonstrated the capacity of human culture to gain control over nature. But as Western culture expanded into a hegemonic force over the nineteenth and twentieth centuries, it morphed into the globalized socioeconomic framework of growth-driven capitalism and consumerism that threatens to undermine the very system of human domination that it successfully fostered.[40]

Such is, briefly and roughly recapped, the unfinished, ironic, in important respects exhilarating, yet potentially tragic tale of humanity's rise to planet-warping power and its recent preparation—by way of inaction—for a fall. By recounting it in these sweeping, unrefined terms, I have repeated a common gesture that serves to distance it from the realities of our daily lives. Granting that the form and timing of the denouement remain unclear, the threat of collapse should at least force us to reckon with the collective history that now confronts us and to ask how we should respond to the possibility of a fallen civilization.

Humanities scholars have done prodigious, heavy-duty work in piecing this lapsarian story together in its complexity and in pointing out its stark implications, yet the versions of the narrative that are ritually retold within the University (treated, as it were, in subfields such as environmental history, environmental philosophy, political ecology, ecocriticism, and in diverse interdisciplinary programs in environmental studies) usually have ambiguous effects. On the one hand, they diffuse a warning that heightens awareness and understanding of the problem. On the other hand, they carry out a translation into scholarly or expert discourse that domesticates—normalizes and technisizes—within institutional confines[41] what should be a burning public issue.

This intra-institutional discursive churn, as I noted in chapters 2 and 3, prompts complaints about co-optation like Justin Stover's in "There Is No Case for the Humanities" (2017), where he asserts that the humanities continue to lend cachet to elitist credentialing and "provide cover for the economic engine that the contemporary university has become."[42] If the humanities are facing an authentic crisis of the kind that demands unconditional judgment and decisive response, it lies here, I submit, in their continuing acquiescence to the academy's standard, well-reasoned, and historically beneficial preference for judicious contextualization and calm analytic detachment. The critical issue—the question of crisis—for the academic humanities is whether their complicity with the status quo will be a permanent condition or a transformative relationship. Given their substantial role in the institutional dilution and/or recuperation of the narrative that turns upon their fundamental core, which is the trajectory of humanity, the current task of the humanities, I believe, is both to make the full story public and to challenge the institutional reflex that tempers that story's urgency. In the fifth and final chapter, I shall try to spell out prescriptively what this should imply for the University.

CHAPTER 5

Public Humanities and the University

What, then, does the urgency of reckoning with climate change mean for the University and the public humanities? To be sure, the orbit of the public humanities as I charted it in chapter 2 is not confined to colleges and universities. Among the explicitly humanities-focused organizations in the United States, for example, it includes the important work of the National Endowment for the Humanities (NEH), the fifty-four state and jurisdictional humanities councils funded by the NEH, and the Consortium of Humanities Centers and Institutes, an international association headquartered at the University of California–Berkeley. The fact remains, however, that the public humanities as a concept and a movement are ultimately defined by the University—by the relation of its teaching and research to the public interest and by the way colleges and universities reach out to study, serve, and influence the public at large. Moreover, important non-academic advocates for the humanities, such as the NEH, the National Humanities Alliance, the American Council of Learned Societies, the American Academy of Arts and Sciences, and the American Philosophical Society, ally and align themselves with the interests and positions of the academic humanities.

At least until recently the emergence of the public humanities movement has been visible primarily in North American higher education, which has doubtless predominated because its institutions have retained commitments to the idea of liberal education at the university level. Tending to delay student specialization longer than their counterparts in other parts of the world, our universities (especially those with humanities centers and institutes) have been the breeding ground of the humanities writ large, conceived as a collaborative transdisciplinary horizon and as a relatively accessible sphere of general learning. Within higher education, their distinctive role is to embrace the entirety of the university's curriculum and research mission by articulating synthetically, for all members of the academic community, a vision of humanity—of its promise and its limits—that the collective work of their institution subsumes and supports. Concomitantly, they uphold an enduring notion of education itself as a basic initiation into the art of learning and the appreciation of intellectual life. As a formative experience available to all students in all fields, they constitute a relatively stable (as opposed to rapidly evolving) educational core that provides for common understanding and cross-disciplinary communication amid all the manifold differences in interest and outlook that the University harbors.

To qualify this overarching, reflexive view of the humanities as *public* is to ascribe to the institutions of higher learning that embody such a vision a responsibility to relate—to connect and to convey—their work to the world through action that goes beyond sending their graduates into society and thereby allowing the benefits of advanced learning to spread haphazardly by osmosis. It is to recognize something on the order of an institutional message, constituted by the community of scholars, about the state of the world and the situation of humanity within it; it is to graft onto the calling of the humanities an imperative to make the message emanating from educational communities *public*, which is to say both to ground it in the public interest and to communicate it freely and widely in intelligible terms, as knowledge worthy of universal attention. Concretely, what do these two facets of the project—constructing collective insight and disseminating it—entail?

The evident thrust of the preceding chapter was to assert an urgent historical necessity. For both individuals and institutions, the implications of environmental degradation—ultimately, the possibility of societal collapse at a planetary scale—must become a central, mission-defining preoccupation. In the universe of higher education, this means that the composite of studies making up the curriculum must be reimagined as a complex organic whole, the numerous, widely varied components of which converge around the challenge—a problematics—of civilization's survival.[1] For students and academic professionals, pursuing a serious understanding of climate change and the interlocking environmental and social problems that it exacerbates will have to become a decisive mandate, a fundamental requirement that orients teaching and research alike.

The possibility of implementing such a prescription across the entire curricular spectrum is already well established. For example, in a long chapter of the 2022 edition of the *Handbook of Climate Change Mitigation and Adaptation* titled "Climate Change Education at Universities: Relevance and Strategies for Every Discipline" (Lackner, Sajjadi, and Chen 2022, 1–62), Petra Molthan-

Hill and colleagues undertake to show what climate change education means concretely by reviewing courses and programs currently offered, primarily in British and American universities, in fifteen disciplinary areas ranging from broad clusters (natural sciences, social sciences, humanities, arts) to narrower, professionally oriented fields (engineering, business, law, agriculture, medicine, etc.).

Similarly, in the remarkably capacious opening chapter of *Education and Climate Change* (Reimers 2021) titled "The Role of Universities Building an Ecosystem of Climate Change Education," Fernando Reimers invokes "the need for systemic, multilevel and multidimensional perspectives in climate change education" (32). He lays out the case for a collaborative interdisciplinary climate change curriculum that introduces students to behavioral as well as environmental sciences, to ethical frameworks, and to "multiple humanistic traditions" (22); he then proceeds to urge faculty "to integrate climate change education into existing courses" (37). The vast scholarly literature on climate change education leaves no doubt that its curriculum has to be thoroughly interdisciplinary and to involve a pervasive change in institutional culture. This same literature, however, recalls ad nauseam the lack of commitment to a full-fledged climate change curriculum both in individual institutions and across higher education in general.[2]

At this point, it is possible to qualify the overall response of the humanities to arguments for a concerted rethinking of educational responsibility in response to climate change as one of significant concern and understanding, yet hardly one of urgency or intense advocacy. At the university level, we can envision the charge of the humanities as that of articulating on behalf of the educational establishment a vision around the core institutional message I evoked above—that is, a unifying outlook born of a communally sanctioned narrative of modern human history and an integrative understanding of personal and social relations. If up to now the process has been largely a matter of recounting individual and collective achievements and associating them with common values and critical perspectives, at this juncture the lessons of earth system science call for a more pointed focus: the University must come fully to grips with the advent of the Anthropocene, with the dynamics of planetary devolution that imperils humanity's future. The imperative, in sum, is to reckon with the revised narrative of the human trajectory that I sketched in chapter 4. Were such a redirection actually to take hold, it would intensify the interest of the humanities in science—especially earth system science—and in society—especially its capacity to respond collectively to the effects of climate change. By the same token, within the University, it would spawn, necessarily, a renewed reflection on the institution's responsibility to a society behooved to undertake a major transformation that will fail if it is not pursued by design and at warp speed.

Against this background that compels the University to ask what it should be doing in response to radical planetary challenges facing humanity, the immediate, near-term role of humanities scholars would have to be far more frontally concerned with raising provocative questions and proposing educational reforms than with promoting traditional culture or skillful communication. This is to say that a rethinking of priorities for the academic humanities would have to be pursued and that it would have to turn on the purpose and enactment of a reconceived public mission of the University. It is doubtless important to recognize, therefore, that the various ideas in the humanities fields and professional organizations about what the public humanities are and how they should be developing still seem nascent and provisional. The fact remains that the efforts undertaken to date do shed helpful light on the hypothetical paradigm outlined in chapter 2 and alert us to the difficulty of elaborating prescriptions for reform.

The Current Horizon

The following four points attempt to summarize in sweeping terms the approaches that are in the air. They reveal both considerable promise and nontrivial limitations.

1. Many discussions and proposed reforms address the apparent decline in humanities enrollments and job opportunities for humanities scholars while bemoaning the escalating flow—detrimental to the humanities and the arts—of undergraduates into programs and majors leading to lucrative business and professional careers. The instinctive ground-level impulse here is to seek ways to reverse the trend, to ask how to restore the lost strength of humanities programs.

At the undergraduate level, changes in the curriculum that would multiply courses designed to appeal to manifest student interests—environmental issues prominent among them—or to attract minority students and others who may prefer a less Eurocentric canon are typically a first response to the decline. For graduate programs, the contents of the curriculum are also at issue, perhaps more radically since the orientation of advanced field-based research is at stake. Emphasis has fallen initially on rethinking the path to the PhD so that the training of doctoral candidates prepares them for non-academic positions as well as for the professoriate—for a diversity of occupations in which skills in research, collaboration, communication, and human relations are essential. The Mellon Foundation's early grants to the American Council of Learned Societies (a vigorous organization strongly supportive of a forward-looking humanities) for placement of new PhDs in public-sector positions assumed that the intervention of the humanities is needed in world-at-large occupations and sought to demonstrate the viability of the extra-academic trajectory.

Yet what the few experiments undertaken so far[3] tell us about the constitution of a curriculum veritably centered on students' needs and attendant to real-world outcomes—as opposed to traditional packages of distribution requirements or to a miscellany of advanced courses reflecting the interests of individual faculty members—remains to be determined. At both the undergraduate and graduate levels, the impetus still waiting to take hold is a sense of crisis and cogent direction that should center not so much on the inward-looking desire to rehabilitate the troubled humanities, but on the public—on confronting the risks before us and engaging with the public interest. From the standpoint of topics to be studied, the curriculum waiting to be developed would reflect a ready alliance of the public humanities with efforts pursued in the environmental humanities and political philosophy in the name of the public interest. The horizon of research to be traced and presented to the world at large would derive from a future-oriented interrogation, somehow informing every field and every course, aimed at understanding what would make it possible for human society to prolong itself as the earth's habitable spaces warm and shrink.

2. Defenders of the humanities have turned with greater sympathy than in the past toward extant outreach efforts by their institutions under the banner of engagement with the surround-

ing community or with the world.[4] To some extent, the early reticence within the humanities about direct social engagement doubtless had to do with a sense that its main thrust was toward economic development and the exploitation of research in domains—science, engineering, city planning, business, agriculture, and so forth—that seemed distant from the humanities.

More recently, the discourse around institutional engagement has often focused on the responsibilities, whether local or global, of the University as a whole, stressing its active participation in the construction of prosperous "knowledge economies" and well-managed communities.[5] Yet there has been a helpful shift away from the narrow association of the term *outreach* with service-learning courses and practical assistance offered by extension programs. Over the last few decades extramural work has become an increasingly valuable option for humanities faculty and students who are prepared to seek out audiences or collaborative groups in the general public and to participate in activities designed to promote cultural enrichment, historical or political understanding, civic responsibility, and social justice. Outreach can also, to be sure, take the form of writing or performing for the general public or, in certain cases, pursuing the public intellectual's role of influencing popular opinion. In the domain of climate change and environmental issues, where much of the public appears to be receptive to the views of experts, a crucial opportunity for representatives of the humanities— doubtless in collaboration with their colleagues in the social sciences—is to convey to the citizenry the narrative about what humans have done to their habitat that I sketched in the final pages of chapter 4. It is not principally, however, to echo the scientific experts who are presenting the relevant facts; it is rather to find ways to engage citizens in dialogue about what individuals, groups, enterprises, and societies can and should do in response to them.[6]

With respect to the full potential of the renewed horizon of public engagement or outreach that I have just noted, the most capacious appreciation that I have encountered is elaborated in a book that is not focused primarily on the humanities, but rather on the university and its need for a transformed academic culture, Kathleen Fitzpatrick's *Generous Thinking: A Radical Approach to Saving the University* (2019). A highly regarded scholar of literature, Fitzpatrick includes a substantial discussion of the humanities in her introduction (16–32), and the book as a whole conjures up a vibrant vision of the public humanities and its potential both for engaging with a range of publics outside of the academy and for promoting a return to the conception of higher education as a public good. In a chapter titled "Working in Public," she focuses insistently on the building of communities, both of scholars among themselves and of scholars interacting with members of the general public who can be interested in the research and writing of academic experts when it is made accessible to them. Access and community-building involve more, to be sure, than making work available to users of the internet's communication platforms and more than translating highly complicated analysis and technically sophisticated language into discourse that is comprehensible and unpretentious; they also require scholars to develop opportunities for interaction, for authentic dialogue, for the bond-forming coproduction of knowledge. Fitzpatrick's reasonable hypothesis is that such collaborative endeavors would counter the tendency, manifest in much of American society and culture, to treat the enclosed and out-of-reach sphere of high-end, high-cost academia as suspect and to resent its apparent elitism.

The overarching argument of *Generous Thinking* is predicated on a forceful critique of *competitive individualism* that Fitzpatrick describes as harmfully dominant in the research university. The competitiveness is exemplified by the drive to originality or divergence from other scholars whose rival views have to be challenged; the race for distinction motivates individual faculty members in their search for tenure and thereafter for professional recognition and rewards. Its hold on the institution's value system goes hand in hand with the privatization of higher education discussed in chapter 3 and with the devaluation of collegial commitments and of public service and engagement within the university hierarchy. The current situation reflects a kind of institutional mission drift away from the training of students as citizens of the state—something of a public orientation—to the credentialing of student consumers as corporate citizens with allegiances to the globalized market. In this context, the practitioners of the humanities can be typecast as individualists or gadflies whose discordant practice of critique and competitive dissensus is primarily of value to the private individual. Since their self-assertive posture consolidates the education their fields impart to them as a private good and defines success as a personal rather than social achievement, it aligns with—indeed instantiates—the systemic privatization that pervades the institution.

If Fitzpatrick envisages an appropriately complex solution to the problem of competitive individualism, it nonetheless seems fair to underscore two essential trajectories toward restoring the priority of the public over the private that *Generous Thinking* traces. One of these is predominantly intra-institutional and would focus on developing a less competitive, more cooperative and empathetic academic culture. The other is tilted toward the extra-institutional and would focus on engaging members of the public-at-large in collaborative projects of the kind that numerous public humanities programs have launched. Both involve the practice of generous thinking and the building of communities. Together they would carry the extant university not so much into a binge of organizational restructuring or a proliferation of new pedagogies as toward what Fitzpatrick characterizes as a paradigm shift, a reorientation of relations and values from the private toward the public, from the economic toward the social, that would generate a new institutional politics or "even a new political unconscious: a turn from privatized, rationalist, competition-based models for knowledge production to ways of knowing, of learning, of being in community that are grounded in an ethic of care" (207–8).

Two remarks are in order here. In the first place, *Generous Thinking* makes an extraordinarily capacious and insistent case for public humanities activity focused on outreach, community building, and collaborative projects designed to repair a troubled relationship between the university and the public it purports to serve.[7] Fitzpatrick's argument takes note of the need to correlate service learning programs with core academic efforts, and for the humanities it articulates a key imperative: in order to emerge from a role of shielding the university from critiques of privatization and to achieve a renewal that is vital to their future, they must become public oriented, must devote themselves to meeting the needs of the public, the entire body politic. In the second place, it seems important to note that, in this discussion, I have banked above all on the dimension of *Generous Thinking* that elucidates the nature and significance of public outreach and engagement. The book's central proposal, calling for a paradigm shift that might save the university, obviously resonates with essentially all of the components of the paradigm outlined in chapter 2. But more importantly, the proposal extends far beyond this discrete umbrella. Indeed, Fitzpatrick's ultimate focus on the university's political substratum anticipates in important respects the fourth category of public humanities work that I shall take up hereafter. It will serve as a comparative foil for my own proposal.

3. The most impressive elaboration of proposals for graduate program reform that I have encountered, *The New PhD: How to Build a Better Graduate Education*, by Leonard Cassuto and Robert Weisbuch (2021), propounds a far bolder set of recommendations for a "public-facing PhD" and for humanities outreach intertwined with "public scholarship" than those that have emerged from the various humanities fields. The authors have looked rather more broadly at the University than have, for example, professional organizations such as the American Historical Association and the Modern Language Association, which have carried out laudable initiatives intended to program into doctoral programs in English and history preparation for non-academic careers. Cassuto and Weisbuch wisely included the STEM fields in their research, and they have not shied away from calling for major across-the-board changes in institutional policy, administrative practice, and faculty behavior. A centerpiece of the remarkably extensive set of proposals *The New PhD* elaborates is the empowerment of graduate school deans, potentially important administrators who typically lack the control of budgets, appointments, and organizational arrangements that enables deans of professional schools and undergraduate colleges to exert a decisive influence in their bailiwicks.

No longer a mere figurehead or an occasional convener/mediator, the graduate deans conjured up by Cassuto and Weisbuch would actually be put in charge of graduate-level education: they would have managerial responsibility for program evaluation, the wherewithal to incentivize the reform efforts of cooperative faculty, the task of promoting interdisciplinary innovation, and the opportunity to exert intellectual leadership. They would be able, in sum, to foster an academic culture in which program curricula would be reshaped on the basis of student interests and in anticipation of diverse professional outcomes. Cassuto and Weisbuch go so far as to explain how a public-facing curriculum could be designed, and by positioning a wide range of carefully enumerated careers to which advanced humanities students can reasonably aspire as an end, they constitute a lever for reshaping courses of study in relation to the market for competent humanists that actually exists. Moreover, their vision of a student-centered doctoral program could readily be converted into a model for rethinking the undergraduate experience in humanities majors.

While the revisionary thrust of *The New PhD* is extraordinarily thorough and decisive, in the main the reinvigorated, public-oriented University that Cassuto and Weisbuch envision would result from what they term a *fix*. An overhaul that would go beyond discrete repairs of glaring defects, the fix would be a combination of strategic reforms sufficient to allow the venerable institution that has long commanded our respect to adapt to current realities as they are widely perceived at this juncture. While making numerous, interrelated changes, it would retain familiar disciplinary structures, operational assumptions, and scholarly mindsets, and along with them an establishmentarian sense of mission-based continuity with the past that is largely of a piece with the classic apology for a liberal education.[8] Insofar as it both preserves and renews traditional models of undergraduate education and graduate-level specialization, it allows faculty members to take part in a transformation that would substantially revamp their approach to teaching and to relations with students, yet also to imagine that their commitments to highly specialized research, their understanding of its value, and their sense of professional identity will remain viable. Since redirecting their work toward a new collective mindset involving responsibility to the future and an axiomatics of survival is not yet a significant feature among the capaciously delineated correctives Cassuto and Weisbuch propose, my task will be to ask what would make their proposals fully commensurate with the central problem to be faced on the horizon of public interest.

4. Finally and crucially, some observers of the linkage between the public humanities movement and the established humanities framework in universities have worried that academics tend to understand the move into the public arena oversimply—condescendingly—as an attempt by experts to edify the ignorant. The risk is that self-possessed academic authorities, upon exiting from the ivory tower into the world at large, might aim merely to instruct, might be content to translate their sophisticated knowledges into forms that would presumably benefit a public in need of enlightenment and encouragement. Such one-way interventions by well-meaning faculty and students would stop short of grasping explicitly the ways in which that extra-academic world complicates their scholarly work and in some respects throws it into question.

Once the agents of the public humanities are outside of the university's walls and caught up in dialogue centered on the public's views and problems, are they not positioning themselves for acts of research and discovery or for looking back from a public vantage point at their protected institutional milieu and situating it in a new light? Should the public humanities not be humanities transformed by experiences that confront the University with its embeddedness in the world, with what Edward Said depicted as its *worldliness* or circumstantiality?[9] In sum, does the encounter of the intramural humanities with the external world—with the public's insights and issues—not impose, for their scholarly work and their institution's mission, something on the order of a far-reaching critical self-reassessment?

The invocation of Said's critical posture as a public intellectual is a telling factor in two recent books that offer, at least implicitly, responses to this all-important question. The first of these, *The Humanities in the Age of Information and Post-Truth* (Lopez-Calvo and Lux 2019) trenchantly advocates for guiding the humanities toward more strongly committed social and political criticism. The background for this collection is a formidable 2014 essay by one of its contributors, David Theo Goldberg, "The Afterlife of the Humanities."[10] Goldberg proposes a "counter-conception" (27) of the humanities or "posthumanities" that would liberate them from disciplinary and institutional constraints and extend their domain to the whole of the human sciences; he conjures up a "reinvented humanities" capable of reckoning with an age of networking or information or big data that is also one of pervasive "worldly uncertainty" (28). His call for reinvention anticipates an impulse to veer toward militancy that permeates much of *The Humanities in the Age of Information and Post-Truth*. In an essay titled "What Kind of Humanities Do We Want or Need in the 21st Century?" (Lopez-Calvo and Lux 2019), David Castillo and William Egginton answer their own question with a clarion call: "In the all-pervasive market society, it is not enough to defend the value of the humanities in an increasingly corporatized university. Instead the humanities can and should go on the offensive to denounce the blinding effects of market fundamentalism and poke holes in the media-framed reality that's coextensive with it" (103). The role of the public humanities movement in such an endeavor is broached explicitly in the book's final essay by Mariët Westermann, "The Humanities in the World" (2019).

Westermann connects her title to Said's contention that it is wrong to separate either the work of scholars in the humanities or the objects they study from their worldliness, from the material and social conditions in which they are produced and disseminated. While cautioning against the facile public humanities I evoked above that would merely dull down the recondite discourse of specialists for public consumption, Westermann argues for a "regrounding of the humanities in the world around us" (114) and points the public humanities squarely toward dialogue with the public about the world's grand political and environmental challenges. The world she invokes extends far beyond that of the non-academics whom scholars typically encounter when they venture into the extramural milieu that lies outside the university's walls; it is the deeply troubled global world that Judith Butler depicts in her brilliant analysis of the COVID-19 pandemic, *What World Is This?* (2022). "This world" is a shockingly unprotected integration made up no less of the violated earth and its multiple habitats than of a stratified human society racked by injustice and inequality. Westermann focuses on the latter dimension. She proceeds to address two telling examples of the challenges that call for deploying "the expertise and methods of the humanities": first, the refugee crisis in the Middle East and Europe, or more generally the human rights of stateless persons in all parts of the world, and second, "the destruction of cultural heritage as an instrument of political and civil war" (117), emblematized by the atrocities committed against minorities by ISIS and the Taliban's obliteration of Buddhist cultural heritage in Afghanistan. The responses of mobilized scholars and cultural institutions that she cites beckon sympathetically toward Said's practice of intrepid political engagement.

The second appeal to Said's foregrounding of worldliness opens a work that I take to be exceptionally significant, a remarkably innovative study by the architect Reinhold Martin, *Knowledge Worlds: Media, Materiality, and the Making of the Modern University* (2021). Owing to the subtlety and intricacy of Martin's perception of the university's embeddedness in the world and of its role in recasting our views of that world, I propose to discuss this work at considerable length. Its title, opening the worldly to a plurality of epistemic worlds and juxtaposing it with media and matter, expands and densifies the thrust of Said's invocation of a world that, in its circumstantial immediacy and complex interactive dynamics, is incommensurable with the simpler world defined or assumed by classic theories and ideologies. The activity we observe in the ins and outs of the university's *making* is, according to Martin, a prolonged process of assemblage or compilation—a *technopoesis*—that constitutes a media complex.[11] Abstractly, we can characterize this mass of networking media as a far-reaching infrastructural web of disparate components, connected and separated by technical practices, arrangements, or devices, that underlie and inform efforts to make sense—knowledge—of our experiences and surroundings and to enable the appropriation and preservation of that knowledge.

But Martin prefers the concrete to the abstract. Looking at the University both from the inside—the sphere of liberal arts education—and from the outside—the more practical order of economics and politics that profits from education and knowledge production—he sets forth on multiple, at times mundane, levels various mediations through which the intramural and the extramural interact. His book juxtaposes a set of case studies, situated loosely in four half-century eras between the late eighteenth and the late twentieth centuries, that leave much to be extrapolated. Its readers are led, chapter by chapter, through genealogical investigations of down-to-earth, often elaborate instances of mediation occurring in a discrete number of exemplary (although for the most part elite or at least highly reputed) colleges and universities.[12]

Genealogy, as advocated and enacted in the work of Michel Foucault, eschews the search for origins, ends, tight causation, teleological lines of evolution, and narrative closure in favor of analyzing what Friedrich Nietzsche called "the endlessly repeated play of dominations" (85) while revealing complex relations of descent and the "singular randomness of events" (88).[13] Martin's genealogies, although verifiably factual, nonetheless have an anecdotal, creatively associative quality. While they do tell revelatory stories about distinctive features of the institutions examined, they reflect the Foucauldian critique of conventional history insofar as they resist classic linear narratives of continuity and unity and show no patience with stories of special commitment and unique achievement of the sort that academic leaders are prone to tell about their institutions. Rather, channeled by the emphasis on media, infrastructure, and architecture, they are multidimensional probes into the emergence and resolution of formative tensions affecting the way knowledge is produced, disseminated, and preserved by the University. Martin consistently treats these tensions or dilemmas as *bound-*

ary problems, among which drawing the proverbial town-gown line separating the university from the world it studies and fecundates is pivotal.

The result is an "off-center" history that bears little resemblance to the approaches of most historians of ideas and institutions (a majority of them from humanities fields[14]) who have studied the University from within, constructing linear narratives that trace the evolution of disciplines, curricula, pedagogies, directions of research, conflicts over governance, financial underpinnings, federal and state regulation, the academic marketplace, and so forth. Moving back and forth between inside (the province of academic humanities and social sciences) and outside (the purview of professions such as architecture, engineering, law, and medicine), Martin analyzes the emergence of intricate, often barely noticed networks that entangle the University with nominally external influences such as religion, industry, large-scale agriculture, geographic frontiers, demographics, and race, class, and gender relations. Each chapter turns on boundaries, interfaces, and knowledge systems that come together in a myriad of concrete technical operations: the design of buildings and campuses, disciplinary and administrative hierarchies, modes and methods of communication, processes of self-monitoring redefined by data collection and statistical analysis, research drivers, the compilation of reading lists, the role of "books, libraries, legal documents, and letters" that are caught up in overlapping media systems, and so forth.

Accentuating details and practical contours of elemental epistemic parameters (such as space, time, scale, discourse, instrumentality, figurability, measurability) while incessantly mixing story lines with elaborate descriptions, each mapping of passages and events discloses within the academic world the centrality of material possibility conditions and organizational machinery, the factors of operative tools, techniques, and technologies that are subsumed under the rubric of *technics*. At every turn the same pervasive connectivity and processuality that ground the University's capacity to become a research machine or knowledge factory provide for its reach into the economic and cultural world at large. Not even the rarefied realm of the most traditional "great books humanities" can escape from its entrenchment in a maze of worldliness.

While offering us an accumulation of genealogies that constitute a view of the University as a corporate body at once separate from the world—a sanctuary preserving spaces for contemplation and free expression—and intricately commingled with it, Martin is shrewdly circumspect when it comes to ascribing a historical trajectory to it, to articulating a critique of its practices and self-representations, or to positioning the humanities within it. Yet in delving into the give-and-take between universities and society, *Knowledge Worlds* repeatedly unveils a dynamics of knowledge-making mastery and mutual dependence that results in renewed complicities between them. The same alternating perspectives that display the University's worldliness beckon toward a public humanities practice that would similarly be capable of integrating views of the University from both inside and outside and addressing the ongoing recurrence of the boundary problems highlighted in Martin's genealogies.

The final chapter of *Knowledge Worlds* offers a clear and relevant case in point. It takes up a mid-twentieth-century situation, the aftermath of World War II and the stark tragedies of Hiroshima and Nagasaki, in which the humanities play a central role and in which the issues resonate with the concerns about planetary degradation confronting us now. The sites of inquiry are two powerful bastions of advanced technology, MIT and Stanford, both of which would enjoy privileged relations with nearby commercial high-tech centers during the ensuing decades. Martin uncovers efforts in each to deploy the humanities for two complementary purposes: to restore a sense of moral order that the war had shaken and to articulate the reintegration of highly compartmentalized fields, focused single-mindedly by the wartime imperatives of applied research, into an institutional whole (*universitas*) that can lay claim to a common intellectual and liberal-educational purpose.

In each of these cases, the pivotal instantiation of the humanities-technoscience alliance is a defining campus monument—the ensemble of the chapel and Kresge Auditorium designed by Eero Saarinen at MIT, the iconic Hoover Tower at Stanford. At MIT, in Martin's reading, the little chapel's soft light and the auditorium's acoustics optimized for the individual voice function as effects linking the "anonymous corridors of big science" (233) to the comforting presence of individual human souls, a frame of reference that reminds us of Helen Small's definition of the humanities "primarily in terms of the individual response and with an ineliminable element of subjectivity" (2013, 23). As for Stanford, Martin's analyses end with the evolution of the Hoover Tower from a library and archive into the home of a neoliberal think tank, the Hoover Institution. The latter represents the interests of *homo oeconomicus*, a real and representative human being of our modern or postmodern era whose engagement in what Philip Mirowski calls a "cyborg science" embodies the melding of the science-and-technology enterprise with a compatible humanities, an updated version primed to appreciate entrepreneurial subjects pursuing "the computer-driven, probabilistic calculus of market optimization, game theory, risk analysis, and systems modeling" (Martin 2021, 248). Both monuments, in sum, incorporate a media complex that consolidates a systemic assimilation or appropriation of cooperative human subjects who contribute to the dominance of the technology-driven knowledge-making machine.[15]

In the epilogue to *Knowledge Worlds*, Martin addresses briefly the apparent outcome of this highly associative genealogical narrative, its recognition of a recuperation of the humanities that both reasserts and redefines their value as institutional capital integral to the ongoing operation of the University's knowledge-producing machinery. The structure of that operation is described more elaborately in chapter 6, which presents the University of Chicago as an "intermedial circuit" in which an aural Protestantism aligned with the lecture format hooked up with a textual/visual secularism aligned with the seminar format.

In the Chicago case, the acoustical design—"a *doubled-up* psycho-acoustic space"(180; my italics here and below)—of another campus religious monument, the Rockefeller Memorial Chapel, delineated a relationship similar to, though a bit more complicated than, the one divulged by the analysis of the listening experience in MIT's Kresge Auditorium. Sophisticated sound engineering allows the authoritative voice from the pulpit in the chapel to be heard clearly by the distant audience, yet also to reverberate back to the speaker in a feedback loop that splits it in two: "The serial voice of reason audible in the pews, and the subtly reverberant voice of a displaced, sublimated god, a master standing at some distance and listening to himself" (180). The feedback heard only by the speaker confirms the authority of the discourse addressed to a passive audience, yet also displaces it toward mindful listening and self-assured mastery.

The point of the Great Books seminars that would become

the university's signature undergraduate program was to switch climactically from the lecture's didactic master-to-listener relationship to the seminar's ostensibly democratic practice of dialogue. The change repositioned professors as both questioners and listeners whose attention was "literally *doubled up*" (183). In humanities seminars held in a room with faculty and students seated together at an oval table, "speaking mouths multiplied and assembled around an infrastructure that *doubled up* the master's voice into a genial dialogue" (181).

The paradox was, then, that the intended democratization of the knowledge-production process—*doubling up* conjoins replication and magnification, amplifying the intermediation that it reproduces—actually restored the discourse of mastery by folding it upward into a different, higher model, that of the textual authority that came to be wielded by the carefully selected, eventually influential list of great books and that positioned professorial mastery as an art of insightful conversation. The new model adroitly instituted this advance while leaving the institution's underlying infrastructural control over its faculty and student agents intact.

Against this background, Martin goes on to describe what he terms the dialectic of the University, using the Hegelian account of the master-slave relation (which the dialectic of the lecture and the seminar "*doubles up*" [188]) and Jacques Lacan's construal of the discourse of the master as his conceptual levers. Lacan's contribution, echoing Nietzsche's perception of the Prussian state as the force behind the university he encountered in the 1870s, was to liken academic discourse to that of a state bureaucracy fulfilling its collective wish for submission to authority. In the long-term context of American higher education, the essential lesson here doubtless points to the quiet, gradual displacement of church authority by the dominance of the state (a force eventually apprehended as the overseer of a research-driving military-industrial-academic complex).

Such a reorientation is discernible in the successful adaptation to the secular seminar model: the University's technocratic mastery over the knowledge-based power produced by the labors of its faculty and students continues to derive from its control of the operative infrastructure, smartly recast in the Chicago case by the list of great books. The rationale for its exercise of that power lies in the lasting value of its established outputs, instrumentalizable research and knowledge that are doubled up, as it were, by the production of competent human subjects whose ability to make and/or apply new knowledges constitutes their status as human capital. As the grounding of this rationale that religion had long bestowed on institutions of higher learning evanesces, the internal genealogical slope becomes clear: the secular humanities inherited, as it were, the role of the sanctioning authority, the task of endowing the administration of the knowledge-power complex with a core of humanity, of validating the place left for human subjectivity and oversight of the University's machinery.

From the short epilogue to *Knowledge Worlds*, it is possible, to some extent in defiance of the author's unerringly artful subtlety and resistance to synthesis or closure, to extract the lineaments of a broad, partially familiar history of the University as we have come to know it. To put it crudely, in the succession of media complexes we can follow a trajectory with four phases: corporate, global, liberal, and neoliberal. Martin persuasively locates the first two much earlier than do commentators who expatiate on the consequences of rampant corporatization and financial globalization in the latter half of the twentieth century. He also defines them differently. The legal incorporation of American colleges during the early decades of the eighteenth century charted a path not only toward a domain-specific corporate structure, but also toward a kind of corporate entity or personhood, a collective body that would evolve into a community made up of individuals who identify with the institution that they cherish.

With respect to globalization, understood as the appropriation of international resources and the formation of worldwide networks of investment required by industrialization, we can now situate its gestation alongside early American imperialism, the development of an economy that relied heavily on the importation of slaves from Africa, and the transnational networks that traversed American agriculture as it spread westward during the nineteenth century. The global connection would be vital, moreover, to the conception and consolidation of the American research university during the late nineteenth and early twentieth centuries.

As for the decisive liberal phase, Martin's conception of its broad meaning and long duration is consistent with the established understanding of a liberal education: an experience of breadth (cultural and historical) and depth (intensive research) that *liberates* individuals, enables them to flourish in the world at large. The progressive arc of education thus complements that of the machinery developed by technology, the indispensable force that enriches the existence of humans by freeing them from various constraints of manual labor and affording them an ever-expanding range of opportunities. In his introduction Martin underscores three forms of the freedom that he associates with the University: free thought and speech, free will, and free markets. It is the last of these three vectors, the market mindset extolling competition, economic growth, and private enrichment, that presides over the sharp turn toward the neoliberal during the final decades of the twentieth century. The bonds that tie neoliberalism and its entrepreneurial human subjects to gainful, instrumentalizable knowledge nourish their affinity with the technocratically shaped University that *Knowledge Worlds* gradually reveals.

Exposure of its neoliberalism opens the University immersed in real-world capitalism and compliant with the promotion of knowledge as power to a certain critique, albeit one that is carefully balanced by a steadfast defense of its truth-telling mission, that *Knowledge Worlds* brings to the surface intermittently. Martin's overarching genealogy invites us to envisage the neoliberal University as the current variant of a media system that reorients a dynamics of separation and connection descended from and parallel to that of its predecessors. Within the protected space of a particular institution, the production of knowledge to be delivered to the world at large and of individual human subjects who are shaped by and collectively responsible for that process appears to be intact. The *dialectic* of the University, to use Martin's term, still does its work.

The evolving technical machinery undergirding this knowledge world has become ever more complex and media centered as cybernetics, information science, digitalization, data mining and analysis, quantum computing, spreading automation, robotics, machine learning, and artificial intelligence, while flowing outward and permeating society at large, have clearly established their hold in and on the universe of higher education. They have infiltrated its infrastructures and weigh heavily on its ongoing transformation. Does this looming knowledge world have a dark side? Can we now glimpse the specter of a technical sublime that is no longer "a technoscientific sublime serviced by the humanities" (Martin 2021, 19), but rather that of a fully reengineered postmodern university armed with the wherewithal to extricate itself from a framework of mastery that assumes direction by a controlling human agency?[16] Do we need to reckon with the possibility of an institution driven by programmed decision-making that ultimately allows technics to take over, to operate as a self-generating, self-governing system for which an autonomous, self-sufficient market, rather than a managed network that facilitates the play of human interactions, would be the model?[17]

For the academic humanities, the immediate concerns that are provoked by nervously speculative "posthuman" scenarios of this sort have to do with widely circulating claims by observers who believe that over the past half century the STEM fields have been taking over both the training of competent human subjects and the task of sustaining an integrative institutional vision of and for the University. This seemingly indomitable technoscientific juggernaut is subject to far more pressure to prioritize its partnerships with business interests than to worry about sanctions (whether supportive or admonitory) emanating from the humanities. Does its ascendancy, which also weighs heavily on the operational infrastructure of educational institutions that function as knowledge factories, signify the definitive marginalization of the humanities? Or is it still possible for specialized humanities fields whose doctoral students are no longer marketable in the academy to adapt inventively to the sobering realities they now face and mount a comeback?[18]

For the public humanities, the questions raised by the plight of the academic humanities do not simply involve their defense and rehabilitation within academia; the issue is also how to represent their role positively in the public arena against the background of their crippled intramural status. This handicap is doubled up, we might add, by the historical complicity of the humanities with the very forces—those of the so-called information economy and of what Martin terms *mediapolitics*—that contribute visibly to their current marginalization. They are, after all, no less enmeshed in their institution's worldliness than are the other academic disciplines. The worry, in other words, is that the public humanities are destined to carry into the extramural sphere the compromise-laden intramural relationship between the humanities and technoscience that *Knowledge Worlds* brings delicately into focus. Hence the discomfiting question: in order to reassert the values of the humanities in the world at large, as the public humanities make their way into extramural spaces, must they resort to articulating critiques of the academic humanities and proposals to reform the very University they undertake to represent? Such is the quandary, I submit, that now confronts advocates of a worldly public humanities.

The four-point overview of the current situation of the public humanities movement that I ventured above was deliberately limited to generic categories of widely visible activity. As such, it could by no means do justice to the variety and merit of many innovative local efforts that are extending connections between colleges and universities and their communities, nor could it begin to appreciate their documented successes in broadening and refining the purview and relevance of the humanities in and for the world at large.[19] While each of the four emphases I included is unquestionably reasonable and constructive, the fact remains that the first three—on revitalizing the humanities curriculum through a turn toward public interest and environmental responsibility, on renewing and expanding traditional outreach programs that address practical needs and public concerns, and on reorienting graduate work in the humanities toward public scholarship and a broad spectrum of professional opportunities—differ significantly from the fourth and final one, which evokes a critical reckoning with higher education's embeddedness in the socioeconomic world that humans have constructed.

The first three approaches share a reformist assumption that reflects an establishmentarian vision of the long-term status of the University. They expect it to endure as a liberal (in the core sense of liberating) and progressive institution that produces knowledge conducive to constructive change as well as human subjects whose capacities will ensure intelligent adaptation to changing conditions. To the extent that they are addressing a situation of crisis in the academic humanities, they tend to portray it as a serious but familiar and manageable problem to be addressed within a stable yet pliable context by incremental adjustments and strategic initiatives. These helpful measures can presumably be implemented gradually and result in needed correctives or enhancements. Their relatively standard and comfortable programmatic goal, in sum, is to revamp and strengthen the existing institutional framework by revitalizing the humanities within it. Accordingly, the degree of urgency and sense of necessity that the proponents of these laudable efforts put into play, while inevitably variable given the size and diversity of the higher education universe, is compatible with a relatively orthodox vision of progress and reform.

Thus the typical public humanities initiative stops short of asking whether the basic mission of the University does not have to be recast in light of the dangers it encounters in the world at large. The reservation I began to formulate in discussing *The*

New PhD actually applies to all three of these laudable approaches: in their public-facing efforts are the academic humanities reckoning as strongly as they should with the issues—with climate change and the whole cluster of calamities it will spawn or aggravate—that are bearing down on the world at large and its billions of inhabitants? Not yet.

The prevailing mindset here is all too predictably the one I underscored in introducing the conundrums of risk and uncertainty in chapter 4: a seemingly natural inclination to assume that higher education will evolve proficiently and enjoy indefinitely, or at least for a good long while, the benefits of stability and prosperity. While such an assumption is entirely understandable and would be defensible on the basis of a centuries-long history that preceded the appearance of the Anthropocene, it is at odds with the physical and social conditions in the present brave new world that the public humanities are destined to encounter and address. Or to put the issue more aggressively, it presumes implausibly the effectiveness of relatively palatable measures of mitigation and dismisses as impracticable programs such as the so-called Green New Deal that would require radical change.

The immediate advantage of the fourth approach that I've begun to delineate lies in its openness to setting aside such reassuring assumptions and to rethinking the role and responsibility of the University through critical analysis of the institution's historical embeddedness in the dense and dynamic world it inhabits. A second asset is its focus on understanding both the reach and the impact of technics[20]—technique and technology—in structuring operations and decision-making in the University as well as in the society that has bred what Langdon Winner terms a "technopolitan culture" (1986, ix). A third and increasingly vital feature is its recognition of a planetary future that is likely to be punctuated by environmental disruptions potent enough to reverse the flow of incremental improvements in living standards that industrialized countries have come to expect. A fourth is a crucial conceptual shift that opens onto the reinvention of the humanities advocated by David Theo Goldberg.

This by no means unprecedented move[21] consists in broadening the domain to which the term *humanities* refers to the whole of the *human sciences*. Indeed, in the conclusion that follows I shall treat the redefined academic Humanities / Public Humanities (henceforth marked by the uppercase H and P) as a public-facing domain in which the arts, traditional humanities, and social sciences are bound together by their interlocking interests in the human species and the future of humanity. Finally, from the sociopolitical standpoint advanced in *The Humanities in the Age of Information and Post-Truth*, it is perhaps possible to envision an activist academic universe in which higher education, as a collective project of producing and preserving life-sustaining knowledge, aims to promote with resolute urgency the development of an environmentally responsible culture in the world at large.[22] I shall attempt to expand on these general claims in the pages that follow.

Beyond the Corporate University

Over the last few decades, American analysts of higher education have often focused their critical lenses on the University's corporatization, that is, not only on its participation in the military-industrial-academic complex as a generator of exploitable knowledge, but also on its adoption of the mindset and operative apparatus of profit-making, metrics-driven business organizations. The tendencies in purportedly public colleges and universities toward privatization and professionalization, discussed in chapters 1 and 3, are conspicuous signs of an institutional willingness to participate in the larger economic regime as an engine of innovation and growth. Together, private and public institutions make up a quite significant business sector in their own right.[23] Their sense of collective self-interest is tied to commercial activities: they sell valuable products, create vital intellectual capital, engage in active competition for customers and resources, and extol the financial benefits of the credentials they award as a primary component of the rationale for attending and supporting them. Upon turning their attention to the vast, amorphous audience located outside of the University, the Public Humanities inevitably encounter both appreciation of this economic rationale and discontent with it, a reaction of resigned acquiescence along with suspicion and complaint.

When critical resistance to this corporatized academic enterprise takes as its starting point the major role of the University in the gestation of the Anthropocene, can it reasonably argue that a radical curtailment or reconstruction of the University is in order? If tempering its corporate turn in order to prioritize the public interest is the imperative at hand, should the consequent change in mission entail a wholesale restructuring of the institution? The essential answer, I believe, has to be a cautiously realistic one. It beckons toward the kind of logic that informs claims according to which crucial industries (automobile manufacturing, pharmaceuticals, banking, electric power) and vital systems (social security, healthcare, law and order) cannot be allowed to fail because the repercussions would be too devastating.

Or perhaps more pertinent to an approach to the climate

emergency, there is the crucial case of the fossil fuel industry: since it cannot simply be phased out, but will have to continue meeting essential needs while alternative energy sources are being developed, its task cannot be simple-minded self-liquidation or abdication; rather, it is behooved to pursue its eventual dissolution prudently by committing to cooperative participation in the energy revolution that climate change has made necessary.

Similarly, since the system of higher education, which is indeed socially and economically indispensable, could hardly justify a turn away from meeting basic educational needs, its task must also be transitional. Given the planetary crisis it has helped, for the most part unwittingly, to create, and given as well the need to respond in a manner commensurable with the threat, it must reshape itself on the basis of the relevant ecological knowledge and understanding it is well positioned to muster. It is not absurd to ask, moreover, whether the University is not the sole major institution capable of rising decisively to meet this daunting challenge. Concomitantly, we can aver that, owing to its incomparable ability to produce knowledge across the full range of relevant inquiry,[24] its responsibility is exceptional as well.

To delineate that responsibility in terms that would give it purchase on what colleges and universities actually ought to do differently, it is necessary to take critical measure both of the institution and the world. Thus, the call of the Public Humanities, as Mariët Westermann insists, is not simply to transmit compelling insights and offer useful assistance and collaboration to such audiences as its practitioners can find in the world, but at the same time to deploy Humanities lenses and practices in an open-minded attempt to understand the world they encounter on its own terms and to determine how to respond to its paramount needs. Hence the audacious duty to be assumed by agents of the Public Humanities would be the distillation, on behalf of the public, of need-based proposals for a responsive, adaptive University to be considered by their colleagues within the university.

Can we specify concretely a framework of ideas and measures that such a public-oriented renovation of the academic industry would entail? With an earnest sense of great urgency, but stopping short of desperation, I have pointed here, in grandiose terms that I would ordinarily eschew, toward a commanding object of reflection on behalf of humanity. At its crux it would consist of something on the order of a climate turn, a conception of worldly reality that grants absolute priority to the need for a concerted reckoning with climate change and the battery of hazards associated with it. This is of course an all too familiar call that innumerable like-minded observers have been articulating for decades. My particular version of that call consists in addressing the appeal for action not merely to the manifestly relevant academic fields and research paradigms, but to the institution, to the University as a whole, to its complex, largely complicitous engagement with the deeply imperiled anthropocenic world that is now before us. More specifically it is to stress the need for a comprehensive account of higher education's responsibility to that world and to point out that, on historical and philosophical grounds, the Public Humanities should be propelling the effort to meet it.

As it reaches out to the chaotic, elaborately mediated world it seeks to serve, the Public Humanities movement encounters in microcosm a humanity that has been plainly unable to deal with the threat to its survival and for the most part inclined to deny it or defer responses to it. The immediate dilemma is obvious. Given that, whatever the context, transmitting urgent messages about the ticking biospheric clock is demonstrably ineffectual, by what means might any progress toward a serious response be achieved? The revisionary thinking that such a question calls for has to be pursued in two orbits or on two levels of persuasion— one that, hinging on purposeful arguments and exchanges among educators and students, takes place within college and university communities and reflects on their relations with a world in crisis, and another that, in a less pointed, more diffuse process of dissemination, extends the acclimation to evolving realities and discourses to the human population at large.

My concern here bears primarily on the first of these processes that would be launched in academic communities and that could develop rapidly. The discussion, which for some might evoke the familiar, often suspect exercise of strategic planning, needs to be pursued in a framework with at least three integrally related yet distinct dimensions. The first, in which historical and moral perceptions converge, involves a critical judgment about institutional or collective responsibility vis-à-vis society and the way we think about our relations to the past and the future. The second would focus on the university's contributions to science and technology and the values that apply to the ways in which research is programmed and technologies are used. The third involves the understanding within the scholarly community about the purpose and structure of education per se, and in particular how that understanding is reflected in the curriculum and the institutional ethos. In each of these zones of intramural reflection, the participation of the Public Humanities would be predicated on a simple premise: the critical feedback gleaned from their encounters with the extra-academic world would beckon toward a revamped remit for the University as a whole.

Assuming Responsibility

As Henry Shue argues in *The Pivotal Generation: Why We Have a Moral Responsibility to Slow Climate Change Right Now* (2022), while the 2020s may already be too late, it is certain that this will be the last decade during which there is a chance to prevent global warming from reaching ecologically untenable levels. It is also the first and doubtless crucial decade when the scholarly community can take on frontally the intellectual challenge of reshaping the global framework in which the flow of world history has long been situated by fusing it with deep—geological or planetary—history. For current generations these destabilizing realizations about a time of crisis—historian Dipesh Chakrabarty (2021) borrows from philosopher Karl Jaspers the term *epochal consciousness* to characterize the encounter with unprecedented timescales—ground a sense of critical conjuncture that confronts us with the apparent precarity and finitude of the human species. A parallel version of the challenge presented by an unsettled, multi-scalar temporal order would call on the Humanities, as I'm defining them expansively here, to take on the task of combating the isolation of new, unfamiliar, and disruptive accounts of nature or planetary evolution advanced in the interdisciplinary framework of earth system science. Such an endeavor to engage in what we might aptly term *planetary thinking*[25] would seek to integrate that cold and hard scientific knowledge into the norm-governed discourse and world-representing imaginary that modulate our assumptions about the future.

The pressures accompanying the need for such historical reframing should at least spur serious attention to the climate crisis and fuel widespread exploration of our discomfited relations to the past, the present, and the future. Since, for example, we did not participate in the development of an energy regime that we now understand to be unsustainable, must we assume the burden of fixing it? Since the affluent zones of industrial civilization have monopolized the benefits of modern technologies while imposing many of the damaging costs on disadvantaged populations, does elemental fairness not oblige rich nations to furnish the victims of this imbalance with most of the resources for mitigation or adaptation? Does the fact that previous generations left us a standard of living that is as good as or better than was theirs imply that we should endeavor to do the same for future generations?

Given that failure to take strong—therefore costly—measures now will make the climate-induced harms to be experienced by our descendants far more difficult and costly to address than they would be if we acted promptly and generously, do we not face a categorical imperative to recognize and assume a large share of the burden here and now? Beyond this concern about the moral stance we adopt vis-à-vis our descendants, does our humanity—a matter not of biological identity, but of solidarity and belonging, of historicity and sociality—not oblige us to engage in an active effort to ward off the possibility that the human civilization now in place on Earth will collapse? In sum, do we not occupy a historical and moral position that imposes on us a responsibility—"epochal consciousness," Chakrabarty declares, "is ultimately ethical" (2021, 197)—to take all-out measures to limit the damage we know climate change will bring?

Over the last several decades, accomplished philosophers in both the analytic and the continental traditions have produced a substantial literature, replete with elaborate analyses and conflicting perspectives, on climate ethics and justice. In lieu of sketching a review of the various claims and tensions within the dominant analytic approach,[26] I propose simply to recognize the somewhat paradoxical understanding that emerges from the intriguing book by Stephen Gardiner and David Weisbach, *Debating Climate Ethics* (2016).

In an early, seminal essay, "A Perfect Moral Storm: Climate Change, Intergenerational Ethics, and the Problem of Corruption" (2006),[27] Gardiner situated climate change as the mainspring of a multidimensional set of ethical quandaries that are compounded when they coincide. Of the three most prominent theoretical perspectives on climate justice, which we might qualify roughly as deontological, utilitarian, and altruistic,[28] it seems fair to grant that to some extent each helps us elucidate the moral problems it addresses, that none appears able to resolve them definitively, and that all are eventually confounded by the difficulty of motivating moral action. When these limitations are reinforced by Weisbach's contention that such insights into climate (in)justice as the competing theories may offer will fail to convince the authorities who would have to respond by instigating effective public policies for coping with climate change, it becomes evident that the debates are destined to continue indefinitely and inconclusively.

The less prominent exploration of climate justice in continental philosophy develops along a trajectory for which the study of science and technology provides the framework. It runs from Hans Jonas's *The Phenomenon of Life* (1966) and *The Imperative of Responsibility* ([1979] 1984) through numerous works by Bruno Latour and Isabelle Stengers to the impressive recent work of Matthias Fritsch.[29] My cautious sense is that up to now the debates in this tradition, which cover a wide spectrum of arguments about the relevance and potential application of ethical thinking to climate change, are no more likely to come to closure or to result in effective governmental responses than those of analytic philosophy. On the other hand, on both of these philosophical horizons the net effect of the accumulated theories of justice and analyses of deontological relations and decisions is nonetheless a general sense that egregious forms of climate injustice exist and should be combatted. If the prevailing admixture of consensus and dissensus at the theoretical level does not yield a decisive injunction that is likely to be heeded by political authorities, it does constitute a horizon of broad argumentative concurrence—a judicious compromise formation—according to which the perpetrators and beneficiaries of climate change ought to assume a major responsibility for dealing with it and that all people have a right to protection of their habitat.

Such an overarching and conciliatory outlook is built into the United Nations Educational, Scientific, and Cultural Organization's *Declaration of Ethical Principles in Relation to Climate Change* (UNESCO 2017),[30] which is accompanied by a substantial statement (eight points, more than nine hundred words) on the application of the six principles. The paradox here is that the bulk, generality, and unwavering diplomacy of this relatively noncontroversial document are signs of its amorphous status and patent inapplicability: far from articulating enforceable imperatives, it rather meekly offers principles to be considered.

What does this unsettled situation, which at every turn drives home the gap between ethical rationales and political action, imply for confrontations with climate injustice within the University? At this juncture, given the formidable sophistication with which academics engage in intellectually robust disagreement and tenaciously defend the status quo, and given as well the endless deliberative complications that the numerous academic fields and institutional interests would put into play, the familiar pattern of protracted discussion and reserved institutional reaction, as opposed to prompt agreement and urgent action, is likely to prevail. The visible trends of the last two decades are clear. An overwhelming majority of American colleges and universities have understood in conventional terms that both their interests and their stated ethical commitments favor the adoption of measures to mitigate global warming. Accordingly, they have aligned themselves with a smart business-largely-as-usual strategy that gradually strengthens prudent current efforts, here to promote greenhouse gas emissions reduction and sustainability practices, and there to expand teaching and research in the environmental sciences and related fields.

A significant, highly visible example of this approach is provided by the Climate Leadership Network that operates under the aegis of the nonprofit organization Second Nature.[31] The network's more than eight hundred institutions have pledged formally to establish climate mitigation and/or adaptation plans for their campuses and to achieve net carbon neutrality by a specified date. In adopting this posture, they are providing the communities they serve with a valuable opportunity to observe and to learn from operational changes and adjusted priorities. So far they do not seem ready, however, for an all-out, all-pervasive game-changing course correction that would reorient higher education across the board, as it were, around an environmental mandate to preserve a viable planetary habitat for future generations. The questions still before us, then, are whether such a pronounced change should occur, how it could occur, and what form it would take.

Adaptation and Resilience

The background hovering over hypothetical answers to these exceedingly demanding questions is the function of the University as a knowledge factory and of higher education as a global institution. The holistic, integrally interdisciplinary insights of earth system science are preponderantly a product of university-based research and reflect the collaborative, broadly international nature of the work carried out in the major academic fields. At least potentially, the elaborately networked superstructure of the global academic world harbors a capacity to organize research, disseminate knowledge, and transform culture that other international institutions cannot hope to match.[32] It is possible to imagine, moreover, that American colleges and universities, which are already linked by robust professional organizations,[33] would take the lead in developing first a national and then a global consortium that would preside over the construction of a new model of the University, one that would embark on an urgent campaign to steer the world's societies onto a path of adaptation and risk reduction.

As I have suggested, to propose that the University should assert such a leadership responsibility is to recognize that science and technology have enabled institutions of higher education to accumulate a broad store of special expertise on the dangers we face as a result of the changing climate and to erect a powerful intellectual syndicate capable of reckoning with them collaboratively. Academia has constructed explanatory contexts and amassed an abundance of technical competencies that are more extensive, more lucid, and, at least theoretically, more disinterested than those we encounter in other broadly influential institutions such as government, business, religion, public health, and philanthropy. By no means, however, does this imply that the knowledge and technological prowess institutions of higher education have at their disposal are already sufficient to address the problems at hand.

A powerfully compelling case in point is the splendid Princeton University report, *Net-Zero America* (2021), produced by a team of seventeen experts, thirteen of whom are academics. It presents in prodigious detail a set of scenarios showing how the United States could reach a goal of net-zero emissions of greenhouse gases by 2050. The report demonstrates masterfully that the economic and technological wherewithal required for such a project could be mustered. Unmistakably, the nation can indeed rely on researchers trained and often based in American universities to develop plausible, concrete measures and elaborate systems to meet the massive infrastructural challenges that would have to be addressed in the 2030s and 2040s. At the same time, the Princeton report points out forthrightly, under the heading "capital mobilization," that carrying out the necessary research and development at sufficient speed would require enormous, unprecedented investments and public commitments. Unlike the dominant science and technology dimension of the report, which yields arguably feasible scenarios for designing and building a clean-energy system based on thoroughgoing electrification and large-scale capture of carbon dioxide, the public investment dimension, while providing a substantial accounting of the necessary funding, skirts the feasibility question. It is devoid of scenarios for consensus building that might make it possible to obtain and invest the capital.

While noting that "investors face deep uncertainty around future technology costs and performance, policy priorities of future governments, investment preferences among peers, customers and competitors, and public acceptance of certain technologies" (252), the *Net-Zero America* study leaves unexamined the nature and feasibility of the daunting public policy initiatives that would have to be pursued.[34] The latter problem would have to be taken on by the conjoined Humanities fields (arts, anthropology, economics, history, literature, philosophy, political science, psychology, sociology, and others) that, up to now, have not risen to the task of developing scenarios for achieving the necessary social understanding and political commitment.

On the contrary, for the Humanities, taking on that monumental burden would require a concerted reorientation of the whole enterprise of research and teaching toward dealing with unanswered questions and setting new goals in a transdisciplinary context. The challenges are formidable. To specify them it suffices to refer back to the obstacles to remedial action (the system, the collective action problem, and unmanageable scale) that I discussed in chapter 4, or alternatively to weigh the structural, political, and psychological pathologies of climate governance explored by Paul Harris in *Pathologies of Climate Governance* (2021).

The understanding of the University through its evolving infrastructural arrangements that unfolds in Martin's *Knowledge Worlds* culminates in its recognition of a neoliberal University caught up in the perpetual generation of technologies and motivations that anchor the growth-exigent dynamics of capitalism and consumerism. For the participants in academic operations, the elaborate infrastructural base that is ensconced in norms and routines has long rested on the two pillars we take for granted, research and teaching. Each of these core functions grounds a complex sufficiently massive and intricate to render wholesale reconstruction virtually unthinkable, yet sufficiently pliable to allow for reactive adjustments to the institutional machinery they employ when they are confronted by disruptions such as the climate crisis or an economic meltdown. This capacity to respond through discrete adjustments, which some observers conceptualize as *resilience*, is essential to institutional stability and durability.

In short, strategic adaptation to exogenous pressure is the name of the game. Engineering a feasible and efficient climate or ecological turn within the monumental academic edifice would necessitate, on the one hand, analyzing and refocusing the fundamental vectors of activity—research and teaching—and on the other hand, persuading armies of administrators, faculty members, and students to cooperate with a rapid transformation of individual and collective intent. A readily plausible objection positing the impossibility of finding leadership for such a project, whether at the level of individual institutions or intercollegiate bodies, could of course be supported by a simple description of the status quo:[35] the size and rigidity of a self-preserving establishment caught up in a powerful, resolutely competitive academic marketplace could be grounds for dismissing the idea out of hand. A somewhat less skeptical tack would qualify the project as improbable until such time as climatic events, by visiting substantial harms on the academic world itself, become directly forcing effects.[36]

My contention is nonetheless that, for the humanities fields that need to relocate themselves in a public-oriented Humanities, it is important to engage without delay in bold reflection on how the University can take measures in response to climate change that are commensurate with the potential harms human society needs to be facing now. At the moment the defense I can offer for this claim is primarily instinctual and secondarily conjectural: instinctual since it derives from a sense of obligation to younger generations whose lot looks grim; conjectural since it involves making a wager on the eventual value of bearing witness to ecological damage and contesting the legitimacy of denying it.[37] Making a theoretical case for this tentative position that is not only cogent, but convincing in the extramural world would be one of the tasks for philosophers in the adaptive University I am trying to imagine.

Reshaping Institutional Culture

Granting, in any case, the potential futility of pointed calls for precisely targeted reforms, can we at least propose a general shift in orientation that the Public Humanities can reasonably prevail upon the University's research complex to enact? Here, and subsequently with respect to the teaching mission as well, the starting point has to be recognition of a general imperative to limit the climate change we have to anticipate, to understand it as well as possible, and to prepare for dealing with all of its ramifications. The immediate challenge is to translate that imperative explicitly, field by field, into programs of both basic and applied research that deserve to be prioritized because of their potential to contribute, whether directly or indirectly, to survival or sustainability. The translation is doubtless easier to render in the domains of science and technology than elsewhere since essentially all STEM fields are already contributing significantly to the interdisciplinary research of earth system science.

To illustrate the general adjustment in emphasis and mindset that would nonetheless be needed in this area, a few examples of redirectional or recalibrational thinking that an ecological turn would trigger should suffice. A key starting point would surely be drastic reinforcement of the funding priority accorded to the development of clean energy and the pursuit of greater efficiency in energy use. This would favor efforts in the physical sciences and engineering to promote such highly publicized objectives as viable long-term management of nuclear waste, affordable hydrogen fuel for powering transportation, achievement of controlled nuclear fusion as an energy source, design of new systems for distributing and storing electricity, exploitation of geothermal energy sources, massified programs for converting leaky buildings into tight ones, and so forth.

The problematics developed by earth system science has reinforced the importance of research in the geological and atmospheric sciences that will allow for enhanced understanding of tipping points and deepened insight into changes in planetary states as well as for further investigating the pros and cons of such geoengineering measures as albedo modification. In the biological and ecological sciences, the immediate question for researchers studying the dynamics of biodiversity and genomics will doubtless be the effects of a warmed world on living organisms and the natural world and on the means of enabling their adaptation to climate change, of enhancing the resilience of life.

Across the full horizon of theoretical and applied research, those processes that have promoted a technology-for-technology's-sake mentality or rationalized an ethos of unconstrained exploration for the sake of innovation or discovery will have to give way to a more focused criterion that orients research investment toward preservation of a viable habitat for humans or for life in general. Such a pragmatic shift toward a horizon of human concern will nudge the STEM community toward responding anew to a familiar criticism—namely, that its message about climate change, while truthful, rigorous, and authoritative, tends to be understated or couched in terms that are scrupulously nonpartisan, guarded in tone, apolitical.[38] The appeal addressed to them by their Public Humanities colleagues will argue essentially that the present conjuncture imperils all research and knowledge and compels them to speak out far more emphatically, to ask if the community of scientists should not undertake to articulate an environmental politics that would relate directly to the mission and organization of colleges and universities.[39]

This is to underscore, in other words, the need for intensified dialogue between representatives of the Humanities and the STEM fields of the kind that can only take place inside institutions of higher education. It is also to prescribe for the STEM fields an analogue to the Humanities imperative to distill and communicate the message of climate science to the public at large. For the experts in science and technology, it is a matter, conversely, of attending to the insights of the Humanities and allowing them not only to affect their actions as individual citizens but also to inflect their collective thinking about the responsibilities of their academic institution.

As I implied above, the University's task of translating the broad imperative to combat climate change would generally ask more of most researchers in the humanities and social sciences fields than of their colleagues in the sciences. The primary reasons for this have to do with the unprecedented objective that comes into play, which is to determine what feasible changes in human culture would improve humanity's chances for survival and how they could be realized at planetary scale. To researchers in the humanities and social sciences would fall not only the burden of synthesizing the findings of their scientific colleagues and inventing means of communicating a confident understanding of them persuasively to the global public at large, but the mission of orchestrating something on the order of a socio-cultural revolution driven by a current of shared collective interest. A ready way to represent the degree of difficulty to be encountered here is to recall once again the obstacles to action noted above: the assumptions and the self-centered, consumptive drives underlying the pathologies at work in human behavior, the pervasiveness of power, complexity and structural injustice in the global economic system, the enormity of the collective action problem, and the huge, unsustainable scale of resource demands.

As Dipesh Chakrabarty has been observing in diverse venues over the last decade, the Humanities have to reckon with accounts of the globalized modern world that differ significantly from the scientific narrative—abstract, data driven, dispassionate—of global warming. The latter story positions the object of climate science as a biogeophysical phenomenon affecting the physical globe as a whole; that phenomenon, better termed planetary than global, is understood through the aggregation of quantitative measures and empirical studies carried out across many fields; the findings coalesce in a strong consensus in the scientific community about what is happening to the planet. This unified body of knowledge reinforces the value of the disciplinary methods and models deployed by the participating STEM fields, which purport to evolve in a scrupulous, verification-based process. While this planetary knowledge provides the basis, in the realm of human affairs, for prioritizing the need for clean energy, Chakrabarty rightly points out that no politics can be directly derived from it. Researchers who militate in favor of preserving a livable environment step laterally into their roles as citizens active in society.

By way of contrast, the heterogeneous global world studied in the broadly conceived Humanities is that of socioeconomic globalization, the worldwide web of connections constructed by humans during the modern era. Far from embracing a unified view, the studies of both causes and effects of global warming from the widely varying standpoints that coexist in this arena do not merely confront us with threats to a viable future. They also remind us of social phenomena that matter greatly to Humanities scholars: otherness, cultural difference, equal opportunity, and attention to multiple, competing perspectives on the world's festering crises.

It is hardly surprising, then, that the disparate, less settled fields of the Humanities, which are challenged by the Anthropocene to rethink deeply held assumptions and to question cherished disciplinary models, have been no more able than the STEM fields to proffer a cogent ecopolitics. From field to field, scholars confront a paradoxical need—to which the Public Humanities have to be acutely sensitive—to respond in unison to the risks and threats associated with climate change, yet also to continue wrestling with the problems of the contemporary human condition and to propose palatable solutions. No field can set aside the at once real and rhetorical questions that have long been manifest. Shouldn't political science propose solutions to the collective action problem? Shouldn't psychology explain how collective interest can achieve priority over individuals' appetite for wealth? Shouldn't philosophy come to closure on issues of climate justice? Shouldn't the practice of history reconstitute itself in the light of geohistory?

Such a stream of critical summonses extends across the many and varied fields of the human sciences. The predicament is exacerbated when representatives of those fields have to confront the planetary outlook articulated by their colleagues in the STEM fields. In the first place, as Chakrabarty notes, the message of climate science "challenges the inherent and deep-set anthropocentrism of the human sciences and calls on humanists to develop new perspectival points from which to comment on the human condition today" (2017, 168). In the second place, the difficulty intensifies once the community of academics in the humanities and social sciences perceive in the message from climate science an urgent call to come collectively to grips with the pressure exerted by the planetary perspective and thus to conceive of a unified Humanities response.

The call, in other words, is to interpret the thrust introduced by climate change into the academic investigation of socioeconomic globalization as an imperative to achieve a transdisciplinary accord commensurable with the commonality of outlook achieved by the sciences. Such an accord cannot, however, be as straightforward as the scientific consensus since it has to maintain, alongside the potentially unifying influence of the planetary perspective, the attention of each field, here to the problems of humans and other forms of life, and there to the ongoing concerns with difference, otherness, critical analysis, justice, open debate, and so forth. The demand, in sum, is for unity in tension and complication, for conciliation of a new and, as it were, higher priority with important ongoing commitments.

One of the University's evident responsibilities is to maintain a space where such an arduous compromise formation can be negotiated. Can we imagine the process in abstract terms that are akin to the generalization I offered above about the conceptual or inflectional adjustments that a planetary or geological turn would stimulate in the sciences? In *History 4º Celsius* Ian

Baucom (2021) elaborates masterfully a multiscaled theoretical superstructure within which the materialist and cosmological discourses that energize planetary thinking are drawn into an entanglement with modes of historical understanding and ethical perspectives that were in place before the emergence of the Anthropocene. While my practical take on the question at hand welcomes such theory,[40] its immediate preoccupation is feasible institutional adaptation. In the zones of the existing arts, humanities, and social science disciplines, at least a portion of the negotiation would occur on the horizon of research. In every field the overarching investigatory challenge is to specify the enabling conditions that would allow a planetary or geological turn to take hold strongly and to bear at least tangentially on ongoing efforts to address existing needs and problems. Or perhaps, more pointedly, it is a search for approaches to existing problems—inequitable distribution of wealth and resources foremost among them—that necessarily include adaptation to climate change as an indispensable objective and, as a corollary, conciliation of that climate-imposed requirement with other, potentially conflicting objectives.

In the many fields that study human behavior and its relations to social organization, adjustment to such a dual principle would obviously entail strengthened emphasis on how to understand and influence long-term collective commitments and how to gain acceptance for unwelcome changes in comfort and lifestyle. In softer areas typified by the arts, language, literature, classics, and some zones of history, it would be a matter of thematic direction, of according persistent attention to the ways in which climate and environment relate to works studied or performed and guide the revision of interests and values.

In generalizing about orienting the University's research mission more explicitly toward the challenges of limiting climate change and adapting to it, I have already ventured onto turf where the activities of research and teaching overlap and interact. One function of an unequivocally "soft" climate-sensitive undergraduate course—say, for example, a course in literature that includes the lenses of ecocriticism among the approaches it deploys in studying lyric poems—is to familiarize its students with concepts and viewpoints drawn from environmental studies and to encourage them to come to grips with ecological insights and values. At the same time, such a course is an occasion for original research on what distinguishes ecocritical interpretations from other common approaches and thus for asking why the accent on the physical environment rather than other contexts may be especially relevant to readers now. In course after course, across the soft-to-hard curricular spectrum, analogous experiences of contextualization could occur, ranging from passing and discrete to reiterative and extensive. Their cumulative effect as an overarching background—a kind of transdisciplinary leitmotif or institutional trademark—would inevitably be reflected in the collegial culture and the discourse by which colleges and universities identify themselves.

The utterly conventional point here is that formal education is an at once variable and programmed process, a practice—under conditions of freedom and constraint—of articulating relationships with the world. We express those relationships in the language we speak, the assumptions we make about the way things work, the viewpoints we adopt, the values we internalize, the habits we form, the skills we develop, and the goals we pursue. Some would qualify this norm-shaping bundle of instincts, beliefs, capabilities, and perceptual filters as an *ideology*, while others would prefer to treat it as an *imaginary*; yet no one, I contend, would deny that the institutionalized experience of study and reflection that members of an academic community pursue together involves an exceedingly complex blend of the suppositional and the intentional, an amalgam to which structured teaching and learning are integral and from which a certain collective mindset or ethos issues.

From the standpoint of education as acculturation or preparation for life in a society, then, what matters are the learned beliefs and practices that are widely shared and that come to form, gradually and quietly, a core of assent: a sense of commonality, a set of norms, an atmosphere of civility, an awareness of societal purpose, a common and secure worldview. Public trust and communal solidarity are path-dependent reflections of this process into which education draws teachers and students alike. The question that climate change compels academia to ponder is to what extent the educational apparatus we now designate with the compound "teaching and learning" could and should incorporate a reinvented conceptual and discursive axiomatics for society, a communicable repositioning of collective outlook that could ramify in the world at large. In other words, can the University be charged with a mission of inducing a designed cultural change in response to the threats and risks that command our attention, and how might such an adaptation or adjustment, which in the final analysis I would qualify as a geological turn, be defined and pursued?

In my comments on academic fields and the curriculum as a whole, I have evoked a change in institutional culture that could, I submit, take the form of a relatively compatible supplement to what is already in place while nonetheless reshaping intellectually the communities of most colleges and universities. In essence, it would simply provide for the systematic integration of the climate factor and the problems caused or intensified by climate change into thinking about the objects and design of research programs and into deliberations on the curriculum's content and structure. Even modest moves in this direction— one can imagine various degrees of individual compliance with the mandated viewpoint, some of which might lie closer to lip service than full-blown engagement—could have a significant effect on the prevailing discourses and attitudes inside a given academic community. The classic dilemma that hangs over the launching of such a deliberate shift is, of course, how far and how fast to go.

Up to now, I have worked with two general, thus imprecise, premises: on the one hand, the academy's responses to the disruptions (to be) caused by climate change have been for the most part prudently cautious and underwhelming, in keeping with similar efforts—significant, yet measured—that we observe in many relatively enlightened enterprises in the business world. On the other hand, the educational establishment's entrenchment in the world of consumerism and excessive extraction of resources precludes the kind of radical restructuring that would set it in forthright opposition to the socioeconomic forces that have long sustained it. The adversarial course would, moreover, jeopardize its multiple opportunities to work for needed changes in the world it purports to serve.

In sum, if the University is to exert a strong, forward-looking influence in and on that world, it will have to uphold a lucid compromise between timid and bellicose gestures. Its posture would be at once far more decisive—indeed, trenchant—in the face of the climate emergency than its current, usually guarded strategy, yet it would also be calculated to maintain and exploit the cultural, intellectual, and political capital it has built up during centuries of participation in what has become a dangerous and endangered global system.

Changing the institutional culture within academia is also a major motif in *Generous Thinking*, the work by Kathleen Fitzpatrick that I discussed early in this chapter. The unquestionably desirable change envisioned by Fitzpatrick would consist of a retreat from competition among colleagues for distinction and among institutions for prestige that would make for more generous human relations and a collective turn toward valuing social responsibility rather than economic advantage. Her call for a paradigm shift dovetails with my proposal here to the extent that it conceives of a networked academic world politically engaged in multiple efforts to engineer a cultural transformation: "Those networks of support are vital, not least because transformational change within universities and in the broader culture they serve—allowing all of us to return to a focus on the public good—will require massive organization and mobilization" (233).

Two principal concerns differentiate our perspectives. The conspicuous difference stems from my claim that confronting climate change as an existential threat to the survival of humanity should be the fundamental priority that motivates the advent of a polemical Public Humanities and an activist rethinking of the University's purpose and public posture. With her compelling case for community-building and for a vision of productive, empathic human relations inflected by an ethics of care, Fitzpatrick does indeed set forth a radical approach to ameliorating the extant academic culture. The laudable paradigm change she prescribes stops short, however, of calling for the singularly targeted revamping of mission and curriculum that my proposed focus on climate change entails.

The second and more complex difference might be expressed in either political or ethical terms. It has to do with the critique of the University that the Public Humanities, as I have situated them, are summoned to carry out on the basis of a history that culminates in our encounter with the Anthropocene. This history calls for future-oriented dialogues, both intramural and extramural, about the University's responsibility to humanity at large.

Like Fitzpatrick, I believe that the prevailing model of the corporate University, driven by the forces of competition and private gain, perpetuates the historical entrenchment of the higher education system in the rise of a global capitalism and a market-supporting consumerism that, in the twenty-first century, appear more and more clearly to be morally and politically untenable. To turn away from that relationship of complacent compromise and toward the adoption of communal values, the University would indeed need to develop a new institutional paradigm, a framework for binding the work of education to the public interest.

The challenge inherent in such a project is to define the public interest in such a way that a new model can be designed and implemented with the eventual acquiescence of the powerful interests whose initial inclination would be to resist it. Can we believe that the prospect of remedying the institution's apparent defects and failures will be an objective strong enough to galvanize a spate of political movements capable of resetting the educational system's compass, of generating the new paradigm or political unconscious that Fitzpatrick calls for? Would an academic workplace organized to respect the principles of an ethics of care[41] provide the public at large with an exemplary model of communal relations from which it could in turn draw the makings of a cultural reformation?

Formulated in its complexity, my hypothesis is not merely that something on the order of a collective drive to survive, aroused belatedly by the threat or fear of human extinction and intensified by massive socioeconomic crisis, is the only potentially sufficient motivation for achieving the kind of universal cultural transformation that the endangered humanity of our anthropocenic world needs to forge.[42] It is also that such a transcendent achievement would have to be an effect of a broadly distributed educational nucleus, of education for survival; it would be the product of a consensual and consortial higher education establishment responsible for promoting a broad public understanding and acceptance of measures and values that would improve humanity's chances for successful adaptation to a less hospitable world. It is, finally, that the function of education, when it is understood as an instrument of cultural transformation, would be a fully conscious, necessarily organized, and political fashioning of a collective worldview. While subject to unlimited local and individual variations, such an impelling framework would be fundamentally unified and unifying in its respect for a decisively defined public interest derived from the geohistorical narrative of humanity that I have highlighted.

Conclusion

So, what components of a worldview should be understood and taught, then carried into the world both by graduating students and by representatives of the Public Humanities? Throughout the chapters in this small book, which are heavily marked by intra-academic circumstance, my aim has been to unveil an imagined narrative of and for humanity, a backward-looking long-term account that could constitute something on the order of a corrective historical context or perhaps a collective framing instrument or even a prototypical lesson in global civics.

The terse sketch of the story's lineaments that I offered in chapter 4 was baldly partial, not only insofar as it held to a high degree of generality that would allow it to include a wide variety of detailed and conflicting narratives, but also insofar as it was limited to modernity, to the era of Eurocentric ascendancy capped by socioeconomic globalization. In this final chapter I have occasionally hinted at the need to extend the panoptic narrative back across the two hundred thousand years of human history and far beyond. The idea, which many others have ventured and explored, is to situate that human history in the context of a planetary mega-history stretching over billions of years during which the earth evolved on its own and life emerged from life-lessness. When humans complicate their understanding of themselves and their significance by setting off the current climate emergency against the planetary (and ultimately cosmic) horizon, many assumptions built into the stories by which we situate ourselves in the world are thrown into question.[43]

For institutions of higher learning, the challenge is to confront these questions strongly, with unprecedented urgency. Doing so would require the University both to formulate the revisions in educational paradigms and to take on the focused sense of the University's mission that the climate crisis imposes. This would entail foregrounding a core of representational parameters that can extend into a population's common understanding of the world at large. To put it in familiar, professional terms, it is a call to determine how such a revised set of assumptions should fit into the worldview or cognitive framework that informs liberal education. The programmatic transformation that I deem imperative is obviously a project that leaders of higher education should elaborate in concert. Here I propose simply to point out three important, typical, yet dubious assumptions for which educators now make allowances. My essential claim is that, as a well-informed and responsible collective body, they need to subject them, along with many other less vital presuppositions that underlie the curriculum, to critique and to reformation.

The first major assumption concerns historical context, which has all too often been limited to human history and the roles of human individuals that unfold along a chain of events. The humbling history that should also be taught is temporally deep and conceptually geological. It is not just human, not just the story of the emergence and evolution of life, not just a recent linear trajectory made possible by intelligence and technology. Earth's history reflects its own self-organizing dynamics and has often been marked by rapid and massive disruptions, including drastic climate changes, that are beyond human control. The earth system is—and will remain—in the driver's seat.

By no means does the Anthropocene thesis that attributes to Homo sapiens the capacity to modify climate or to strip the planet of essential resources imply that the earth system would have remained a stable environment for human society had the proliferation of greenhouse gases been avoided. Crucial planet-shaping forces that lie outside the sphere of human influence (changes in its solar orbit and axial tilt, solar radiation, meteor strikes, the movement of tectonic plates, [de]glaciations, altered ocean currents, thawing permafrost, and so forth) augur eventualities that are unpredictable and have the potential of shifting the earth system into another state. The record of previous geological changes imposes the recognition that human history is finite and thus that the basic—and demanding—questions before us are why and how to prolong it.

The second major assumption concerns the possibility conditions under which societies can be formed and human relations can be shaped. We have become too accustomed to imagining that the terrestrial habitat can be open to unlimited growth in population and economic activity, without regard for the effects of this "progress" on the natural environment and the planet's ability to support its inhabitants. The delicate questions that are rarely if ever asked outside of science fiction are how biodiversity loss could actually be arrested and how the excessive human population could decline to a level dictated by the earth's carrying capacity, which is perhaps one-fourth of the current eight billion.

The reigning counter-assumption has been instead that only robust growth can generate solutions to intractable human problems such as inequitable distribution of wealth and opportunity and that such growth can continue indefinitely without exhausting extractable resources. If the ultimate value recognized by institutions of education and built into their discourse is the survival or at least the prolongation of life on Earth more or less as we have known it during the last four millennia (the Meghalayan period of the Holocene epoch), the vector of teaching and learning pursued on behalf of humankind will have to turn toward investigating not only the possibility of adapting to ongoing climate changes but also toward the task of managing a process of global contraction.

The third and final major assumption I propose to highlight

concerns thinking about the future of institutions. It is already clear that academic institutions will not be able simply to go on expanding their accumulated knowledges about the past and present and treating their obviously necessary educational enterprise as an indefinitely viable and incrementally renewable operation. Instead, the University will have to face up boldly to its irrevocable embeddedness in the imperiled global ecosystem and its long-term dependency on that system's durability. Since institutions of higher learning are destined to evolve in tandem with that system, their self-interest dictates that their mission no longer be confined to anticipating and mapping out a sustainable future for humanity on the basis of established and emerging knowledges. Rather, compelled by the earth system to be mindful of insuperable unknowns that complicate the task, they shall have to come to grips with diverse plausible scenarios of future deterioration and hypotheses about how to respond to them humanely.

In sum, at every turn, in all quarters, contingency planning for a problematic, rather than promising, future will have to be the order of the day. Visions of the future that include scenarios of possible survival and possible collapse will need to be articulated, assessed, and understood as grounds for mitigation efforts in the present. At the outset this necessary effort to rethink the future has to exclude the idea that humanity can simply cling to the status quo and bank on reproducing and improving the insecure trappings of civilization that are in place. The University will inevitably be a key site for managing the public representation of what lies ahead. Up to now the motor behind many optimistic visions of the future has been our confident reliance on human invention, the ever-expanding technological prowess that has over and over yielded major enhancements of the human condition. It underlies the popular notion according to which technology, smartly developed and deployed, will produce the wherewithal to "save us," even as it also provides cover for carefree carpe diem voices who exalt the present and would leave the presumably resourceful inhabitants of a super-high-tech future era to deal with the problems of their time.

That fatuous optimism will, I submit, have to be toned down. The arc of geohistory that belies such comforting claims about human ingenuity is doubtless best exemplified by the grimly unequivocal prediction that the climate-forcing effects of greenhouse gases already in the atmosphere are sure to worsen steadily for decades, if not centuries or millennia.[44] This *certitude*, implying that over an extended temporal horizon we should prepare to cope with a range of catastrophes, is the sober counterpoint to the insurmountable *uncertainty* about looming environmental changes: When will they occur? How severe will they be? Will crossing a given tipping point trigger a cascade of calamities? Will technologies of mitigation be efficacious? And so forth.

Against this sober background of duality—a certainly uncertain future—the realistic assumption that needs to take hold, projecting neither a utopic nor a dystopic future, is not that technology will save us from the catastrophes that lie ahead. Rather, it should be appropriated as an invaluable tool of adaptation, one that is capable, for example, of helping our descendants meet their energy needs as they are forced to face up psychologically and politically to a menacingly unpredictable future.

Much of this sternly guarded take on our worldly future can be applied to the University itself when it is grasped as a knowledge factory or an infrastructural complex with evolving technological machinery that harbors a proven capacity for adaptation and change. The neither/nor position I'm espousing—neither that "we're definitively doomed" nor that "we're sure to be saved," but that navigating in between those poles we must face up to urgent needs for change in order to have a chance to survive— was lucidly anticipated by a book first published in 2017 that does not address the climate problem frontally, but does deal capaciously with the full range of the University's multilayered infrastructure and with its anachronistic components, its lack of acclimation to the needs of a technologized world that is lurching out of control. Cathy Davidson's *The New Education: How to Revolutionize the University to Prepare Students for a World in Flux* ([2017] 2022) brilliantly explores existing and potential teaching and learning arrangements and practices in this powerful, but incongruous, institution. Juxtaposing chapters titled "Against Technophobia" and "Against Technophilia," Davidson treats excessive hostility to and enthusiasm for our technoculture as "twin pitfalls" (132) that have to be judiciously avoided by serious educators. Their task is both to appreciate the opportunity for remodeling of the University that new techniques and inventions open up and to hold the new models that emerge up to critical scrutiny from the standpoint of their students' needs and aspirations. Recognizing that efforts to revamp the institution's educational practices and to recast its worldly mission will reinforce one another, my contention here is that, in a University devoted to the public interest, climate change should be recognized as the pivotal driver of both reformation and critique.

Epilogue

My conclusion amounts to a proposal that the Public Humanities—a coalition of the arts, traditional humanities, and social sciences—press the University toward what I chose to term a reformation. For the institution, the somewhat implausible objective of such a reformation would be to convert its mission and curriculum into a project of cultural transformation. At the core of such a movement, the universal impact of climate change would position a new human perspective on the world, conceived no longer as an external object but rather as the intertwining of an inhabitable earth with a humanity committed to its preservation.[1] At its core there would be a consensual bond—something on the order of a prevailing outlook, a unifying framework, a common horizon of experience, a shared set of values, a conceptual paradigm. Such a mental infrastructure or perceptual complex would be subtended by the cumulative work of education; it would consist of what would become implicit assumptions about the human condition and explicit principles governing human relations. Their elaboration within the University would not be derived directly from the store of knowledge about climate change that reveals their necessity; it would be rather a product of informed human judgment about what society must do to maximize the chances of sustaining the planet's habitability.

Readers who have followed the elaboration of this scheme will have been well aware of two inevitable questions that I have seeded but left largely in abeyance: can one really imagine the University, under pressure from the Public Humanities, incorporating the geological turn and pursuing a cultural reformation? If experience tells us that the prospects for such a turn are virtually nil, and if, moreover, humanity's chances of avoiding a civilizational collapse are similarly dim, why should the Public Humanities (why should anyone?) advocate for protective and adaptive changes in public policy and personal lifestyle at all? In other words, given that we have arrived at a state of crisis consciousness too late to take corrective measures that could have been effective if they had been enacted decades ago, is it not more reasonable simply to let the inevitable play itself out and to define the task of education as that of preparing coming generations to endure the consequences of our inadequate response?

In light of higher education's stunningly rapid, far-reaching, and convention-breaching response to the coronavirus pandemic, one has to wonder whether such resignation should not be resisted. As Cathy Davidson points out in the preface to the 2022 edition of *The New Education*, the numbers of smartly conceived, often overdue changes and the fact that "higher ed responded at a scale that literally no one would have imagined possible" (xx) revealed the system's formidable capacity to adapt to an unprecedented emergency. At least under some plausible scenarios for the future, betting on institutional resilience is an option that can reasonably be tried.

On this topic there is surely much to say and there are many observers much better qualified than I am to address it. Drawing solely on the lineaments of a response that I've presented in this book, at least a brief comment on both questions—the University's potential as a prime institutional mover of political action, on the one hand, and the citizen's responsibility to support collective well-being, on the other—is in order. A key question for the University to ponder is whether any approach other than the one I've suggested has any chance of success.

As soon as we grant that international political solutions to the climate change problem are overwhelmingly unlikely in the absence of a massive cultural shift away from consumerism and competition for wealth and status, the burden of developing sociopolitical conditions conducive to such a shift—presumably something on the order of a mass movement of unprecedented scale—falls on the global educational establishment. It seems evident enough that the University, perched at the top of that establishment, would have to take the lead. The inescapable specter of uncertainty that enshrouds the future precludes any unqualified claim that, since failure is certain, it makes no sense to try.

Beyond that, the possibilities for stimulating resilience in the face of harmful change are real and lie clearly within the purview of the institution's research mission. In this same vein, the possibility of lessening the intensity and extent of suffering by humans and other living beings is a worthy motive for research and reflection in essentially all academic fields. Accordingly, even if a full-blown project with global reach is not feasible, I submit that the University should still heed the urgent call and move as far and as fast as it can.

As for the citizenry at large, on both collective and individual horizons, the argument that matters is already in place in the societies we inhabit. While it takes diverse forms that I shall not rehearse here, it is embodied in the very theories of justice and human rights that command broad support and to which even those who, on humanitarian grounds, resist drastic measures to limit climate change can subscribe. Moreover, the call to prioritize the objective of survival and to act to achieve it is implicit in the principle according to which it is necessary to conciliate measures adopted in response to climate change with efforts to improve the lot of the disadvantaged. The point is that, while at every level the process of mitigation should be subject to lucid, responsible balancing of the pros and cons, overall, its personal and social benefits are likely to be preferable to the payoffs of material enrichment.

Even when it involves sacrifice, participation in an enlightened collective venture can make the experience of life more satisfactory than it would be otherwise. By the same token, those who refuse to join in such altruistic commitments place themselves in a morally antipathetic position that, in the long run, is unlikely to be a recipe for happiness. Even under dire conditions, asserting a responsibility to do what one can to make life better for others is a more promising path to human dignity and self-respect than resignation or abdication.

NOTES

Preface

1. Under the suggestive title "The Future of the Liberal Arts in America and Its Leadership Role in Education around the World," the very successful symposium, organized by Daniel Weiss and Rebecca Chopp, resulted in a well-wrought, richly insightful book, *Remaking College* (2013).

1. The Big Picture

1. The original version of the text was circulated as background to participants in a seminar, "Modeling the Humanities in Higher Education," organized by Professors Christie McDonald (Harvard) and Gary Wihl (Washington University, St. Louis) and hosted by the Radcliffe Institute in the spring of 2016.

2. Although approximate, this number is based on research that former colleagues at the Mellon Foundation, Donald J. Waters and Susanne Pichler, were able to carry out with astonishing rapidity. They responded to a casual query from me by running searches of books published in 2015, using the databases of books in print available online and searchable by categories such as higher education. While I lacked the time to examine five hundred plus books in detail, by printing out the list and examining the titles, I was able to verify at least superficially the aptness of the list obtained by using the Dewey decimal system's number for higher education.

3. In this chapter I rely primarily and heavily on the capacious,

remarkably thoughtful history by John Thelin, *A History of American Higher Education* ([2004] 2011). Working in the wake of Frederick Rudolph's *The American College and University* (1962), Thelin provides a compelling account of the dimension of student life, which I neglect here (see note 5); he also provides an invaluable appendix with an "Essay on Sources" (433–51) and an excellent topical index. Geiger's much cited essay, "The Ten Generations of American Higher Education" (2016b), appears as the first chapter of *American Higher Education in the Twenty-First Century* (Bastedo, Altbach, and Gumport (2016).

4.   Veysey's work stresses intellectual history, especially the thinking of faculty involved in the celebrated, well-endowed universities highlighted in Edwin Slosson's 1910 volume, *Great American Universities*. Thelin and others rightly cite these books as the source of a dubious tendency to treat the development of higher education as a top-down, trickle-down process in which most powerful, wealthy universities that sprang up at the turn of the century quickly established the frameworks and approaches that the whole universe of higher education would then emulate. For example, according to Thelin (2011, 151–52), the notion that the liberal arts college and its liberal arts degree constitute the foundational core of the academic enterprise emerges decades later and not solely in the prestigious institutions. In chapters 3 and 4, I shall refer to a remarkable historical account that had not appeared in 2015 when I wrote this essay; see Labaree (2017).

5.   A well-founded objection here would be that I am omitting a quite major fifth category that contributes a great deal to the distinctiveness of US higher education, that of student life and cocurricular activity. Or one could envisage a broadly defined domain that would embrace the whole extracurricular establishment, including student life, alumni relations, athletics, community relations, and so forth. While I shall take note of this zone in describing the system's financial pressures and budgetary trade-offs, I do not think it is commensurable with the other categories because there is so much variation among institutions in their degree of commitment to the residential experience of undergraduates, to the cultivation of alumni networks, and so forth. In the history I sketch, the four factors I deal with are constants that shape a model to which all degree-granting institutions have to relate; one cannot say that about the student life factor, which hardly enters at all into the budgetary picture of for-profit institutions and ranges from minimal to modest in

many urban institutions and community colleges. Similarly, many institutions do not take on the heavy-duty costs of big athletics programs.

6. The current version has six basic types: doctoral universities, master's colleges and universities, baccalaureate colleges, baccalaureate/associates colleges, associates colleges, and special-focus institutions. Within each type, subgroups are distinguished on the basis of student numbers, degrees awarded at various levels, and so forth. The classification moved from the Carnegie Foundation for the Advancement of Teaching to the University of Indiana in 2014. The website maintained by the Indiana University School of Education remains a valuable basic resource: http://carnegieclassifications.iu.edu/.

7. For a revisionist view of the German influence, see Habinek (2010). The standard view that relates the implementation of a Humboldtian scheme is well summarized in Fallon (1980).

8. In his analysis of substantive and reactive development, Clark deployed the terms developed by another distinguished authority on US higher education, Walter Metzger, who coauthored (with Richard Hofstadter) an important historical work, *The Development of Academic Freedom in the United States* (1955), that deploys precisely the macro-distinction I shall appropriate here between "the age of the college" (Hofstadter's part) and the "age of the university" (Metzger's part).

9. The American Council of Learned Societies offers us a good example of this phenomenon. Founded by thirteen member organizations in 1919, it has grown to seventy-four member organizations today, of which at least three-fourths represent humanities fields (the remainder are in the social sciences and area studies). The two largest and most influential associations within the ACLS, the American Historical Association and the Modern Language Association, both date from the 1880s.

10. These numbers are based on the tabular account provided in Clark (1987, 39).

11. The institutional distribution of bachelor's degrees in the humanities is presented in the fifth set of tables (especially II-3a and II-3b) under the heading "undergraduate education" in the Humanities Indicators, http://www.humanitiesindicators.org/content/indicatorDoc.aspx?i=9.

12. While this simple and favorable view of advancing scientific research seems to me to be widely accepted in the humanities, it should be noted that historians and sociologists of science paint a passably more

complicated picture in which the economic dynamics of big science some-times undermine its claims to scholarly disinterest. Beyond this concern about the tension between the practice and the financing of science, there is also more epistemological complication than my simpleminded formulation suggests. For an accessible account of the consensus that has emerged since the work of Thomas Kuhn on paradigm change and Chaïm Perelman on argumentation theory in the 1960s, which recognizes the role of vision and language in the perception of the natural world while retaining objective reality and verification by experiment as indispens-able grounds of research practice, see the first two chapters of Steven Mailloux's *Disciplinary Identities* (2006).

13.　Of the twelve contributors to the volume (including Kernan), on the basis of their essays at least three—Carla Hesse, Lynn Hunt, and Louis Menand—cannot be said to subscribe to this view.

14.　See, in particular, Bérubé's introduction and chapter 1, "Value and Values" (written solo) in the book coauthored with Jennifer Ruth, *The Humanities, Higher Education and Academic Freedom* (2015).

15.　A helpful resource for appreciating this dynamic domain of ac-tivity is the website of the Center for Research on Teaching and Learning at the University of Michigan: http://www.crlt.umich.edu. Two influen-tial books by Cathy Davidson (2011, 2022) make the case for reform in this area with remarkable eloquence and rigor.

16.　A salient example of this discourse that stresses the globaliza-tion of the academic marketplace is provided by Wildavsky (2010).

17.　For discussion of redesigned pedagogies and the promised efficiencies that many courses (especially large introductory ones) can attain by using digital technology in the delivery of instruction, auto-mated evaluation of students' work, and so forth, see Bowen (2013). For a discussion of the MOOC (massive open online course) phenomenon, see Davidson (2022, 101–24). Another, far more complicated concern stems from the appropriation of digital tools in research, although the hurdles may be lower in STEM fields than elsewhere. It involves the knowledge explosion that digital technology makes possible and, in the humanities, the enormous difficulty of reckoning with the masses of data in textual form that technology has put at the disposal of research-ers. Over and beyond the work of data collection, the digital humanities and corpus linguistics have undertaken to develop means of analyzing huge corpora by focusing on phenomena that computers can count. The question is not merely what can be done with results obtained by such analysis, but also whether the very form of the analysis distorts the aims and values of traditional interpretation in the humanities, and thus how important it may be to cling to these values.

18. American Academy of Arts and Sciences, "Humanities Indicators Project," www.humanitiesindicators.org. While the statistics collected here are invaluable, it should also be noted that the succinct overviews and commentary supplied by the team of researchers are remarkably astute.

19. The kinship between Leitch's book and the *Norton Anthology of Theory and Criticism* (2010) of which he is the general editor is unmistakable (he discusses the anthology at some length in *Literary Criticism in the 21st Century* [2014]) and calls for a remark about the wide range of disciplines covered by the *studies* phenomenon: these accounts of theory are interdisciplinary and not at all limited to literature or to literary criticism or literary theory. Since they span the humanities and related social sciences, it is reasonable to grasp in Leitch's work an overview that deals with the humanities writ large.

20. Historically, the conceptualized need for academic freedom appears to relate directly to the emergence of the research university and its mission of discovering or creating new knowledge, as opposed to the more conservative mission of transmitting established truths to the younger generation that was primary during the age of the colleges. The open-minded search for new, potentially unsettling and controversial truths entailed a willingness to overturn received ideas. That potentially subversive attitude needed protection.

21. In the field of higher education studies, attention to the rise of faculty influence was galvanized by a 1968 study by Christopher Jencks and David Riesman, *The Academic Revolution*.

22. In their recent short book *Lesson Plan* (2016), William Bowen and Michael McPherson argue for a change in graduate programs that would allow students to opt for two tracks as they pursue advanced degrees, one that would prepare them for a career primarily in teaching, the other essentially the current track that leads to a research-dominated orientation.

23. The strong identification of graduates with their undergraduate institution is a significant feature that distinguishes US higher education from the national systems that developed in Europe and in many other

countries around the world. In the classic European system, faculty and staff understand themselves to be employees of the civil service striving to succeed in the national system rather than appointees beholden to the university in which they labor. Strong loyalty to one's home institution is rare. In the American system, the four-year experience of undergraduates in residence and caught up in extracurricular activities with their peers channels them into an experience of identity and community that often endures for a lifetime. Without it the reliance of many upper-level colleges and universities on alumni support would not be possible.

24.   The department's account of its marginal status prior to the establishment of the Department of Health, Education and Welfare in 1953 can be found at US Department of Education, "An Overview of the U.S. Department of Education," https://www2.ed.gov/about/overview/focus/what_pg2.html. The Department of Education and the Department of Health and Human Services became separate entities in 1979.

25.   The observation of declining state support has occasionally been contested by officials who point to level or increasing total appropriations for higher education in state budgets, but numerous empirical studies of the period from 1975 to the present show declining appropriations per student and major cuts when widespread economic downturns have occurred. In Bastedo, Altbach, and Gumport (2016), chapters 9 ("The States and Higher Education") and 11 ("Financing American Higher Education") provide serious accounts of the financial issues and the negative effects on student access that result from reducing subsidies and increasing the contributions required of students and their families.

26.   The federal share of research and development costs in science and social science (the humanities do not figure in the data published by the National Science Foundation's National Center for Science and Engineering Statistics) has been a fairly steady 60% in recent decades. A helpful account of the overall picture is accessible on the website of the American Association for the Advancement of Science, while a basic explanation of the issues surrounding indirect cost recovery and aggressive supervision of grants by federal agencies (NIH, NSF, DOD, DOE, et al.) is offered on the site of the American Association of Universities.

27.   The compelling book by Slaughter and Rhoades (2004) describes at great length the gradual emergence during the second half of the twentieth century of an "academic capitalist knowledge/learning regime" that, in their view, comes to coexist with—thus not to replace—the earlier

"public good knowledge / learning regime." The term *academic capitalism* effectively subsumes the tilt toward privatization that occurs when entrepreneurial universities move to commodify new knowledge and promote its development in the private sector. The move to exploit new knowledge justifies itself not simply as a source of revenue for the institution but as a contribution to the generation of economic growth that benefits society at large. Hence its retention of a certain public good rationale. Among other sobering books that deal critically with academic capitalism, I would recommend Bok (2003) and Washburn (2005).

28.   In *Locus of Authority* (2015) William Bowen and Eugene Tobin offer a cautious argument in favor of reinvigorating the idea of shared governance and building new bridges between faculty and administration.

29.   "In an unheralded academic revolution, there has been an increase in the authority of administrators and unprecedented bureaucratic control over working conditions on campus." Altbach (2016, 93). Altbach's essay is the best short, synthetic account I have found to date of current conditions in American higher education. For a more polemical view of the faculty's waning influence, see Ginsberg (2011).

30.   When writing this chapter in 2016, I was not yet aware of the intriguing interplay presented in chapter 4 of Labaree (2017). Labaree depicts the subversion of the liberal by the professional at the lower end of the higher education pecking order and conversely the invasion of the professional zone by the liberal at the higher end.

31.   Scholars tend to be much more aware of learned societies than of these professional organizations, most of which were founded more recently than the academic associations noted earlier and draw their members from staff and administrative constituencies. The following examples suggest the types of concerns around which they develop common interests and policies: Association of Public and Land-grant Universities, the National Association of College and University Business Officers, American Association of Collegiate Registrars and Admissions Officers, Association of Governing Boards of Universities and Colleges, American Association of State Colleges and Universities, American Association of Community Colleges, National Association of Student Personnel Administrators, State Higher Education Executive Officers Association, Association of American Colleges & Universities, Association of University Technology Managers, and so on.

32.   A formidable case for the claim that students in American

higher education are not getting their money's worth is offered by Arum and Roksa (2011).

33. See Caplow and McGee (1958).

34. The rapid proliferation of national and international rankings has resulted in a veritable rankings market with competition among the varying approaches. The rankings game and the endless debates about the criteria and methods used constitute a significant complication for administrations and trustees. At minimum, decisions about whether to cooperate with the rating organizations are necessary, and many believe that the desire to secure higher rankings contributes to questionable budgetary commitments that intensify the escalation of already high costs.

2. Paradigms for the Public Humanities?

1. My remarks here were conceived some seven years before the publication of Kathleen Fitzpatrick's remarkable book *Generous Thinking* in 2019. Fitzpatrick makes a well-wrought, persuasive case for subjecting higher education as a whole to a paradigm shift, understood as "a turn from privatized, rationalist, competition-based models for knowledge production to ways of knowing, of learning, of being in community that are grounded in an ethic of care" (207–8). I shall look closely at her analysis in chapter 5.

2. Here I allude lapidarily to a complex historical and sociological horizon, the significance of which is probed in depth in Calhoun (1994).

3. Of late, this point, which Butler was making vigorously some years ago, has been buttressed judiciously in Muller (2018).

4. For an excellent, concise overview of the environmental humanities, see Ursula Heise's introduction to Heise, Christensen, and Niemann (2017).

5. The presumable relations of kinship and cooperation between the public humanities and the two subfields I have mentioned here, the digital humanities and the environmental humanities, are evident. Moreover, thanks in part to the semantic reach of the term *public*, the broad horizon of the public humanities also covers significant aspects of numerous interdisciplinary areas of inquiry that I associated with the "studies" label in chapter 1, among which cultural studies, media studies, performance studies, gender studies, and visual studies are prominent examples. Within most of these interdisciplinary clusters, one encounters a combination of well-theorized claims about their special relevance

and a firm resolve to guard the independence they have achieved in the academic establishment. Accordingly, while it is possible to imagine the public humanities as a unifying force behind a coalition of existing fields and programs, the movement's continued development will be subject to the same institutional dynamic that kindles the aspiration to independent status.

6. Since I was the Mellon officer who worked with the American Academy on the funding but had no direct involvement in the work of the commission, I allow myself both this glowing qualification of the report and a supportive response to the critique advanced by Gordon Hutner and Feisal G. Mohamed, the editors of *A New Deal for the Humanities* (2016). Hutner and Mohamed object to the "nearly complete absence of professors from public institutions" in the membership of the quite large commission (fifty-two members). The critique is sound and significant insofar as it underscores the predictable dominance of an academic elite whose outlook reflects the mindset of an establishmentarian private sector. Its pertinence is limited, however, by the drift of public institutions into the modus operandi of the private sector that I take up in chapter 3.

7. This proposition echoes uncannily Helen Small's insistent assertion that, on the horizon of public goods, basic human and social needs take priority over the five arguments she invokes in support of the humanities (2013).

8. Published in 2011 by the Woodrow Wilson International Center for Scholars under the pseudonym "Mr. Y."

3. Public Humanities and the Privatized Public University

1. This chapter revises and extends a paper delivered on April 16, 2015, at a conference titled "Humanities and the Public University" hosted by the State University of New York at Buffalo.

2. Danielle S. Allen, the James Bryant Conant University Professor at Harvard University, became chair of the Mellon board in 2015 and completed her ten-year term on the board in 2019.

3. Earl Lewis completed his five-year term in 2018. He is now director of the University of Michigan's Center for Social Solutions.

4. Small's position on the humanities and the paradigmatic framework I established on the basis of it are set forth in chapter 2.

5. Dewey's emphasis falls heavily on the problems of communicating with the public. If he nonetheless holds out some hope for a better

informed public, he is hardly less preoccupied than Lippman with the difficulties of democracy that stem from a distracted or indifferent citizenry.

6.   I have omitted from the plurality of existing publics under consideration here (essentially those envisioned by the leaders of public and private universities) the rarefied conception of an imagined, astutely critical public that, according to Mark Greif, university-based intellectuals should aspire to construct. Greif's vision does resonate cannily, however, with the project of an activist public humanities that I shall invoke in chapter 5. See Greif (2015).

7.   For key contributions to the conference, see Lye, Newfield, and Vernon (2011).

8.   See chapter 1.

9.   It is doubtless noteworthy that some private and public universities do demonstrate a certain capacity for growth by adding satellite campuses, but the incidence of such expansion is modest and the typical rationale for it, while not devoid of market-based considerations, is passably complex.

10.   See notably Slaughter and Rhoades (2004).

11.   Low-cost areas identified by Newfield are business, education, arts, humanities, and qualitative social sciences; high costs are concentrated in the STEM fields.

12.   Newfield cites data provided by Eugenie Samuel Reich in a preliminary report on American research universities ("Thrift in Store for US Research," *Nature* 476 [August 25, 2011], https://www.nature.com/articles/476385a.pdf?origin=ppub) by a panel of the National Academy of Sciences (2012, Research Universities and the Future of America: Ten Breakthrough Actions Vital to Our Nation's Prosperity and Security, https://nap.nationalacademies.org/download/13396). The sixth of the 2012 report's recommendations (p. 15) addresses the cross-subsidization issue.

13.   The locus of enactment for the last measure here, reconstruction of the productivity wage, is rather more society at large than the public university. The case within the university that Newfield appropriately cites (2016a, 293) as an example of the missing linkage between productivity and remuneration is that of the adjunct professorial corps. The adjunct is typically a highly trained, technically skilled performer but

receives pay much lower than that of a similarly qualified tenured professor in the same department.

14.   The assumption about future employment is subject to significant reservations. A snapshot of the complexity one encounters in this domain is provided in the third section, "Workforce," of the Humanities Indicators (https://www.amacad.org/humanities-indicators) and by a recent study published by the Humanities Indicators Project, "State of the Humanities 2021."

15.   See Bérubé (2013). For recent, exceedingly intelligent and provocative contributions to the debates about crisis, see Schmidt (2018) and Reitter and Wellmon (2021). A far more provocative—indeed, politically radical—position is advanced by Boggs and Mitchell (2018).

16.   To justify this claim, it suffices to observe the strong positions occupied by major public universities in the National Research Council and *U.S. News* rankings of graduate programs in the humanities.

17.   The notion of "friends" includes not only individuals (e.g., parents who are not alumni), but also professional and corporate connections.

18.   Note that the private sector is stratified and has a significant number of relatively poor institutions that attend to a financially challenged public by veering away from liberal education toward vocationalization. But this underprivileged layer in the private sector is unable to do very much for affordable access for want of resources, whereas the affluent layer makes a token contribution while siphoning off special talent.

19.   See chapter 2.

20.   For tabular enrollment figures for 1995–2017, see NCES (2017).

21.   See chapter 2.

4. The Real Humanities Crisis

1.   There are innumerable accounts of the acceleration. For a particularly helpful overview, see Will Steffen et al. (2015).

2.   For a brief, radical, and caustic statement of the full-blown apocalyptic view, see "A Grim New Definition of Generation X" by the far-left editorial cartoonist and columnist Ted Rall (2020).

3.   For an excellent introduction to this transdisciplinary sphere of inquiry, see Steffen et al. (2020). On the future of the field, see National Academies of Sciences, Engineering, and Medicine (2022).

4.   My minimalist summary here draws from the thorough, systematic work of David Wallace-Wells (2019). The twelve sections of his second chapter describe in detail the principal impacts of global warming. In the aggregate, we have to expect a veritable reshaping of the planet as species are forced to migrate to cooler habitats at higher elevations. For a succinct account, see McKibben (2022).

5.   The Stern report to the British House of Lords dates from 2005, a time parallel to Diamond's *Collapse* (2005). Stern provides an update in *Why Are We Waiting?* (2015).

6.   "The larger point is that scholarship in the humanities is defined by its concern with the subject of humanity" (Harpham 2011, 29).

7.   Among dozens of possible references here, one deserves special mention: Vollmann (2018, *Carbon Ideologies*, in two volumes: *No Immediate Danger*, vol. 1; and *No Good Alternative*, vol. 2). In this huge and laborious compendium of information that forces recognition of the harm that burning fossil fuels and relying on nuclear power inflict on the planet, Vollmann addresses himself in a steadfastly pessimistic voice to future readers who will blame us for subjecting the earth to irreparable devastation.

8.   Latour was by no means alone in this effort. Alongside the work of his colleague and kindred spirit, the French anthropologist Philippe Descola, I would place that of the American political theorist, Langdon Winner, whose analysis of technoculture in *The Whale and the Reactor* (1986) includes a chapter, "The State of Nature Revisited," that anticipates Latour's objections to the idea of progress as the mastery of nature by humans. "The ecological persuasion," Winner writes, "in both its survivalist and deep ecology versions, has challenged an idea long prevalent in Western culture, an idea that portrays nature as an object of control and source of wealth. The alternative model now proposed holds that nature be seen as a system, an incalculably intricate, delicately balanced aggregate of interdependent parts and processes" (136).

9.   A nontrivial component of this triumph is, to be sure, the naturalist's conciliation of an artistic and cultural fabrication of idealized nature—at once winsome and sublime, and commonly associated with European romanticism—with the cognitively and technologically mastered nature that we associate with a scientific rationalism bolstered by the Enlightenment and its vision of progress. By dint of this convenient alliance, a beautiful, endearing nature is also a knowable, exploitable

object in the real world. One contemporary analogue of this convergent trajectory is doubtless what has become the harmonious interaction or cross-fertilization of evolutionary biology and molecular biology, distinct horizons of interest in (and strands of inquiry into) nature that ecology situates in a vital relation of complementarity.

10.   While considerable ink has flowed questioning the aptness of this concept, I take the case for using it to designate the current period of planetary crisis that the Canadian Marxist Ian Angus makes in part 1 of *Facing the Anthropocene* (2016) to be definitive. In discussing the problems we have with facing it (the term facing, used by Angus and also by Bruno Latour, contrasts tellingly with practices of avoidance or denial that we must also size up), I shall of course allude to the conditions that prompt some scholars to adopt narrower markers such as Capitalocene, Econocene, and Urbanocene that I would place within the broadly integrative category of the Anthropocene.

11.   "The total amount of energy delivered by the sun to the Earth is approximately a million trillion (10^{18}) kilowatt hours a year, compared with our 'measly' needs (on this scale) of 150 million (1.5×10^{14}) kilowatt-hours we collectively use each year" (West 2018, 240).

12.   The basis of this assumption is not that fossil fuel sources (coal in particular) will be exhausted, but the effects of extracting and burning them on temperatures and air quality will no longer be tolerable. This entails supposing that technologies of carbon capture and geoengineering will not succeed in restoring fossil fuel viability. A thorough and cautious discussion on which I base this supposition is elaborated in Lawrence et al. (2018).

13.   The discussion here omits a theme that is unmistakably important in published work on climate change, the widespread incidence of explicit and aggressive denial to which the findings and projections of earth system science have been subjected. The constructive task of the public humanities, as I am elaborating it, is to defend rigorous research and to support action on the basis of science; it is neither to explain nor to dismiss denial, even when the impulse that informs it has a clear connection to the morally contestable self-interest that impedes individuals from making sacrifices for the purpose of preserving an inhabitable planet; it is rather to address the claims of denialism seriously and reason with its proponents respectfully.

14.   In these paragraphs that evoke the assumptions and behaviors

of individuals, I barely scratch the surface of the compelling discussion of consumptive practices provided by Paul G. Harris in chapter 7, "Pathologies of Human Nature," of *Pathologies of Climate Governance* (2021) or of the superb overview of the forces that block remedial action on climate change elaborated in this book.

15.   The necessity, the limits, and the retreat from overconsumption that come into play at this simultaneously abstract and concrete level are ultimately consequences of Earth's carrying capacity in relation to the human population. This complex but quantifiable factor is a function of both the resources required to meet basic needs and the damage from excess use and pollution that the global environment can withstand. Vaclav Smil's short book *How the World Really Works* (2022) lays out economically the components of the macro-scale framework within which the idea of carrying capacity becomes meaningful.

16.   My brief discussion of these terms draws primarily on the incisive essay by Raymond Murphy, "Managing Risk under Uncertainty" (2012). An exceptionally helpful introduction to contemporary theories of risk and accounts of risk perceptions is provided by Ursula Heise in chapter 4 of her still very compelling 2008 study, *Sense of Place and Sense of Planet*. Among the many valuable perspectives on risk that she covers, two are particularly pertinent to my discussion of the obstacles to action on climate change: the difference between lay views of risk and those of experts who calculate risk levels, and the gap between political and sociocultural responses to risk that needs to be closed.

17.   The objections that I evoke lapidarily here are reviewed thoroughly and rigorously in chapter 2 of Hartzell-Nichols (2019).

18.   The aim of Bayesian inference is to move from an uncertain understanding based on limited information or simply on belief to a more plausible view by factoring in data that becomes available. A clear and simple comparison of Bayesian statistics to classical frequentist statistics is offered in *Bayesian Statistics: A Beginner's Guide* (Anonymous 2022). A more capacious account of Bayesian approaches to decision-making is provided in volume 1, chapter 13 of Roeser et al. (2012).

19.   The estimates are tabulated in figure 6.1 of Ord (2020, 167).

20.   Weitzman's 2007 review of the 2005 Stern report launches an argument, developed and refined over the next decade, that emphasizes the uncertainty of the probabilities that extreme events will or will not

occur and the real possibility (on the order of 10%) that temperature increases will reach 6° C or higher by the end of the current century. Mitigation efforts would respond to a need for insurance against irreversible tragedy. See Weitzman (2007); and in Wagner and Weitzman (2015, see especially chapter 3, "Fat Tails," 48–79). In this vein, I note that the 2021 IPCC report *Climate Change 2021: The Physical Science Basis* echoes this concern: "Low-likelihood outcomes, such as ice-sheet collapse, abrupt ocean circulation changes, some compound extreme events, and warming substantially larger than the assessed very likely range of future warming, cannot be ruled out and are part of risk assessment" (27).

21.   The conception of that long-term potential becomes subject to dispute, to be sure, when the possible effects of runaway artificial intelligence are brought into accounts of the future. Does it suffice to require that smart, decision-making machines be programmed to act in accord with human values? Could the potential of humanity be a posthuman intelligence generative of its own values? Instances of the technoscientific sublime to which I allude in chapter 5 can actually be found in texts such as philosopher Nick Bostrom's famous "Letter from Utopia" (2008). Its fictional author, writing to humans from the future, evokes "possible artificial persons" and moments of inexpressible wonder.

22.   Each chapter of the report includes a specification of "knowledge gaps" and needed research. The most substantial case is section 4.6, "Knowledge Gaps and Key Uncertainties," of chapter 4, "Strengthening and Implementing the Global Response," which includes the following illustrative questions:

> How much can be realistically expected from innovation and behavioural and systemic political and economic change in improving resilience, enhancing adaptation and reducing GHG emissions? How can rates of changes be accelerated and scaled up? What is the outcome of realistic assessments of mitigation and adaptation land transitions that are compliant with sustainable development, poverty eradication and addressing inequality? What are life-cycle emissions and prospects of early-stage CDR options? How can climate and sustainable development policies converge, and how can they be organised within a global governance framework and financial system, based on principles of justice and ethics (CBDR-RC), reciprocity and partnership? To what extent would limiting warming to

1.5° C require a harmonization of macro-financial and fiscal policies, which could include central banks? How can different actors and processes in climate governance reinforce each other, and hedge against the fragmentation of initiatives?

23. The term refers to the global circulation of ocean water. A prominent example of its effect on climate is the Gulf Stream, the loss of which would result in a quite consequential cooling of northern Europe.

24. To some degree the imaginable optimistic scenario circumvents the indecision that plagues political negotiations among nation states. It would entail a norm-resetting intervention by multinational business and finance organizations to redefine and protect their interests on the basis of a judgment that long-term survival requires socially responsible corporate governance and behavior. For discussion of this possibility, see Ruggie (2022). The unanswered question is of course how such a transformation could be sufficiently rapid and extensive.

25. Predictions of the time required for an eventual transition to green energy are problematic. Bill Gates (2021) and many others plausibly argue that it cannot be achieved at the needed pace without heavy investments in nuclear power—for the time being in fission, but perhaps after midcentury in fusion.

26. Here I make the standard assumption that there cannot be free riders because noncompliance by one or more significant participants would cause those who are willing to cooperate to refuse to make the needed commitment.

27. For a brief history of UN-sponsored meetings and agreements, see Center for Climate and Energy Solutions (2022).

28. "The Climate Action Tracker (CAT) estimate of the total warming of the aggregate effect of Paris Agreement commitments and of real-world policy shows little change. If all governments achieved their Paris Agreement commitments the world will likely warm 3.0° C—twice the 1.5° C limit they agreed in Paris." (CAT 2018) .

29. I take the term from Franz Mauelshagen's chapter title, "The Age of Uncertainty: The Challenge of Climate Change for the Insurance Industry," in Leggewie and Mauelshagen (2018).

30. See, for example, the observations in Fukuyama (2020, 15–16).

31. Notwithstanding the early references to Elinor Ostrom's account of trust and cooperation in *Governing the Commons* (1990), I qualify this claim because later parts of the book beckon toward the relevance of her

insistence on complexity and her proposal of a polycentric approach in "Beyond Markets and States" (2010).

32. Smil's monumental work (twenty-one books published over the last fifteen years) is a singular contribution to the study of the Anthropocene era.

33. The order of generality here makes for theory—a mechanistic science—in the strongest sense. West posits fundamental rules of scalability and network structures that are at work in the growth of all living organisms; subsequently, he deploys the same paradigm in considering the growth of cities and companies and ultimately the question of global sustainability.

34. For explanation of the theory's claims about accelerating cycles of innovation, see West (2018, 415–26).

35. It should be noted that Smil's views on population growth and eventual decline are cautious and far less alarmist than some of the striking but sketchy projections in *Ten Billion*. See the precautionary segment on "failed predictions" and ill-conceived forecasting in Smil (2022, 205–38).

36. For example, Smil expresses unqualified skepticism about the prospects for reversing the growth of consumer demand: "Hopes for an early end to this demand are unrealistic because the growth of material consumption is a universal and durable phenomenon: objects of desire change, desire remains" (2019, 501).

37. See Ord (2020, 39–40). If I hesitate to voice here the necessarily tentative guess that I expressed in early 2021, it is because any gesture toward prediction has to be qualified by attention to the many uncertainties and unknowns, especially those that have to do with tipping points and the planet's long-term carrying capacity that I have stressed. It is arguable, I would readily grant, that the imagination of a "likely" climate-changed future that David Wallace-Wells (2022) has ventured is somewhat more plausible than the fully apocalyptic visions that he downplays. I would qualify the overall thrust of his claims, however, as misleading and ill-advised insofar as they discount critical risks that need to be faced. The issue is whether the optimistic edges of the adaptation Wallace-Wells foresees, by outweighing his reminder "that the likeliest futures still lie beyond thresholds long thought disastrous" (44), will temper the drive to urgent action that we need to be strengthening. For a somewhat diffuse but apposite (worth reading to the end) critique of his revised outlook,

see Bendell (2022). For a sober counterpoint, cited by Bendell, that reckons appropriately with the importance of dealing with severe climate collapse scenarios, see Steel, DesRoches, and Mintz-Woo (2022).

38.   My thinking about the benefits of facing up to a dire future and focusing on how the effort to limit climate change could result in a better world echoes that of Halstead (2019).

39.   The term *collapsologie*, coined by Pablo Servigne and Raphaël Stevens in their book *Comment tout peut s'effondrer* (2015), belatedly translated as *How Everything Can Collapse* (2020), refers to a process, but is not predictive or "catastrophist." The activist movement that deploys it in France parallels in many respects the "deep adaptation" movement in the United Kingdom and United States. See Bendell and Read (2021).

40.   I must acknowledge a certain intersection of the exceedingly condensed narrative I have outlined here with the brilliant recasting of modern global history that has been elaborated during the past decade by the distinguished historian Dipesh Chakrabarty. His influential inquiry into the significance of the Anthropocene culminates in *The Climate of History in a Planetary Age* (2021). In that book, Chakrabarty envisages a "negative universal history" (47) of the Anthropocene that goes much further than my skeletal, present-focused revision toward reintegrating the human species into the profoundly complex lifeworld disclosed by earth system science and by the arc of geological history that spans billions of years. This background will complicate the narrative I have sketched when it is recast in my concluding chapter, which focuses on the future of higher education.

41.   "Scientific resources for producing and regenerating expertise, access to which is meticulously controlled and embedded in networks of academic laboratories, methods, technologies, engineers, scientists, institutions and careers, afford organizational bases for manufacturing knowledge about disastrous disruptions. Climate change, extinction level events, global epidemics and other potential yet invisible or never to be seen disruptions thus are transformed into facts, and are able to withstand efforts at deconstruction waged against them by laypersons or by experts from competing fact-building networks" Vollmer (2013, 6).

42.   In "Stop Defending the Humanities" (2014), Simon During voices a comparably pungent, if less dismissive, complaint about defenses of the humanities based on their values, interests, or methods, arguing

that the case for them should be a minimal one that protects access to them by those who lack it.

5. Public Humanities and the University

1. *Civilization* is of course a potentially objectionable term that, for some critics, conjures up the harmful effects of conventional humanism (positioning the human as the measure of all things), colonialism (the hegemonic imposition of a European value system), and capitalism (the ascendancy of economic growth and consumerism). A critical project can promote the survival of the human species at the global scale as a fundamental priority only by subscribing to a less anthropocentric notion of civilization that respects nonhuman forms of life and promotes the preservation of a viable earthly habitat.

2. Since the launching of the American College & University Presidents' Climate Commitment in 2006, we have, to be sure, witnessed a concerted movement within US higher education to confront the challenges of climate change both by bolstering fields in which study of the state of the biosphere is central and by adopting commitments to green practices—most notably to reaching carbon neutrality by a given date—on their campuses. The website of the Second Nature organization, with programs for higher education in the Climate Leadership Network and the University Climate Change Coalition, provides a helpful overview of this laudable effort (Second Nature, n.d.). My argument here will be simply that the commitments to climate education, research, and institutional action need to become far more urgent and systematic than they have been to date.

3. For a particularly compelling model of a successful experiment (a graduate seminar at Emory University), see Leonard et al. (2020).

4. For a substantial overview, see the foreword (xi–xix) by Ahmed Bawa and Ronaldo Munck and introduction (1–11) to McIlrath, Lyons, and Munck (2012).

5. See Grau (2018).

6. The exemplary case that I cited in chapter 2 is discussed in Woodward (2009).

7. Consider, for example, this comment, under the subheading "public scholarship," about the need to go beyond traditional extension programs and continuing education: "But it is crucial today that we think about what an extension program embracing the entire university, including the humanities and social sciences, might look like, and the ways that

public universities might play a key role in bringing not just technical knowledge to the public but the liberal arts as well: not just tools for production, but tools for living" (Fitzpatrick 2019, 180).

8. An exceptionally capacious reflection on the humanities and liberal education is offered by Anthony Appiah in a volume I shall take up shortly, *The Humanities in the Age of Information and Post-Truth* (Lopez-Calvo and Lux 2019).

9. While Said uses the concept of worldliness, as elaborated in the introduction to *The World, the Text, and the Critic* (1983, notably on pp. 22–27), primarily to situate texts, these pages indicate clearly that it underlies his opposition to what he calls "the Eurocentric model for the humanities" (22).

10. The text lays out in detail the questions to be addressed during Goldberg's tenure as director of the University of California Humanities Research Institute.

11. It is important to understand that the wide semantic spectrum of the term *media*—not merely organs or systems of mass communication and material in or of which things are made or stored, but anything in between two entities that connects them or opposes them—makes for a great many forms of mediation. The latter is an act or process of making connections that range from often overlooked infrastructures of buildings and organizations to modalities of conciliation between differing parties in human societies.

12. They are named in a seven-line list in the preface.

13. The quoted phrases are from Foucault (1971) 1984.

14. A well-wrought overview of the relevant studies is provided by the lengthy footnote 29 (Martin 2021, 259). The introductory chapter I composed for this book falls into the institutional category.

15. I focus on the architectural examples because the analysis of their symbolic position in an overarching signifying network leads into the articulation of Martin's general thesis about the neoliberal university we have come to know over the past half century. It is noteworthy, however, that the chapter contains parallel analyses of two important wartime inventions, stroboscopic (ultra-high-speed) photography at MIT and the klystron tube at Stanford, that are likewise at the center of media complexes and illustrative of the sociotechnical conception of humanity that emerges in Martin's analyses of the human-machine interface.

16. Futurist speculations about a "fourth industrial revolution"

resulting from combinations of new technologies waver between perilous scenarios in which humans allow themselves to be robotized or reduced to "quantified" selves and liberating visions that move us toward reasserting control as biotechnology and AI "compel us to redefine our moral and ethical boundaries" (Schwab 2016, 5). For a curiously optimistic view of a planetary future in which the earth system (Gaia) is regulated by a world of cyborgs, see Lovelock (2015).

17.   For a sober and sobering introduction to the issues surrounding the projected achievement of an *artificial general intelligence* that surpasses human abilities but functions with goals and incentives that are misaligned with human values, see the segment in Ord (2020) headed "Unaligned Artificial Intelligence" (138–52).

18.   The question is raised forcefully by Eric Hayot (2018): "We cannot go on allowing ourselves to accept students who believe that they will be the ones to make it, when we see so clearly that the job market is a matter not of individual talent but of structural violence, of a system whose primary ideological function is to absolve the individuals who participate in it from any moral responsibility for its effects."

19.   An impressive compendium of examples of engaged public humanities work is provided on the website of the National Humanities Alliance under the heading "Humanities for All." See https://humanities forall.org.

20.   This broad concept was central to my early scholarly work on the war of the ancients and moderns in seventeenth-century France. Its use in accounts of the relations between technology and culture has been prominent in the wake of Lewis Mumford's influential and controversial *Technics and Civilization* (1934).

21.   The principal precedent here is less the traditional notion of the *sciences humaines* that I invoked in chapter 1 than the recent appropriation by traditional humanities fields of research methods and of social and political perspectives that were elaborated in the social sciences. While the enlarged purview is perhaps most spectacularly visible in the hybrid field of science and technology studies and in the cross-disciplinary orbit of critical theory, its interest and importance have long been recognized by academic historians who have wavered among three options: locating the practice of history in the humanities, in the social sciences, or in both. My conception of a broadened Humanities closely parallels Ian Baucom's expansive conception of Philosophy in *History 4° Celsius* (114).

22.   The case for activism on the part of individual researchers and teachers that departs from professional norms is elaborated thoughtfully by Jessica F. Green (2020).

23.   For a venerable—thorough and still valid—account of the business, see Weisbrod, Ballou, and Asch (2008).

24.   The point is not that the University's contributions to the growth of energy consumption make its responsibility comparable to or greater than that of other institutions, but that it is better equipped than others to play a key role in the reckoning with climate change. Awareness of this singular capacity to pursue a well-informed, comprehensive response should entail a heightened sense of responsibility.

25.   I can recommend strongly one ambitious and remarkably astute experiment in this vein: Clark and Szerszynski (2021; see especially the dense and far-reaching discussion of time and futurity at the start of the final chapter, 169–76). Concomitantly, for a superb, deep-historical account of biocultural evolution, I recommend Tomlinson (2018).

26.   For a skillful overview and compendious bibliography, see Simon Caney's (2020) entry on climate justice in the *Stanford Encyclopedia of Philosophy*.

27.   Chapter 4 of the very valuable collection *Climate Ethics* (Gardiner et al. 2010). The argument is developed fully in Gardiner's important book *A Perfect Moral Storm* (2011), which makes the strategic case for an "ethics of transition," aimed at influencing social policy, as opposed to a grand integrative theory of ethics.

28.   For an account of these positions in relation to problems of motivation and application, see André and Bourban (2016).

29.   Most notably in *Taking Turns with the Earth* (2018b). Fritsch's essay "An Eco-Deconstructive Account of the Emergence of Normativity in 'Nature'" (2018a) provides an exemplary introduction to what the author terms "Continental-European resources" (280).

30.   The document offers the following abstract titles to the six principles it defines: (1) prevention of harm; (2) precautionary approach; (3) equity and justice; (4) sustainable development; (5) solidarity; and (6) scientific knowledge and integrity in decision-making.

31.   Second Nature (n.d.).

32.   On this capacity, in addition to the aforementioned essay by Fernando Reimers (2021, esp. 34–37), see the remarkable theorization of the "global university" carried out in the essays of de Bary (2010).

33. See, for example, "List of Higher Education Associations and Organizations in the United States," Wikipedia, https://en.wikipedia.org /wiki/List_of_higher_education_associations_and_organizations_in _the_United_States.

34. A boldly ambitious, extensively researched proposal that parallels the Princeton report in many respects is elaborated in Doerr (2021). To his great credit, Doerr not only takes seriously the challenge of explaining concretely what scaling up rapidly to the required level of clean energy would entail. He also addresses the investment issue in considerable detail and does at least recognize in broad, somewhat cursory terms the kind of collective mobilization—"a climate Marshall Plan" (304)—that enactment of his plan would require. Yet how the business-oriented scheme he constructs could be engineered politically and culturally remains far from clear, and the book elides the long-term difficulty of maintaining a flow of resources—that is, avoiding their exhaustion after a massive scaling-up—sufficient to support the transformed world of the future that he projects.

35. For an overview of the status quo that points out the inadequacies of current efforts, see "Climate Change Education: An Overview of International Trends and the Need for Action," the introductory chapter in Leal Filho and Hemstock (2019). For a more recent complementary study led by Leal Filho, see Leal Filho et al. (2021).

36. For the time being, my guarded hypothesis about the effects of the COVID-19 pandemic is that they do indeed serve to alert the educational establishment to the possibility of severe disruptions of the academic marketplace and perhaps to long-term trends that will dramatically alter the landscape of competition in international education, especially at the graduate and professional levels. On the other hand, severe strains are not necessarily large-scale forcing effects. The impact of COVID on the delivery of instruction has reinforced the appreciation of in-person, on-campus educational experiences, and up to late 2022 systemic effects that would devalue postsecondary education across the board and force a thoroughgoing revision of its glaringly problematic cost structure do not appear to be on the near-term horizon.

37. The rationale and value of bearing witness are explored in "Witnessing Climate Change," the remarkable fall 2020 issue of *Daedalus*. See especially the probing introduction by the issue's guest editor, Nancy L. Rosenblum, "Paths to Witnessing, Ethics of Speaking Out" (6–24).

38.   For a more nuanced and strategic view of the climate expert's public role, see Oreskes (2020).

39.   Not in question here is the formidably intelligent and valuable work of the National Academies of Science, Engineering, and Medicine and of the Union of Concerned Scientists. These strong and effective national organizations maintain impressive commitments to an environmental politics, developed over decades of interdisciplinary activity, that seeks to influence public opinion and public policy. If the extent of their influence is subject to debate, neither their responsiveness nor their ability to operate in the public policy arena is in doubt. I am focusing on what happens in particular academic institutions and assuming that, in most cases, organizing politically in that intramural context would be quite complicated, akin to taking on an insoluble or "wicked" problem.

40.   Much of Baucom's integration of human and nonhuman timescales into an epochal totality, as well as his location of its development in the university community and its linkage with civil society, meshes well with the imperative of relating planetary thinking to existing work toward amelioration of the human condition that I have articulated here. Pursuant to his meticulous and penetrating critique (44–51) of Chakrabarty's *The Climate of History in a Planetary Age* (2021), however, Baucom makes a move that strikes me as dubious and unnecessary. To the set of timescales or temporal layers that he puts in a knotted or braided relationship, he appends a dimension, beyond cosmic history or cosmological ontology, that he terms, citing Walter Benjamin's "Theses on the Philosophy of History," messianic or theological.

41.   I take the ethics of care, as it has been refined over the last three decades, to be clearly relevant to a project of ridding academic culture of excessive competitiveness and judge that its proponents have responded effectively to certain critiques that treat it as apolitical (see, for example, Laugier 2015, 236). I am not persuaded that care ethics can contribute significantly to the rearticulation and validation of collective institutional interests that the critique of the corporate University calls for.

42.   I shall not argue with proponents of responses to climate change that stop far short of a full-blown cultural transformation. Their judgment that such a thoroughgoing response would be far-fetched and unachievable may be sound. I should at least note that my conception of such an overarching and deep-rooted transformation is not original. The works of Félix Guattari in the 1980s and early 1990s evoke the necessity

of what he calls, in the final pages of *Les Trois Écologies* (1989), a tri-ecological vision, including far-reaching, if not worldwide, mental and social ecologies—a new conception of subjectivity, the self and self-interest and a new understanding of social relations and societal viability—without which the achievement of a viable environmental ecology at the planetary level would be impossible.

43.   While urging the importation of planetary thinking into the discourse of the Humanities and about the University, I have refrained from taking up explicitly the relationship of earth system science (or more narrowly, of evolutionary biology and ecological history) with the kind of neo-materialist, object-oriented outlook that one encounters in books such as Bennett (2010) and Morton (2013). This adventurous theoretical work seems likely to inflect the recasting of epistemological norms in various academic disciplines eventually, but within the institutional culture that concerns me here, it would appear unlikely to gain purchase in the near term.

44.   Among many relevant accounts, I would emphasize Wilder and Kammen (2017): "The truth is that humanity's continuing failure to bring our enormous carbon emissions under control will have planet-altering impacts that could continue not just for hundreds, but thousands of years." See also Branch and Plummer (2021).

Epilogue

1.   Judith Butler (2022) propounds a similarly sweeping version of this claim: "Only a global commitment can honor global interdependency. To undertake such a task, we have to renew and revise our understanding of what we mean by a world, an inhabitable world, one understood as a way of already and always being implicated in each other's life" (64).

WORKS CITED

Altbach, Philip. 2016. "Harsh Realities." In Bastedo, Altbach, and Gumport 2016, 84–109.

American Academy of Arts and Sciences. 2013. *The Heart of the Matter: Report of the Commission on the Humanities and Social Sciences.* https://www.amacad.org/publication/heart-matter.

American Association of University Professors. 1940. *Statement of Principles on Academic Freedom and Tenure.* https://www.aaup.org/file/1940%20Statement.pdf.

Anderson, Amanda. 2005. *The Way We Argue Now.* Princeton, NJ: Princeton University Press.

André, Pierre, and Michel Bourban. 2016. "Éthique et justice climatique: Entre motivations morales et amorales." *Les ateliers de l'éthique* 11 (2–3): 4–27. https://www.erudit.org/en/journals/ateliers/2016-v11-n2-3-ateliers03246/1041764ar.pdf.

Angus, Ian. 2016. *Facing the Anthropocene: Fossil Capitalism and the Crisis of the Earth System.* New York: Monthly Review Press.

Anonymous. 2022. *Bayesian Statistics: A Beginner's Guide.* https://www.quantstart.com/articles/Bayesian-Statistics-A-Beginners-Guide/.

Arum, Richard, and Josipa Roksa. 2011. *Academically Adrift: Limited Learning on College Campuses.* Chicago: University of Chicago Press.

Ayers, Edward J. 2009. "Where the Humanities Live." *Daedalus* 138 (1): 24–34.

Barnett, Ronald (2011). "The Coming of the Ecological University."

Oxford Review of Education 37 (4): 439–55. https://doi.org/10.1080
/03054985.2011.595550.

Bastedo, Michael N., Philip G. Altbach, and Patricia J. Gumport, eds.
2016. *American Higher Education in the Twenty-First Century: Social,
Political, and Economic Challenges*, 4th ed. Baltimore, MD: Johns
Hopkins University Press.

Baucom, Ian. 2021. *History 4° Celsius: Search for a Method in the Age of the
Anthropocene*. Durham, NC: Duke University Press.

Baucom, Ian, and Matthew Omelsky, eds. 2017. *Climate Change and the
Production of Knowledge*. Special issue, *South Atlantic Quarterly* 11 (1).

Bendell, Jem. 2022. "Climate Honesty—Are We 'Beyond Catastrophe'?"
Professor Jem Bendell (blog), November 6. https://jembendell.com
/2022/11/06/climate-honesty-are-we-beyond-catastrophe/.

Bendell, Jem, and Rupert Read, eds. 2021. *Deep Adaptation: Navigating
the Realities of Climate Change*. Cambridge, UK: Polity Press.

Bennett, Jane. 2010. *Vibrant Matter: A Political Ecology of Things*. Durham,
NC: Duke University Press.

Bérubé, Michael. 2013. "How We Got Here." *PMLA* 128 (3): 530–41.

Bérubé, Michael, and Jennifer Ruth. 2015. *The Humanities, Higher Education and Academic Freedom: Three Necessary Arguments*. New York:
Palgrave Macmillan.

Boggs, Abigail, and Nick Mitchell. 2018. "Critical University Studies and
the Crisis Consensus." *Feminist Studies* 44 (2): 432–63.

Bok, Derek. 2003. *Universities in the Marketplace: The Commercialization
of Higher Education*. Princeton, NJ: Princeton University Press.

Bok, Derek. 2012. *Higher Education in America*. Princeton, NJ: Princeton
University Press.

Bostrum, Nick. 2008. "Letter from Utopia." *Ethics, Law, and Technology* 2
(1): 1–7. https://doi.org/10.2202/1942-6008.1025.

Bowen, William G. 2013. *Higher Education in the Digital Age*. Princeton,
NJ: Princeton University Press.

Bowen, William G., and Michael S. McPherson. 2016. *Lesson Plan: An
Agenda for Change in American Higher Education*. Princeton, NJ:
Princeton University Press.

Bowen, William G., and Eugene M. Tobin. 2015. *Locus of Authority: The
Evolution of Faculty Roles in Higher Education*. Princeton, NJ: Princeton University Press.

Branch, John, and Brad Plummer. 2021. "Climate Disruption Is Now

Locked In. The Next Moves Will Be Crucial." *New York Times*, October 7. https://www.nytimes.com/2020/09/22/climate/climate-change-future.html.

Brooks, Peter, ed. 2014a. *The Humanities and Public Life*. New York: Fordham University Press.

Brooks, Peter. 2014b. "Introduction." In Brooks 2014a, 1–14.

Butler, Judith. 2014. "Ordinary, Incredulous." In Brooks 2014a, 15–38.

Butler, Judith. 2022. *What World Is This? A Pandemic Phenomenology*. New York: Columbia University Press.

Calhoun, Craig, ed. 1994. *Habermas and the Public Sphere*. Cambridge, MA: MIT Press.

Calhoun, Craig, and Diana Rhoten, eds. 2011. *Knowledge Matters: The Public Mission of the Research University*. New York: Columbia University Press.

Calvin, William H. 2002. *A Brain for All Seasons*. Chicago: University of Chicago Press.

Caney, Simon. 2020. "Climate Justice." In *Stanford Encyclopedia of Philosophy*. https://plato.stanford.edu/archives/win2021/entries/justice-climate/.

Caplow, Theodore, and Reece J. McGee. 1958. *The Academic Marketplace*. New York: Basic Books.

Cassuto, Leonard, and Robert Weisbuch. 2021. *The New PhD: How to Build a Better Graduate Education*. Baltimore. MD: Johns Hopkins University Press.

Castillo, David, and William Egginton. 2019. "What Kind of Humanities Do We Want or Need in the Twenty-First Century?" In Lopez-Calvo and Lux 2019.

Center for Climate and Energy Solutions. 2022. "History of UN Climate Talks." https://www.c2es.org/content/history-of-un-climate-talks/.

Chakrabarty, Dipesh. 2017. "Afterword." *South Atlantic Quarterly* 116 (1): 163–68.

Chakrabarty, Dipesh. 2021. *The Climate of History in a Planetary Age*. Chicago: University of Chicago Press.

Chomsky, Noam, and Robert Pollin. 2020. *Climate Crisis and the Global Green New Deal*. London: Verso.

Clark, Nigel, and Bronislaw Szerszynski. 2021. *Planetary Social Thought: The Anthropocene Challenge to the Social Sciences*. London: Polity Press.

Clark, Burton R. 1987. *The Academic Life: Small Worlds, Different Worlds*. Princeton, NJ: Carnegie Foundation for the Advancement of Teaching.

Climate Action Tracker (CAT). 2018. "CAT Warming Projections Global Update." https://climateanalytics.org/media/cat_temp_upadate _dec2018.pdf.

Cramton, Peter, David J. C. MacKay, Axel Ockenfels, Steven Stoft, Richard N. Cooper, and Christian Gollier, eds. 2017. *Global Carbon Pricing: The Path to Climate Cooperation*. Cambridge, MA: MIT Press.

Davidson, Cathy N. 2011. *Now You See It: How the Brain Science of Attention Will Transform the Way We Live, Work, and Learn*. New York: Viking.

Davidson, Cathy N. (2017) 2022. *The New Education: How to Revolutionize the University to Prepare Students for a World in Flux*. New York: Basic Books.

de Bary, Brett, ed. 2010. *Universities in Translation: The Mental Labor of Globalization*. Hong Kong: Hong Kong University Press.

Deleuze, Gilles and Félix Guattari. 1980. *Capitalisme et schizophrénie 2: Mille plateaux*. Paris: Editions de Minuit.

Dewey, John. 1927. *The Public and Its Problems*. New York: Henry Holt.

Diamond, Jared. 2005. *Collapse: How Societies Choose to Fail or Succeed*. New York: Viking.

Doerr, John. 2021. *Speed and Scale: An Action Plan for Solving Our Climate Crisis Now*. Edmonton, Alberta: Penguin Portfolio.

During, Simon. 2014. "Stop Defending the Humanities." *Public Books*, March 1. https://www.publicbooks.org/stop-defending-the -humanities/.

Eagleton, Terry. 2003. *After Theory*. New York: Basic Books.

Emmott, Stephen. 2013. *Ten Billion*. New York: Vintage Books.

Fallon, Daniel. 1980. *The German University*. Boulder: Colorado Associated University Press.

Finkelstein, Martin J., Valerie Martin Conley, and Jack H. Schuster. 2016. *The Faculty Factor: Reassessing the American Academy in a Turbulent Era*. Baltimore, MD: Johns Hopkins University Press.

Fitzpatrick, Kathleen. 2019. *Generous Thinking: A Radical Approach to Saving the University*. Baltimore, MD: Johns Hopkins University Press.

Flaherty, Colleen. 2018a. "The Evolving English Major." *Inside Higher Ed*,

July 18. https://www.insidehighered.com/news/2018/07/18/new
-analysis-english-departments-says-numbers-majors-are-way-down
-2012-its-not-death.

Flaherty, Colleen. 2018b. "The Vanishing History Major." *Inside Higher
Ed*, November 27. https://www.insidehighered.com/news/2018/11
/27/new-analysis-history-major-data-says-field-new-low-can-it
-be-saved.

Foucault, Michel. (1971) 1984. "Nietzsche, Genealogy, History." Translated by Donald F. Bouchard and Sherry Simon. In *The Foucault
Reader*, edited by Paul Rabinow, 76–100. New York: Pantheon.

Fritsch, Matthias. 2018a. "An Eco-Deconstructive Account of the Emergence of Normativity in 'Nature.'" In *Eco-Deconstruction: Derrida
and Environmental Philosophy*, edited by Matthias Fritsch, Philippe
Lynes, and David Wood, 279–302. New York: Fordham University
Press.

Fritsch, Matthias. 2018b. *Taking Turns with the Earth: Phenomenology,
Deconstruction, and Intergenerational Justice*. Palo Alto, CA: Stanford
University Press.

Fukuyama, Francis. 2020. "30 Years of World Politics: What Has Changed."
Journal of Democracy 31 (1): 11–22.

Gardiner, Stephen M. 2010. "A Perfect Moral Storm: Climate Change,
Intergenerational Ethics, and the Problem of Corruption." *Environmental Values* 15 (3): 397–413. Reprinted in Gardiner et al. 2010.
https://doi.org/10.1093/oso/9780195399622.003.0012.

Gardiner, Stephen M. 2011. *A Perfect Moral Storm: The Ethical Tragedy of
Climate Change*. Oxford: Oxford University Press.

Gardiner, Stephen M., Simon Caney, Dale Jamieson, and Henry Shue.
2010. *Climate Ethics: Essential Readings*. Oxford: Oxford University
Press.

Gardiner, Stephen M., and David Weisbach. 2016. *Debating Climate
Ethics*. Oxford: Oxford University Press.

Gates, Bill. 2021. *How to Avoid a Climate Disaster*. New York: Alfred A.
Knopf.

Geiger, Roger. 2016a. "From the Land-Grant Tradition to the Current
Crisis in the Humanities." In Hutner and Mohamed 2016, 18–30.

Geiger, Roger. 2016b. "The Ten Generations of American Higher
Education." In Bastedo, Altbach, and Gumport 2016, 3–34.

Ginsberg, Benjamin. 2011. *The Fall of the Faculty: The Rise of the All-*

Administrative University and Why It Matters. New York: Oxford University Press.

Goldberg, David Theo. 2014. *The Afterlife of the Humanities*. Irvine: University of California Humanities Research Institute. https://issuu.com/uchri/docs/afterlife.

Gollier, Christian, and Jean Tirole. 2017. "Effective Institutions against Climate Change." In Cramton et al. 2017. muse.jhu.edu/book/60847.

Grau, Francesc Xavier. 2018. "The 'Glocal' University." Global University Network for Innovation. https://www.guninetwork.org/articles/glocal-university.

Green, Jessica. 2020. "Less Talk, More Walk: Why Climate Change Demands Activism in the Academy." *Daedalus* 149 (4): 151–62.

Greif, Mark. 2015. "What's Wrong with Public Intellectuals?" *Chronicle Review* 61 (23): B6–9.

Guattari, Félix. 1989. *Les Trois Écologies*. Paris: Éditions Galilée. English translation by Ian Pindar and Paul Sutton. https://www.academia.edu/30403909/Guattari_Felix_The_Three_Ecologies.

Guattari, Félix. 2013. "Pour une refondation des pratiques sociales." In *Le Monde diplomatique* (October 26, 1992). Reprinted in *Qu'est-ce que l'Écosophie?* Texts compiled by Stéphane Nadaud. Paris: Éditions Lignes, 589–609.

Habinek, Jacob. 2010. "State-Building and the Origins of Disciplinary Specialization in Nineteenth Century Germany." http://www.irle.berkeley.edu/culture/papers/habinek10.pdf.

Halstead, John. 2019. *Another End of the World Is Possible*. N.p.: Lulu.

Hamilton, Clive. 2010. *Requiem for a Species: Why We Resist the Truth about Climate Change*. London: Routledge.

Hamilton, Clive. 2017. *Defiant Earth: The Fate of Humans in the Anthropocene*. Cambridge: Polity Press.

Harpham, Geoffrey. 2011. *The Humanities and the Dream of America*. Chicago: University of Chicago Press.

Harpham, Geoffrey. 2013. "Finding Ourselves: The Humanities as a Discipline." *American Literary History* 25 (3): 509–34.

Harris, Paul G. 2016. *Global Ethics and Climate Change*, 2nd ed. Edinburgh: Edinburgh University Press.

Harris, Paul G. 2021. *Pathologies of Climate Governance: International Relations, National Politics and Human Nature*. Cambridge: Cambridge University Press.

Hartzell-Nichols, Lauren. 2019. *A Climate of Risk: Precautionary Principles, Catastrophes, and Climate Change*. London: Routledge.

Hayot, Eric. 2018. "The Humanities as We Know Them Are Doomed. Now What?" *Chronicle of Higher Education*, July 1. https://www.chronicle.com/article/the-humanities-as-we-know-them-are-doomed-now-what/.

Heise, Ursula K. 2008. *Sense of Place: The Environmental Imagination of the Global*. Oxford: Oxford University Press.

Heise, Ursula K., Jon Christensen, and Michelle Niemann, eds. 2017. *The Routledge Companion to the Environmental Humanities*. New York: Routledge.

Hertsgaard, Mark. 2012. *Hot: Living through the Next 50 Years on Earth*. New York: Houghton Mifflin Harcourt.

Hofstadter, Richard, and Walter Metzger. 1955. *The Development of Academic Freedom in the United States*. New York: Columbia University Press.

Humanities Indicators Project. 2021. "State of the Humanities 2021: Workforce and Beyond." American Academy of Arts and Sciences. https://www.amacad.org/publication/humanities-workforce-beyond.

Hutner, Gordon, and Feisal G. Mohamed, eds. 2016. *A New Deal for the Humanities: Liberal Arts and the Future of Public Higher Education*. New Brunswick, NJ: Rutgers University Press.

Intergovernmental Panel on Climate Change (IPCC). 2018. "Strengthening and Implementing the Global Response." Chapter 4 in Special Report: *Global Warming of 1.5 °C*. https://www.ipcc.ch/sr15/chapter/chapter-4/.

Intergovernmental Panel on Climate Change (IPCC). 2021. *Climate Change 2021: The Physical Science Basis*, edited by Valérie Masson-Delmotte, Panmao Zhai, et al. Cambridge: Cambridge University Press.

Jamieson, Dale. 2014. *Reason in a Dark Time: Why the Struggle against Climate Change Failed—and What It Means for Our Future*. Oxford: Oxford University Press.

Jencks, Christopher, and David Riesman. 1968. *The Academic Revolution*. Garden City, NY: Doubleday.

Jonas, Hans. 1966. *The Phenomenon of Life: Toward a Philosophical Biology*. New York: Harper and Row.

Jonas, Hans. (1979) 1984. *The Imperative of Responsibility: In Search of an Ethics for the Technological Age.* Translated by Hans Jonas with David Herr. Chicago: University of Chicago Press.

Kahn, Paul. 2014. "On Humanities and Human Rights." In Brooks 2014a, 116–22.

Kamuf, Peggy. 1997. *The Division of Literature: Or the University in Deconstruction.* Chicago: University of Chicago Press.

Kernan, Alvin, ed. 1997. *What's Happened to the Humanities?* Princeton, NJ: Princeton University Press.

Kuhn, Thomas. 1962. *The Structure of Scientific Revolutions.* Chicago: University of Chicago Press.

Labaree, David F. 2017. *A Perfect Mess: The Unlikely Ascendancy of American Higher Education.* Chicago: University of Chicago Press.

Lackner, Maximilian, Baharak Sajjadi, and W. Y. Chen, eds. 2022. *Handbook of Climate Change Mitigation and Adaptation.* New York: Springer.

Latour, Bruno. 1991. *We Have Never Been Modern.* Translated by Catherine Porter. Cambridge, MA: Harvard University Press.

Latour, Bruno. 2017. *Facing Gaia: Eight Lectures on the New Climatic Regime.* Translated by Catherine Porter. Cambridge, UK: Polity Press.

Latour, Bruno. 2018a. "Bruno Latour Tracks Down Gaia." Translated by Stephen Muecke. *Los Angeles Review of Books*, July 3. https://lareviewofbooks.org/article/bruno-latour-tracks-down-gaia.

Latour, Bruno. 2018b. *Down to Earth: Politics in the New Climatic Regime.* Translated by Catherine Porter. Cambridge, UK: Polity Press.

Laugier, Sandra. 2015. "The Ethics of Care as a Politics of the Ordinary." *New Literary History* 46 (2): 217–40.

Lawrence, Mark G., Stefan Schäfer, Helene Muri, Vivian Scott, Andreas Oschlies, Naomi E. Vaughan, Olivier Boucher, Hauke Schmidt, Jim Haywood, and Jürgen Scheffran. 2018. "Evaluating Climate Geo-engineering Proposals in the Context of the Paris Agreement Temperature Goals." *Nature Communications* 9 (1): 1–19. https://doi.org/10.1038/s41467-018-05938-3.

Leal Filho, Walter, and Sarah L. Hemstock, eds. 2019. *Climate Change and the Role of Education.* Cham, Switzerland: Springer Publishing.

Leal Filho, Walter, Mihaela Sima, Ayyoob Sharifi, Johannes M. Luetz, Amanda Lange Salvia, Mark Mifsud, Felicia Motunrayo Olooto, et al.

2021. "Handling Climate Change Education at Universities: An Overview." *Environmental Sciences Europe* 33 (109). https://doi.org/10.1186/s12302-021-00552-5.

Leggewie, Claus, and Franz Mauelshagen, eds. 2018. *Climate Change and Cultural Transition in Europe*. Leiden: Brill.

Leitch, Vincent, ed. 2010. *Norton Anthology of Theory and Criticism*, 2nd ed. New York: W. W. Norton.

Leitch, Vincent. 2014. *Literary Criticism in the 21st Century: Theory Renaissance*. London: Bloomsbury.

Leonard, Sophia, Benjamin Reiss, Victor Antonio, and Makenzie Fitzgerald. 2020. "Public Humanities in the Reconstructed University." *American Literature* 92 (4): 781–90.

Levin, Simon. 2000. *Fragile Dominion: Complexity and the Commons*. Cambridge, MA: Perseus Publishing.

Lifton, Robert Jay. 2017. *The Climate Swerve: Reflections on Mind, Hope, and Survival*. New York: New Press.

Lippman, Walter. 1925. *The Phantom Public*. New York: Harcourt Brace.

Lopez-Calvo, Ignacio, and Christina Lux, eds. 2019. *The Humanities in the Age of Information and Post-Truth*. Evanston. IL: Northwestern University Press.

Lovelock, James. 2015. *A Rough Ride to the Future*. New York: Abrams Books.

Lye, Colleen, Christopher Newfield, and James Vernon, eds. 2011. *The Humanities and the Crisis of the Public University*. 2011. Special issue, *Representations* 116 (1).

Mailloux, Steven. 2006. *Disciplinary Identities: Rhetorical Paths of English, Speech, and Composition*. New York: Modern Language Association.

Martin, Reinhold. 2021. *Knowledge Worlds: Media, Materiality, and the Making of the Modern University*. New York: Columbia University Press.

Mauelshagen, Franz. 2018. "The Age of Uncertainty: Challenges of Climate Change for the Insurance Business." In Leggewie and Mauelshagen 2018, 301–19.

McIlrath, Lorraine, Ann Lyons, and Ronaldo Munck, eds. 2012. *Higher Education and Civic Engagement: Comparative Perspectives*. New York: Palgrave Macmillan. https://www.academia.edu/5308845/Higher_Education_and_Civic_Engagement?email_work_card=view-paper.

McKibben, Bill. 1989. *The End of Nature*. New York: Random House.

McKibben, Bill. 2010. *Eaarth: Making a Life on a Tough New Planet*. New York: Time Books.

McKibben, Bill. 2019. *Falter: Has the Human Game Begun to Play Itself Out?* New York: Henry Holt.

McKibben, Bill. 2022. "Where Will We Live?" *New York Review of Books* 69 (October 6): 6–10.

Measham, Thomas, and Stewart Lockie, eds. 2012. *Risk and Social Theory in Environmental Management*. Clayton, Australia: CSIRO Publishing.

Molthan-Hill, Petra, Lia Blaj-Ward, Marcellus Forh Mbah, and Tamara Shapiro Ledley. 2022. "Climate Change Education at Universities: Relevance and Strategies for Every Discipline." In Lackner, Sajjadi, and Chen 2021, 1–64. https://link.springer.com/referencework entry/10.1007/978–1–4614–6431–0_153–1.

Morton, Timothy. 2013. *Hyperobjects: Philosophy and Ecology after the End of the World*. Minneapolis: University of Minnesota Press.

Mr. Y [pseudonym of Colonel Mark Mykleby and Captain Wayne Porter]. 2011. *A National Strategic Narrative*. Washington, DC: Woodrow Wilson Center. https://apps.dtic.mil/sti/pdfs/ADA543772.pdf.

Muller, Jerry. 2018. *The Tyranny of Metrics*. Princeton, NJ: Princeton University Press.

Mumford, Lewis. 1934. *Technics and Civilization*. New York: Harcourt Brace.

Murphy, Raymond. 2012. "Managing Risk under Uncertainty." In Measham and Lockie 2012, 17–26.

National Academies of Sciences, Engineering, and Medicine 2022. *Next Generation Earth Systems Science at the National Science Foundation*. Washington, DC: National Academies Press. https://doi.org/10.17226/26042.

National Center for Education Statistics (NCES). 2017. "Digest of Education Statistics." Institute of Education Sciences. https://nces.ed.gov/programs/digest/d17/tables/dt17_303.20.asp?current=yes.

Net-Zero America Study. 2021. *Net-Zero America: Potential Pathways, Infrastructure, and Impacts*. Princeton, NJ: Princeton University. https://netzeroamerica.princeton.edu/the-report.

Newfield, Christopher. 2008. *Unmaking the Public University*. Cambridge, MA: Harvard University Press.

Newfield, Christopher. 2016a. *The Great Mistake: How We Wrecked Public*

Universities and How We Can Fix Them. Baltimore, MD: Johns Hopkins University Press.

Newfield, Christopher. 2016b. "What Are the Humanities For? Rebuilding the Public University." In Hutner and Mohamed 2016, 160–78.

Ord, Toby. 2020. *The Precipice: Existential Risk and the Future of Humanity*. New York: Hachette.

Oreskes, Naomi. 2020. "What Is the Social Responsibility of Climate Scientists?" *Daedalus* 149 (4): 33–45.

Ostrom, Elinor. 1990. *Governing the Commons: The Evolution of Institutions for Collective Action*. Cambridge: Cambridge University Press.

Ostrom, Elinor. 2010. "Beyond Markets and States: Polycentric Governance of Complex Economic Systems." *American Economic Review* 100 (June): 1–33.

Rabinow, Paul, ed. 1984. *The Foucault Reader*. New York: Pantheon.

Rall, Ted. 2020. "A Grim New Definition of Generation X." Common Dreams, January 1. https://www.commondreams.org/views/2020/01/01/grim-new-definition-generation-x.

Readings, Bill. 1996. *The University in Ruins*. Cambridge, MA: Harvard University Press.

Reimers, Fernando M. 2021. "The Role of Universities Building an Ecosystem of Climate Change Education." In *Education and Climate Change: The Role of Universities*, edited by Fernando M. Reimers, 1–44. New York: Springer. https://link.springer.com/book/10.1007/978-3-030-57927-2.

Reitter, Paul, and Chad Wellmon. 2021. *Permanent Crisis: The Humanities in a Disenchanted Age*. Chicago: University of Chicago Press.

Riesman, David, Nathan Glazer, and Reuel Denney. 1950. *The Lonely Crowd*. New Haven, CT: Yale University Press.

Robbins, Bruce, ed. 1993. *The Phantom Public Sphere*. Minneapolis: University of Minnesota Press.

Roeser, Sabine, Rafaela Hillerbrand, Per Sandin, and Martin Peterson, eds. 2012. *Handbook of Risk Theory: Epistemology Decision Theory, Ethics, and Social Implications of Risk*. Dordrecht: Springer Science and Business Media.

Rosenblum, Nancy L. 2020. "Paths to Witnessing, Ethics of Speaking Out." In "Witnessing Climate Change." Edited by Nancy L. Rosenblum. Special issue, *Daedalus* 149 (4): 6–24.

Rudolph, Frederick. 1962. *The American College and University: A History*. New York: Vintage Books.

Ruggie, John. 2022. "Corporate Globalization and the Liberal Order." In *The Downfall of the American Order*, edited by Peter J. Katzenstein and Jonathan Kirshner, 144–64. Ithaca, NY: Cornell University Press.

Said, Edward. 1983. *The World, the Text, and the Critic*. Cambridge, MA: Harvard University Press.

Schmidt, Benjamin. 2018. "The Humanities Are in Crisis." *Atlantic*, August 23. https://www.theatlantic.com/ideas/archive/2018/08/the-humanities-face-a-crisisof-confidence/567565/.

Schwab, Klaus. 2016. *The Fourth Industrial Revolution: What It Means and How to Respond*. World Economic Forum, January. https://weforum.org/agenda/2016/01/the-fourth-industrial-revolution-what-it-means-and-how-to-respond/.

Scranton, Roy. 2018. *We're Doomed. Now What?* New York: Soho Press.

Second Nature. n.d. "What We Do." https://secondnature.org/wp-content/uploads/Second-Nature-One-Pager_final.pdf.

Sennett, Richard. 1974. *The Fall of Public Man*. New York: W. W. Norton.

Servigne, Pablo, and Raphaël Stevens. 2015. *Comment tout peut s'effondrer*. Paris: Seuil.

Servigne, Pablo, and Raphaël Stevens. 2020. *How Everything Can Collapse: A Manual for Our Time*. Translated by Andrew Brown. Cambridge: Polity Press.

Shue, Henry. 2022. *The Pivotal Generation: Why We Have a Moral Responsibility to Slow Climate Change Right Now*. Princeton, NJ: Princeton University Press.

Slaughter, Sheila, and Gary Rhoades. 2004. *Academic Capitalism and the New Economy*. Baltimore, MD: Johns Hopkins University Press.

Slosson, Edwin E. 1910. *Great American Universities*. New York: Macmillan.

Small, Helen. 2013. *The Value of the Humanities*. Oxford: Oxford University Press.

Smil, Vaclav. 2019. *Growth: From Microorganisms to Megacities*. Cambridge, MA: MIT Press.

Smil, Vaclav. 2022. *How the World Really Works*. London: Viking.

Steel, Daniel, C. Tyler DesRoches, and Kian Mintz-Woo. 2022. "Climate Change and the Threat to Civilization." *Publications of the National*

Academy of Sciences, October 6. https://doi.org/10.1073/pnas
.2210525119.

Steffen, Will, Wendy Broadgate, Lisa Michele Deutsch, and Owen
Gaffney. 2015. "The Trajectory of the Anthropocene: The Great
Acceleration." *Anthropocene Review* 2 (1): 81–98.

Steffen, Will, Katherine Richardson, Johan Rockström, Hans Joachim
Schellnhuber, Opha Pauline Dube, Sébastien Dutreuil, Timothy M.
Lenton, and Jane Lubchenco. 2020. "The Emergence and Evolution
of Earth System Science." *Nature Reviews Earth and Environment* 1
(January): 54–63.

Stern, Nicholas. 2007. *The Economics of Climate Change: The Stern Review*.
Cambridge: Cambridge University Press.

Stern, Nicholas. 2015. *Why Are We Waiting? The Logic, Urgency, and Promise of Tackling Climate Change*. Cambridge, MA: MIT Press.

Stover, Justin. 2017. "There Is No Case for the Humanities." *American
Affairs* 1 (4): 210–24.

Thelin, John R. (2004) 2011. *A History of American Higher Education*. Baltimore, MD: Johns Hopkins University Press.

Tomlinson, Gary. 2018. *Culture and the Course of Human Evolution*. Chicago: University of Chicago Press.

United Nations Educational, Scientific, and Cultural Organization
(UNESCO). 2017. *Declaration of Ethical Principles in Relation to
Climate Change*. Paris: UNESCO. https://unesdoc.unesco.org
/ark:/48223/pf0000260129.

Veysey, Laurence. 1965. *The Emergence of the American University*. Chicago: University of Chicago Press.

Vollman, William T. 2018. *Carbon Ideologies*. 2 vols. New York: Viking.

Vollmer, Hendrik. 2013. *The Sociology of Disruption, Disaster, and Social
Change*. Cambridge: Cambridge University Press.

Wagner, Gernot, and Martin L. Weitzman. 2015. *Climate Shock: The
Economic Consequences of a Hotter Planet*. Princeton, NJ: Princeton
University Press.

Wallace-Wells, David. 2019. *The Uninhabitable Earth*. New York: Tim
Duggan Books.

Wallace-Wells, David. 2022. "A Tour of the New World: Envisioning Life
after Climate Change." Climate Issue, *New York Times Magazine*,
October 30, 24–60.

Washburn, Jennifer. 2005. *University Inc.: The Corporate Corruption of Higher Education*. New York: Basic Books.

Watts, Robb. 2017. *Public Universities, Managerialism, and the Values of Higher Education*. London: Palgrave Macmillan.

Weber, Samuel. 2001. *Institution and Interpretation*. Stanford, CA: Stanford University Press.

Weisbrod, Burton A., Jeffrey P. Ballou, and Evelyn D. Asch. 2008. *Mission and Money: Understanding the University*. Cambridge: Cambridge University Press.

Weiss, Daniel, and Rebecca Chopp. 2013. *Remaking College: Innovation and the Liberal Arts*. Baltimore, MD: Johns Hopkins University Press.

Weitzman, Martin L. 2007. "A Review of the *Stern Review on the Economics of Climate Change*." *Journal of Economic Literature* 45 (September): 703–24.

West, Geoffrey. 2018. *Scale: The Universal Laws of Life, Growth, and Death in Organisms, Cities, and Companies*. New York: Penguin Books.

Westermann, Mariët. 2019. "The Humanities in the World." In Lopez-Calvo and Lux 2019.

Wildavsky, Ben. 2010. *The Great Brain Race: How Global Universities Are Reshaping the World*. Princeton, NJ: Princeton University Press.

Wilder, Rob, and Dan Kammen. 2017. "Taking the Long View: The 'Forever Legacy' of Climate Change." *Yale Environment 360*, September 12. https://e360.yale.edu/features/taking-the-long-view-the-forever-legacy-of-climate-change.

Winner, Langdon. 1986. *The Whale and the Reactor: A Search for Limits in an Age of High Technology*. Chicago: University of Chicago Press.

Woodward, Kathleen. 2009. "The Future of the Humanities—in the Present and in Public." *Daedalus* 138 (1): 110–23.

INDEX

Consortium of Humanities Centers and Institutes, 66, 141
consumerism, 119, 139, 225n36
corporate university, 164–65, 171–72, 196
COVID-19 pandemic, 110, 231n36
cultural heritage: destruction of, 156–57
curriculum: classic, 6; on climate change, 144; debate about, 27–28; evolution of, 8–9, 20, 194; modernization of, 6–7; specializations, 9–10; standard base, 9; students' needs and, 147
cyborg science, 161

Davidson, Cathy: *The New Education*, 203, 205
dead public space, 66
Debating Climate Ethics (Gardiner and Weisbach), 178
"deep adaptation" movement, 226n39
democracy: theories of, 67
Department of Education, 25, 29
Descola, Philippe, 220n8
Development of Academic Freedom in the United States, The, 211n8
Dewey, John, 217n5; *The Public and Its Problems*, 67
Diamond, Jared: *Collapse: How Societies Choose to Fail or Succeed*, 97–98
digital humanities, 46, 52, 84, 87, 212n17
digitization, 20
disciplines: categories of, 16; digital tools and, 14; as institutional formations, 39; reactive and substantive development of, 7–8, 10; research paradigms and, 39
Doerr, John, 231n34
During, Simon, 226n42

Eagleton, Terry: *After Theory*, 15
earth system, 199–200

earth system science, 99, 105, 145, 176, 181, 186, 219n3, 226n40
education: goals of, 92, 192–93, 197
educational attainment, 81–82
Education and Climate Change, 144
Egginton, William, 155
Emergence of the American University (Veysey), 2
Emmott, Stephen: *Stephen Emmott*, 131
energy: global demand for, 107, 133, 136; sources of, 106–7, 119; transition to clean, 224n25, 231n34
entrepreneurial university, 73, 78, 85
environmental future: uncertainty of, 109–10, 202
environmental humanities, 52–53, 87, 96, 97, 139
environmental politics, 187, 232n39
epochal consciousness, 176, 177
ethics of care, 195, 196–97, 232n41
European Union: decision-making model, 112
existential risk, 112–13

faculty: administrative functions, 18, 21, 27; career path, 17–18; distribution across the fields, 10, 20; growing numbers of, 10, 19; non-tenure-track, 34; part-time, 21; productivity and remuneration of, 218n13; professionalization of, 18, 19; at small colleges, 17; status of, 3, 17–18, 19, 22; stratification of, 21; teaching specialists, 35; tenure track, 21; training programs for, 20
Faculty Factor, The (Finkelstein, Conley, and Schuster), 20–21
financial crisis of 2008, 69, 70, 110, 121
Finkelstein, Martin J., 20
Fitzpatrick, Kathleen, 196; *Generous Thinking: A Radical Approach to Saving the University*, 149–52, 195, 216n1

Flaubert, Gustave, 101
fossil fuel consumption, 106–7, 127, 220n7, 221n12
fossil fuel industry, 173
Foucault, Michel, 158
fourth industrial revolution, 228–29n16
freedom: forms of, 165
free rider problem, 125–26
French identity, 58
Fritsch, Matthias, 178

Gaia hypothesis, 104–5
Gardiner, Stephen, 178
Gates, Bill, 224n25
Geiger, Roger, 2, 101, 102
Generous Thinking: A Radical Approach to Saving the University (Fitzpatrick), 149–52, 195
German model of higher education, 4
GI Bill, 5, 24
Global Carbon Pricing: The Path to Climate Cooperation, 125, 126
global economy, 105, 109
globalization, 20, 118, 119
global population forecasts, 133
global system, 119, 120, 121
global warming: acceleration of, 127; causes of, 100, 107, 134, 189; cost of acting on, 100; cultural norms and, 116; effects of, 99–100, 105, 110, 189, 220n4; efforts to prevent, 115, 123, 176; IPCC special report on, 115–16; knowledge gaps and, 115–16; mitigation of, 97; projections of, 137, 223n20, 224n28. *See also* climate change
Goldberg, David Theo, 171; "The Afterlife of the Humanities," 155
Gollier, Christian, 126
graduate deans: responsibility of, 152–53
graduate programs: reform of, 146–47, 152–54, 213n22

grand challenges of the twenty-first century, 59, 95
grants, 25, 26, 64–65
Great Acceleration, 95, 99, 138
greenhouse gas emission, 123, 202, 233n44
Green New Deal, 121–22, 170
"green" political parties, 108
Greif, Mark, 218n6
growth: anthropogenic impacts of, 134–35; of biological organisms, 129; of cities, 129; of economies, 120, 129; forms of, 128; global sustainability and, 225n33; innovations and, 130–31; limits of, 129–30, 135–36; of population, 129, 225n35; scale and, 127, 128, 132–33, 136; as solution to human problems, 200; theory of exponential, 128–29; uncertainty after, 135
Guattari, Félix, 232n42

Habermas, Jürgen, 48
Hamilton, Clive, 106, 117; *Defiant Earth,* 103
Handbook of Climate Change Mitigation and Adaptation, 143
Harpham, Geoffrey, 49, 57, 102; "Finding Ourselves: The Humanities as a Discipline," 38, 39; *The Humanities and the Dream of America,* 101
Harris, Paul, 124, 183
Harvard College, 1
Hayot, Eric, 229n18
Heart of the Matter, The (report), 57, 59, 60, 61, 93
Heise, Ursula, 222n16
Hertsgaard, Mark, 99; *Hot: Living through the Next Fifty Years on Earth,* 98
Higher Education Act (HEA) of 1965, 25
history: as discipline, 229n21; recontextualization of, 198, 199

Holocene epoch, 104, 117, 200
Holquist, Michael, 52
homo oeconomicus, 161
Hoover Institution, 161
horizon of research, 147, 191
humanities: anthropocentrism and, 189–90; claims about the value of, 43–45, 49, 93; community engagement, 147–48; conception of, 9, 170–71, 229n21; crisis of, 12, 13, 15, 16, 34, 38–39, 85, 100–102, 140, 146; critique of, 90, 168; curriculum, 146, 168; definitions of, 40–42, 161, 171; digital technology and, 212–13n17; ecological responsibility of, 102–3; emergence of, 142; enrollment decline, 101; evolution of, 10–12, 13–14, 160–61; funding of, 101; genealogical narrative of, 162; globalized modern world and, 188–89; graduate studies in, 146–47, 169; institutional approach to, 46, 56–57, 164; instrumental justification of, 35, 57; knowledge evaluation in, 43; liberal education and, 35, 161; marginalization of, 167, 168; non-academic advocates for, 141–42; openness of, 39; outreach programs, 168–69; paradigm for, 45; privatization of public universities and, 83, 84–85, 87; programs and specializations, 11, 12, 13, 33–34, 90; promotion of, 142; public sphere and, 40, 46, 47–48, 51–52, 91, 93, 101, 147, 149, 183, 184; reinvention of, 155–56; research in, 11, 86–87, 91–92, 147; secular, 164; statistics of degrees, 85, 86; tasks of, 48–49, 59; technoscience and, 161–62, 168, 187–88; vocationalism and, 101
Humanities and Public Life, The (Brooks), 40, 46, 48, 49, 50, 51
humanities centers, 46, 47, 65–66, 87

Humanities Indicators, 15, 49–50, 86, 213n18
Humanities in the Age of Information and Post-Truth, The, 155, 171
humanities report card, 50
humanity: commitment to self-preservation, 204, 233n1; long-term potential of, 114, 223n21; uncertain future of, 107–8
human sciences, 171
Hutner, Gordon, 217n6

impact philanthropy, 64–65
Imperative of Responsibility, The (Jonas), 178
institutional culture: problematics of changing, 180–85; reorientation of, 185–97
intellectual property rights, 72
interdisciplinary studies, 15, 39, 47, 213n19
international agreements, 124–25
IPCC special report *Global Warming of 1.5°C*, 115, 223n22

Jamieson, Dale, 117
Japan: population and economic stagnation, 133
Jaspers, Karl, 176
Johns Hopkins University, 4
Jonas, Hans, 178

Kahn, Paul: "On Humanities and Human Rights," 50
Kernan, Alvin, 11, 12, 13
knowledge: commodification of, 77; forms of, 73; production of, 163
knowledge economies, 148
knowledge gaps, 115–16, 223n22
knowledge society, 73
Knowledge Worlds: Media, Materiality, and the Making of the Modern University (Martin), 157–60, 162, 164–65, 183
Kuhn, Thomas, 38, 212n12
Kyoto Protocol, 123, 127

Ord, Toby, 113, 114, 137; *The Precipice: Existential Risk and the Future of Humanity,* 112
Ostrom, Elinor, 125

paradigm: definition of, 37–38, 39; for the public humanities, 40
paradigm shift, 80–81, 130–32, 151, 195, 216n2
Paris Agreement, 115, 123, 125, 224n28
Perelman, Chaïm, 212n12
Phantom Public Sphere, The, 67
PhDs: in humanities, path to, 146–47; new curriculum for, 152–53
Phenomenon of Life, The (Jonas), 178
physical sciences, 9
Pichler, Susanne, 209n2
Pivotal Generation, The (Shue), 176
planetary thinking, 176, 230n25
Pollin, Robert, 121
Porter, Wayne, 60, 61
postcapitalist university, 82
posthumanities, 155
"post-theory" era, 15–16
precautionary principle, 111–12, 114, 134
Princeton University: *Net-Zero America* report, 182–83
private universities: affordability of, 72; capacity for growth, 218n9; humanities programs, 90; publics of, 88–89; relations with donors, 81; research advantages, 80–81; statistics of, 72; system of interests and values, 88–90
professional disciplines, 9
professoriate: characterization of, 23
progress, 109, 127, 135, 138, 139, 200, 220n9
public: types of, 68, 218n6; will of the people and, 67
public good, 45, 217n7
public history, 53, 64

public humanities: centers for, 64; collaborative approach, 53–54; community-building with, 149, 151; concept of, 37, 141, 204; connotations of the term, 63–64; definition of, 54, 55, 68–69, 171; development of, 52, 146, 195; guidelines for, 53–55, 68; humanities framework and, 154–55; institutions and, 62; interdisciplinary horizon of, 54, 55; international scope of, 54, 55; master's programs, 64; objects of inquiry, 54; potential for, 149; problematics for, 53–55; publications in, 64; public outreach of, 93, 151, 155, 169–70, 173, 175; in public universities, role of, 87–88; recognition of, 142–43; reinvention of a public narrative, 57–58, 59; scholarly debates on, 55–56; scope of, 216–17n5; support of, 57, 64; tasks of, 67, 68, 93–94, 189, 221n13; transition to, 185
public intellectuals: criticism of, 155
public interest, 61–62
public/private dichotomy, 68
public scholarship, 53, 227n7
public sphere, 48, 51–52, 66–67, 68
public universities: academic traditions and, 75–76; access to, 78; budget cuts, 75, 79–80; capacity for growth, 76, 218n9; competition between, 76; criticism of, 79; current state of, 77–78; decline of, 82–83, 92; educational attainment, 81–82; elitist, 70; financial crisis and, 69, 70; funding model, 77–78, 80; golden age of, 71–72; humanities programs, 89–91; mission of, 72–73, 77, 93; pedagogical practices, 81; *vs.* private universities, 74; privatization of, 71, 72, 74–75, 78–79; public humanities movement and, 87–88; publics of, 88; "recovery cycle" of, 82;

US higher education (*cont.*)
  authority in, 163–64; sociology of,
  7; stakeholders, 32; state authority over, 4, 214n25; stratification
  of, 3, 210n5; studies of, 1–2,
  209n2; systemic structure of,
  22–33; technology and, 166–67

Veysey, Laurence, 210n4; *The Emergence of the American University,* 2
vocationalism in higher education,
  14, 20, 34, 85, 86, 101

Wallace-Wells, David, 220n4,
  225n37
Waters, Donald J., 209n2
Watts, Rob: *Public Universities, Mana-
  gerialism, and the Values of Higher
  Education,* 75

Weisbach, David, 178
Weisbuch, Robert: *The New PhD:
  How to Build a Better Graduate
  Education,* 152–54
Weitzman, Martin, 113
West, Geoffrey, 129, 130, 136; *Scale:
  The Universal Laws of Life, Growth,
  and Death in Organisms, Cities, and
  Companies,* 128
Westermann, Mariët, 173; "The
  Humanities in the World," 156
Westphalia treaties, 124
What's Happened to the Humanities?,
  11, 12
Winner, Langdon, 115, 170; *The
  Whale and the Reactor,* 220n8
Woodward, Kathleen, 46
worldliness: concept of, 155, 156,
  157, 160, 228n9, 233n1